UK ELECTION LAW
A CRITICAL EXAMINATION

Contemporary Issues in Public Policy Series

Series editors: David Downes and Paul Rock

This series of books offers straightforward, informed and comprehensive analyses of topical policy issues, from national health to women's work to central issues of crime and criminal justice – a welcome antidote to the treatment by the mass media, which can be sensationalist, limited or simply factually incorrect. Observers and other commentators often have a political or professional stake in writing. By contrast, what is offered here is dispassionate and accessibly-written expert commentary laid out in a non-technical and usable manner. Providing an excellent core for teaching in social policy, criminology, politics and sociology of contemporary Britain, these books also have a key target audience among politicians, policy-makers, journalists and informed people who wish to know more about the world they are inhabiting today.

UK ELECTION LAW

A CRITICAL EXAMINATION

Bob Watt

London • Sydney • Portland, Oregon

First published in Great Britain 2006 by
Glass House Press, The Glass House,
Wharton Street, London WC1X 9PX, United Kingdom
Telephone: + 44 (0)20 7278 8000   Facsimile: + 44 (0)20 7278 8080
Email: info@cavendishpublishing.com
Website: www.cavendishpublishing.com

Published in the United States by Cavendish Publishing
c/o International Specialized Book Services,
5824 NE Hassalo Street, Portland,
Oregon 97213-3644, USA

Published in Australia by Cavendish Publishing (Australia) Pty Ltd
45 Beach Street, Coogee, NSW 2034, Australia
Telephone: + 61 (2)9664 0909   Facsimile: + 61 (2)9664 5420
Email: info@cavendishpublishing.com.au
Website: www.cavendishpublishing.com.au

Watt, Bob, 1953 –
UK election law: a critical examination
1.Election law – Great Britain
I.Title
342.4'107

Library of Congress Cataloguing in Publication Data
Data available

ISBN 10: 1-89541-916-X
ISBN 13: 978-1-85941-916-8

1 3 5 7 9 10 8 6 4 2
Printed and bound in Great Britain

Contents

Preface |

The study of electoral law and its underlying policy has been neglected. There have been but a handful of books on the subject published in the last two decades. Almost no law schools offer a course on election law, and few legal practitioners are interested in the subject. It is difficult to see why this should be the case. The right to vote lies at the heart of a democracy and the right is, at least to all appearances, strictly regulated by the law. One might say that more people come into personal contact with election law than with criminal law. Each year a form arrives through our letterbox requiring us, by law, to register to vote. It is invariably followed, over the ensuing months, by election leaflets soliciting our vote in parish or town, district, county, parliamentary and European parliamentary elections. Some of us vote in those elections, or for a directly elected mayor. Perhaps these are supplemented by elections to a devolved parliament or assembly. All, or at least we hope all, elected politicians have gained their positions by means of victory in a free and fair election. We have been promised referendums on the European Constitution and upon joining the euro-zone. All of these ballots (ie, elections of politicians and referendums) are, or will be, regulated by legislation and subject to scrutiny by the courts. Yet we do not seem to notice the law that regulates these ballots.

It is suspected that one reason for this invisibility is because all, or most, of us in the UK believe that our election law is of ancient provenance and is somehow perfect and unchanging. It is supposed to tick on, unchallenged and unchallenging, for centuries. Nothing could be further from the truth. Prior to 1872, propertied men voted by show of hands; the ballot was introduced in that year, but the property qualifications did not disappear until, at the earliest, 1918. Women could not vote on the same terms as men until 1928. The plural franchise ended in 1948. The voting age was reduced from 21 years of age to 18 years in 1970. The years since 1997 have seen radical changes. This book charts and analyses these developments. The book does not claim to be comprehensive. It contains an examination of selected areas of the law and the policy governing elections. These areas have been chosen in order best to illustrate some themes in the law. The book is up to date at the beginning of October 2005.

Secondly, academic lawyers have traditionally kept away from 'political law'. At least they have said that they have avoided 'political law', but this has not prevented colleagues from writing about social security law, immigration law, family law, health care law, environmental law, employment law or property law – all of which seem pre-eminently political. All law is 'political law'; for law (or at least, legislation) is the lever of political power. However, election law is explicitly political law. Much of it governs the activities of politicians. Whenever one writes about electoral law, one writes about politics. That is not to say that the book is politically partisan. Footnote 68 in Chapter 7 reveals (or confirms) my past political party membership, though I left that party at the end of 1995 and I am not sure whether I would vote for it today. I will say (along with Aristotle) that man is a political animal and I am still fascinated by the subject. A strong political preference is revealed here and that is for democracy. That is the underlying subject of this book; it presents a *democratic* theory. In accordance with that theory, I convinced myself that I should vote in the general election, though I did not vote in the last two.

I endeavoured to use a wide variety of sources when researching for this book. I have looked at the law, at political science, at political theory and at history. The first and the last made most impression. The prominence given to the law goes without saying. One cannot understand electoral law without looking at its history and I have tried to place the development of the law within the contexts of the period between 1429 and early 2005. Clearly, this survey must be partial and many things are omitted or they are given less prominence than would be the case in a much longer book and in one which was not focused on '"Contemporary" Issues in Public Policy'. The importance of Leveller thought may have been underestimated both in this book and more generally. The Levellers were a group of radical dissenters in the English Civil War. Whilst I have referred to the Putney Debates and, in particular, the debate between Maximilian Petty (a Leveller) and Henry Ireton (*not* a Leveller) in Chapter 2 and again, in passing, in Chapter 7, the significance of the Levellers' contribution to democratic thought is often overlooked. Possibly this is because the Levellers acquired a particular *cachet* during the late 1970s and the 1980s and their contribution to the English constitution was, in some circles, overstated. Whilst I was an undergraduate student, a friend of mine – likewise a mature student though somewhat older than me (many working-class people managed to get higher education in the 1980s because student grants were freely available) – was an enthusiast for the political thought of the Levellers.

Given the politics of the 1980s I was very unenthusiastic about both the Levellers and their 1980s adherents, so I now surprise myself in quoting the words of Anthony Wedgwood (Tony) Benn from his speech in Burford churchyard on 15 May 1976. In discussing the legacy of the Levellers Mr Benn said:

> The Levellers might see in the immense influence of the educational establishment, under the titular leadership of the universities, a new class of rulers in self-perpetuating hierarchy, aiming to establish a claim to the 'private ownership of knowledge' which, by rights, is part of the 'common store house' belonging to us all.

Whilst I am now much more sympathetic to the ideas of the Levellers themselves; Mr Benn proved remarkably prescient in one respect – the establishment of the private ownership of knowledge. The baleful influence of the Research Assessment Exercise turns the universities inwards so that most books written by academics are now read only by academics, if at all. I have tried to write for both academics and a wider audience. I hope I have satisfied both audiences and not fallen into the central pit; but, in any event, Cavendish Publishing is to be commended for their boldness in producing the 'Contemporary Issues in Public Policy' series. I trust neither audience will judge this book too harshly.

The Levellers' contribution to the democratisation of Britain is, as Andrew Sharp demonstrates in his Introduction to *The English Levellers* (Cambridge: CUP, 1998), difficult to chart. Sharp's view (*ibid*, p xiii) is that:

> [i]t is not all that misleading to describe them as liberal democrats. But they were such in conditions where to be one, for those with the temperament, was a standing temptation to rebellion and a mutiny. They exemplify the difficulties of being democratic in impossible circumstances.

Nowadays it is difficult not to be a democrat; following Sir William Harcourt we say, 'We are all democrats now.' However it is argued in this book that we need to be clear what we mean by *a democrat*; we need to distinguish between *democratic citizens* and *market citizens*. Here I argue for democracy – the people's informed choice of representatives elected in accordance with a law designed to ensure a free and fair election.

I have a long list of thanks. I would like to thank the series editors and all the staff at Cavendish Publishing. Beverley Brown commissioned the book and read the first draft, providing me with a number of valuable comments. The task of responding to her comments has improved the book enormously. Thanks to Sarah Birch with whom I have collaborated in the past. She inspired me to follow up some ideas. The staff of the Sir Albert Sloman Library was extremely helpful and remained good-natured despite having to search the archives for rather dusty books on a number of occasions. Thanks to my students over the past few years, upon whom many of the ideas were tested, especially Abdullah Al-Remaidhi, Margaret Anderson, Lee Biddle, George Hargreaves, and Friday Ogazi.

Many of my colleagues at the University of Essex helped me in a variety of ways, so I would like to thank Steve Anderman, John Bartle, Geoff Gilbert, Sheldon Leader and Albert Weale. However, I must give special thanks to Maurice Sunkin, Peter Luther and Brigid Hadfield. All read most of the chapters and made helpful comments throughout. Maurice discussed a number of cases and arguments with me, and Peter helped my historical understanding. They both have heavy administrative loads (as Dean of the Law School and Head of the Department of Law respectively) and I trust that my interruptions proved a welcome respite from the bureaucratic load, rather than a distraction from their academic work. Brigid read the first six chapters with great care. Thanks to Yvonne Cattrall, Sally Painter and Liz Coussell for administrative help. Many thanks to Charlotte (Charlie) King who helped me greatly with the final preparation of the text for submission. The remaining errors of substance and style are all mine.

Finally, the book is dedicated to my children, Graham, Elaine and Fiona, and to my wife Gillian. Gill had to put up with me getting up unconscionably early to work on many occasions. She (together, over the summer holidays, with Elaine and Fiona) suffered much questionable cooking on my part, whilst too many of the meals she cooked for me were swallowed unthinkingly in the race to get back to the text. Her question, 'What are you thinking about?', was answered far too frequently by the words – 'My book.'

So, with much love to Graham, Elaine, Fiona, and especially Gill.

Bob Watt

Table of Cases |

UK cases

Table of Statutes

(Including abbreviations for frequently cited Acts)

Statutory instruments

Chapter 1:
Law, Public Policy
and Ideology

Introduction

This book is about UK election law and policy. It is also, perforce, about
ideology. However, it is not a book about ideology, public policy, or
political theory in general; it is a book about the ideology of election law,
which is a branch of applied political theory. This book is not neutral.
Books of political theory rarely are; they may be liberal, communitarian,
socialist, libertarian, republican, postmodern, or conservative. This book
claims to be democratic; it posits a *democratic theory* against a *market
theory*. That having been said, the balance of the book is towards a legal,
rather than a political, analysis. The most important legal analysis
undertaken in this book is an attempt to measure election law in the UK
against the standards set by the European Convention of Human Rights
and its fast-developing jurisprudence. The European Convention
imposes a normative standard – a democratic standard.

    The starting point is that election law is not black letter law; it always
has a political purpose. It is designed to control the franchise in at least
two dimensions. First, it controls the *breadth* of the franchise; who can
vote? Secondly, it regulates the *method* of voting, how shall people vote,
what safeguards are provided to protect the security of their vote? Each
of these dimensions has their ideological components.

    If we look first at the breadth of the franchise, we can see that it was
contested from the middle ages. From Norman times until the beginning
of the 20th century there were two basic forms of franchise[1] – the
borough and the county franchise. Borough franchises were granted on a
complex basis to townsmen (see Chapter 2), but the county franchise was
originally exercisable by all male freeholders in the county. However in

---

1   Although, as we shall see, university franchises were introduced and the middle of
    the 19th century was marked by proposals to introduce all sorts of 'fancy franchise'.
    These matters, including the 'fancy franchise' are discussed in Chapter 2.

1429–30,[2] the county franchise was restricted to freeholders of substantial freehold properties (worth more than 40 shillings *per annum*) by virtue of the Act of Parliament numbered 8 Henry VI cap VII and entitled *What sort of men shall be choosers and who shall be chosen knights of the parliament.* This restriction on the county freehold and thus the franchise (known as the 40 shilling franchise) continued until the 19th century. The reason for this restriction is given in the preamble to the statute:

> Whereas the elections of the knights of the shires to attend the parliaments of the King have in several counties of England recently been made by very large and excessive numbers of people living within the same counties the greater part of whom were of little or no means but everyone pretending to have an equivalent voice in the election to the most worthy knights and esquires living in the same shires will very likely cause homicides riots batteries and divisions between the gentlemen and other people living in the said counties unless a convenient and due remedy is provided.[3]

Whether the fear of murders, riots, batteries and any such divisions between the gentlemen and the ordinary people were real or conveniently imagined, the effect was plain; the franchise was restricted in late medieval times on the basis of the ownership of real property. As we shall see in Chapter 2, this restriction was not finally swept away until 1918, indeed it could plausibly be said that it was killed off in 1918,

---

2   The regnal year (8 Henry VI, dating from the anniversary of Henry's coronation), the legal year (counted from Lady Day – the Feast of the Annunciation – 25 March), and the calendar year obviously do not coincide so some texts give the date of the Act as 1430 whilst others give 1429. The consensus seems to be 1430, but Pickering's authoritative *Statutes at Large* (1762–1807) gives the date as 1429. That having been said, the conventional date of 1430 is adopted in this book.

3   The original text was in law French. It is unusual to find a statute passed as late as 1429–30 written in law French, especially as England was at war with France at the time. Law French was, by this date, much debased in spelling, grammar and syntax. The probable reason for it being written in law French is that the statute was addressed to lawyers in particular, ie the sheriffs, who were given the responsibility of checking that the voters were qualified. The original text was: '*Item come lez elections dez chevalers dez countees esluz a venire as parlements du Roi en plusours countees dEngleterre ore tarde ount estefaitz par trop graunde & excessive nombre dez gentz demurantz deinz mesmes les counts dount la greinde partie estoit par gentz sinon de petit avoir oude null valu dount chescun pretender davoir voice equivalent quant a tielx elections faire ove les pluis valantz chivalers ou esquires demurrantz deinz mesmes les countes dount homicides riotes batteries & divisions entre les gentiles & autres gentz de mesmes les countes verisemblablement fourdront & ferront si covenable remedie ne soit purveu en celle partie ….*' The translation is based on that given by Pickering (op cit, fn 2), but the text is unclear. The word '*valantz*' translated as 'worthy' is problematic. JAF Thomson (*op cit*, fn 5) appears to translate it as '*valiant*', but this is without foundation. JH Baker (1990) translates '*vaillance*' as 'value' and '*vaillant*' as 'worthy or mighty'. 'Worthy' is no more than a compromise and could refer to the knights and esquires being of great moral worth or of great financial worth. The context indicates that it is the latter.

but, as it were, failed to lie down flat until the decision in *Hipperson v ERO Newbury*[4] in 1984 or even the amendments to electoral registration brought in by the Representation of the People Act 2000. In various ways between 1429–30 and 1918, the franchise was certainly restricted to men on the basis of an estate in land (the ownership of a freehold or leasehold) despite a number of high profile political campaigns, which are considered in Chapter 2.

Thomson comments upon the 1430 changes as follows:

> It is clear that Parliament was representative, above all of the landed class, both through its control of the shire seats, with their greater prestige, and by its infiltration into the boroughs. Changes in electoral law were aimed at preserving its (ie, the landed class) authority against both the Crown and its inferiors.[5]

This clearly demonstrates that political ideology was a major driving force in electoral law from the earliest stages of development.

To give a more modern example is easy. A restriction of the franchise to the relatively wealthy reputedly has a political effect, although the magnitude and direction of the actual effect has been doubted by political scientists.[6] The reputed political effect of property ownership was stated in ringing tones by Sir Harold Bellman, one of the pioneers of the Building Society movement shortly after the 1926 General Strike:

> The working man who is merely a tenant has no real anchorage, no permanent abiding place, and in certain circumstances is fair prey for breeders of faction and revolutionaries of every sort and condition. Home ownership is a civic and national asset. The sense of citizenship is more keenly felt and appreciated, and personal independence opens up many an avenue of wide responsibility and usefulness. The benefits of home ownership are not merely material but ethical and moral as well. The man who has something to protect and improve – a stake of some sort in the country – naturally turns his thoughts in the direction of sane, ordered and perforce economical government.[7]

Whether or not the property qualification had a real effect upon the outlook of the electorate, all that really matters is that important opinion formers and parliamentarians thought that it did, and this induced them to design electoral law in accordance with their own interests.

---

4 *Hipperson and others v Electoral Registration Officer for the District of Newbury and another* [1985] 1 QB 1060.

5 Thomson, 1983, p 281.

6 See, eg, Crewe, 1988, p 31. 'Panel surveys refute the idea that voters switch from Labour to Conservative after buying their council house, or for that matter, their shares. House- and share-owners do not become Conservatives; rather Conservatives become house- and share-owners.'

7 Bellman, 1927, p 53.

BREADTH

If we wish to trace the development of election law and think of the endpoints of franchise reform as being 1430 and 2000, we can count a number of legislative milestones along the way. These are not the only markers, but they seem to be the most significant and they are discussed in more detail in Chapter 2, together with some of the reasoning underlying the reforms. *What sort of men shall be choosers and who shall be chosen knights of the parliament* set the standard for the county franchise from 1430 until 1832, whilst the borough franchise remained fragmented. The first major reform to the 1430 legislation was accomplished by the Reform Act of 1832, which widened the property-based franchise enjoyed by men over 21 years of age in both the county and the borough seats. These reforms were extended in 1867 and 1884, whereby the franchise was again extended to adult men lower down the property ladder. The major departure from the property-ownership principle came in 1918 when the franchise was extended to all men over 21 years of age and all women over 30 years of age. This was further reformed in 1928 when the voting age was reduced to 21 for women. The next major milestone was the reform in 1969–70, which reduced the age of majority (and hence the voting age) to 18 years of age. The final legislative reform came in 2000 when the move away from the franchise being dependent upon a person living in at least some form of identifiable property was completed. This is a brief sketch and the description will be completed in Chapter 2, but it is sufficient to show that the ideological premises upon which the franchise is based have (unsurprisingly) changed over the centuries. In 1430 only reasonably well-to-do adult men had the vote; by 2000 the franchise extended to all 18-year-olds.

METHOD

The development of the method of voting can similarly be traced, although the milestones are fewer and more dramatic. Until 1872 voting was in person and in public. The Ballot Act 1872 introduced the secret ballot conducted by means of the polling station, the polling booth, the secret (but numbered) ballot paper, and the ballot box. Why was this system introduced? During the period 1832–72, with the increase of the number of electors and the decline of the old methods of rigging elections effected by patronage, friendship and kinship, vote buying and voter coercion became more prevalent.[8] During this period a number of measures were introduced to control ballot rigging; the election petition procedure was updated and legislation was introduced to outlaw bribery (in its various forms) and coercion (again, in its many forms). The critical

---

[8] For a careful study of 19th century electoral corruption, see Seymour, C, 1915. Seymour discusses corruption and its control in four chapters; 'Electoral morality before 1854' (Chapter VII); 'The attack upon corruption 1832–54' (Chapter VIII); 'Electoral morality after 1854' (Chapter XIII); and 'The final attack upon corruption and excessive election expenditure' (Chapter XIV).

steps can be seen as the Corrupt Practices Act of 1854 and the Corrupt Practices Act of 1883, the 1868 Act and the 1872 Act. Seymour comments that:

> The Corrupt Practices Act of 1854 was a step of real importance towards the elimination of corruption. Like the Reform Act of 1832, it may claim the significance that attaches to the first in a series; without this rather halting attempt to meet the difficulties at hand the more successful legislation of later years would have been impossible. With all its weak points it indicated a possible solution of the problem and one which, when completed, was destined to prove satisfactory; namely the publication and examination of election expenses. The Corrupt Practices Act of 1883 was, it is true, so much stricter in degree as to almost differ in kind from that of 1854; but it rested, after all upon the principles introduced by the earlier legislation.[9]

It is argued that the same comment, *mutatis mutandis*, can be made about all three pieces of legislation. The 1854 Act[10] introduced the principle that certain electoral practices (bribing, treating – bribing by means of food and, especially, drink – and intimidation) were outlawed. This was extended by the Corrupt and Illegal Practices Act 1883, which also required candidates to account for their election expenditure.

The Parliamentary Elections Act 1868 is an important piece of legislation and it provides the foundation of the modern law of election petitions. An 'election petition' is quite simply a legal challenge to an election. It was introduced in its current form by the 1868 Act. It has a curious name because of its history. Originally an 'election petition' was an actual petition to the House of Commons from a disgruntled elector or candidate asking the House of Commons to overturn the result of an election. In *Ashby v White*,[11] the jurisdiction was firmly established to lie in the House of Commons; it being said that, according to the Bill of Rights of 1689, Parliament was the only body that could determine its own proceedings. However this meant that the House of Commons could, by the simple production of a parliamentary majority, determine whether an election was fairly conducted. This was hardly satisfactory. Clearly members of the parliamentary majority would be, at the least, predisposed to assist their own party members in a disputed election and hinder their opponents. By the early 19th century this politicisation of electoral challenges had proved so controversial that attempts were made to pass the jurisdiction to the ordinary common law courts. By the

---

9 Seymour, 1915, p 385.

10 Corrupt Practices Prevention Act 1854, 17&18 Vict. ch 102.

11 (1703) 2 Ld Raym 938, but see the discussion in Chapter 2.

1860s, the desire for change had grown to be irresistible, not least because, as Seymour pointed out in the following passage:

> ... by 1868 it was the general opinion in the country that the committees of the House [of Commons] must inevitably err on the side of leniency, even if they possessed the requisite legal ability. They would never be willing to put a stigma upon a gentleman, or convict and sentence him, after he had 'parted freely from his money' [in bribing electors].[12]

The 1868 Act provided a method of challenging election results through the ordinary courts. The procedure was, and remains, simple. An elector who believes that an election was not properly conducted can go to a specially convened court – for a parliamentary election, a special court (an Election Court) within the Administrative Court,[13] for a local election, a Commissioner – and provided that the elector has complied with certain, rather onerous, procedural rules, the elector can ask the court to overturn the result of the election and require that it be rerun. The current procedure is now set out in Pt III of the Representation of the People Act 1983.

The Ballot Act 1872 introduced the principle of the secret ballot. The intention behind the Act was to free electors from bribery and intimidation so that they might freely cast their votes.[14] The actual passage of the Act was extremely interesting. Seymour wrote, illustrating his view from a contemporary account, that:

> The final stages were passed without enthusiasm, and the great institutional change was completed, according to a contemporary account, 'in spite of the all but unanimous hostility of the House of Lords, the secret disapproval of the House of Commons and the indifference of the general community'.[15]

The dislike of the secret ballot was, of course, due to the fact that rich, powerful people and the political party organisations found it much more difficult to suborn voters when and where they could not see the actual ballot being cast. The degree of corruption in some boroughs had been so marked that those boroughs were deprived of representation after inquiries by Parliamentary Commissioners.[16] The long-running

---

12 Seymour, 1915, p 422.
13 After the original transfer to the courts, the Petition was tried, of course, on the Crown side of the Court of Queen's Bench.
14 See Seymour, 1915, pp 427–28.
15 Seymour, 1915, pp 431–32. Seymour quotes the *Annual Register* of 1872 p 72.
16 See Seymour, 1915, pp 421–22, who draws attention to the disenfranchisement of the boroughs of Reigate, Yarmouth, Totnes, Lancaster, Beverly (*sic*) and Bridgwater. For full details see *Parliamentary Papers*, 1867 3774, 3775, 3776, 3777, and 1870, c10, c15.

battle for the secret ballot, as outlined in Chapter 2, would seem to question whether the indifference was really as marked as Seymour's source believes. Clearly there were huge shifts in the governing ideology over the course of the 19th century. At the beginning of the period, public voting was usual and generally by the beginning of the 20th century everyone voted in secret.

When looking at the few examples given so far, one cannot fail to be struck by the fact that the powerful people who ruled the country were always ready to try to use the law – either by passing or declining to pass legislation – to buttress their power. In the 19th century the manoeuvres were explicit; we shall see that there was a more subtle approach in later years.

In any event, the basic legislation governing modern election procedures was firmly in place by 1900 and it remained fundamentally unaltered until 1998. The centrepiece of the modern law of election procedure remains the Representation of the People Act 1983 (RPA 1983), although it has been supplemented by legislation introduced by the Labour government following their initial victory in 1997. Many, but not all, of the legal rules discussed in this book are to be found in the 1983 Act. Richard Clayton, then the editor of *Parker's Law and Conduct of Elections*,[17] wrote shortly after the 1997 general election, as follows:

> The RPA 1983 consolidates the RPA 1949 and various enactments amending it. That Act of 1949 was itself a consolidation of earlier legislation. A consolidation cannot alter the substance of the earlier law. Accordingly much of the 1983 Act derives from legislation enacted in the 19th century. As respects parliamentary elections the three principal Acts were the Ballot Act 1872 (from which the rules in Schedule 1 to the 1983 Act derive), the Parliamentary Elections Act 1868 (from which much of Part III of the 1983 Act derives) and the Corrupt and Illegal Practices Prevention Act 1883.[18]

Since 1997 the position has changed, there has been a flurry of legislation and the RPA 1983 is now joined by the Representation of the People Act 2000 and the Political Parties Elections and Referendums Act 2000 Act (which re-enacts the Registration of Political Parties Act 1998). These three Acts (the 1983 Act and the two 2000 Acts) now contribute to the foundation of the modern law of elections.

The 1983 Act, as amended, contains most of the fundamental legislation covering the administration of elections. Part One of the Act continues the system of registration of electors first established by the Reform Act 1832. It also sets out the method of voting to be used in parliamentary and local government elections – providing for the

---

17 *Parker's Law and Conduct of Elections*, 1996 (plus updates).
18 See s 1.2.

appointment of returning officers, the provision of polling places etc – and defines a number of election offences. Most notably, s 66 of the Act provides for secrecy of the ballot.

Part Two of the amended 1983 Act sets out the scheme of the election campaign. It regulates the appointment of election agents (where candidates choose to have them), and contains the outline of the regulation of election expenditure. These provisions also regulate the categories of people who may lawfully be engaged as election workers. It contains provisions for the control of election publicity and election meetings. The most important election offences are set out in this part of the Act.

Part Three of the Act contains the provisions for challenging the result of an election – the election petition procedure – which, as we have seen above, was established as a legal (as opposed to a parliamentary) procedure by the Parliamentary Elections Act 1868. There are a number of other provisions in the Act, but they are of lesser importance.

The Representation of the People Act 2000 is important in that it brought in a new system of voter registration. This will be described below. The main importance of the 2000 Act is that it amended the 1983 Act in a number of ways, rather than bringing in wholly novel provisions.

The Political Parties, Elections and Referendums Act 2000 (PPERA) is of far greater significance. The Act is divided into 10 parts. Part I of the Act establishes the Electoral Commission and sets out some of its general functions. Those functions include reporting on particular elections and referendums and reviewing electoral law. The Commission is also responsible, under this part of the Act, for promoting understanding of electoral and political matters and administering the provision of policy development grants to qualifying political parties. Part I also transfers to the Commission the functions of the four Parliamentary Boundary Commissions and of the Local Government Commission for England and the Local Government Boundary Commissions for Scotland and Wales.

Part II of the Act re-enacts the Registration of Political Parties Act 1998 (RPPA 1998), which is discussed in detail in Chapter 4. It modifies the registration scheme by providing accounting and funding regimes with which registered political parties must comply. These regimes are set out in Pts III and IV of PPERA 2000. Controls on national election campaign expenditure are established by Pt VI of the PPERA 2000.

Part VIII of the Act makes a number of amendments to the RPA1983. It imposes controls on donations to candidates, increases the limit on expenses that may be incurred by a candidate at a parliamentary by-election, clarifies the meaning of 'election expenses', amends the law in relation to election petitions and clarifies the law in respect of the consequences of the commission of corrupt and illegal practices. The other parts of the Act (VII, IX and X) do not require discussion. It should be pointed out from the beginning that this is not a textbook of election law. The most comprehensive text is *Schofield's Election Law* (here referred to as *Schofield*) and extensive references are made to that encyclopaedic loose-leaf work.[19]

Schofield takes up approximately 6,000 pages of text. It must be supplemented by law reports, notably by O'Malley and Hardcastle's Reports (usually abbreviated as O'M & H), which contain reports of election petitions from the end of the 1860s to the beginning of the 1930s. There are many other single reports of election cases spread throughout the law reports. These cases come from all over the United Kingdom; indeed, some useful cases are Irish and date from the time when the island of Ireland was part of Britain. Other powerful cases come from the European Court of Human Rights, and useful illustrative cases can also be found in a number of jurisdictions, most notably, the United States of America and the Republic of Ireland. The body of UK election law is vast, but surely it must have some underlying principles. It does, so what are the main principles underlying the law – what is its ideology?

This question can be answered very shortly in the words of Art 3 of the 1st Protocol to the European Convention of Human Rights.

> The High Contracting Parties undertake to hold free elections at reasonable intervals by secret ballot, under conditions which will ensure the free expression of the opinion of the people in the choice of the legislature.

In the *Greek* case,[20] the European Commission of Human Rights made an important observation that goes toward explaining Art 3. Article 3 'presupposes the existence of a representative legislature, elected at reasonable intervals, as the basis of a democratic society.' Thus free and fair elections are the mechanism which underpins a democratic society. What is a 'democratic society'? We should start with a formal description.

Democracy – a formal description

The central notions of modern democracy are:

* popular sovereignty
* political equality

---

19 Mates, Scallan, and Gribble, 1996 (plus updates).
20 12YB 1 (1969) Eu Comm HR.

- moderated majoritarianism;

and these lead into the practice of:

- political representation;

and thus into the practice of:

- voting in elections.

All of these ideas and practices need some explanation, and the explanation of the last – voting in elections – will take up nearly this entire book. However, and for present purposes, the others may be explained much more succinctly. The principles are set out rather thinly and no defence is offered for the descriptions. They are certainly not secure against strong attack; indeed one of the characteristics of democracy, which seems to distinguish it from other political systems, is that even its central notions are contestable in principle and are contested in fact.

Popular sovereignty means, at its simplest, that, save where the people are wholly self-governing, as in, for example, those in the position of citizens in an Athenian democracy, the governors gain their authority from those whom they govern. A free person is, within the constraints of their capacities – physical, mental, social and economic – a self-governing person. If self-governing people give up part of their self-governance to others, whether merely to secure co-ordination of their activities, to secure defence from aggression from neighbours near or far, or to secure their greater positive freedoms, their governors must remain accountable to them. This notion is therefore linked to the practice of political representation.

Political equality means simply that, provided citizens fall within a broad range of capacities, defined by, for example, age, mental capacity, and freedom from legal disability such as imprisonment, all may take part on an equal footing in the choosing of the governors, and have an equal opportunity of themselves becoming a governor. Clearly the 'content' of political equality is strongly contested. For example, it is only in comparatively recent times that women have been enfranchised in Britain. People did disagree over the question as to whether women and men ought to be politically equal citizens and, whilst this question is now resolved with a resounding 'yes', other questions of equality remain unresolved.

Moderated majoritarianism, as a general principle, simply holds that in a democracy, as opposed to, say, an oligarchy or a monarchy, the expressed view of a numerical majority of citizens prevails over the view of a minority. If there were 100 electors and, in a vote as to whether a new bridge should be built, 30 voted for the Bridge-building Party, whilst 20 voted for the 'No Bridge Here Coalition', and the remaining 50 did not vote, majoritarianism would decree that the bridge be built. The bridge would be built irrespective of the view of the monarch, the priest or the plutocrat. However, there is an exception to this principle. Following the introduction of human rights legislation, certain 'super-laws' have been embedded into national legal systems which preclude certain types of decision in the face of a majority, super-majority or even unanimity of the electorate. Majoritarianism may be said to be moderated by these special rules (or super-laws) that give protection to minorities.

These three central concepts, when taken together, seem to result in a practical definition of democracy, which should serve to support the rest of the debate in this book.

The practice of *political representation* or parliamentary democracy is of fundamental importance to voting; it provides a reason for voting. In a large modern state there is simply too much governing to be done to leave it in the hands of the people; they must choose representatives to do the work for them. As we have seen above, the notions of popular sovereignty and political equality demand that the representatives are chosen from the people, by the people, and remain in some way accountable to them.

The phenomenon of citizens *voting in elections* is the distinguishing characteristic of a democracy. In a parliamentary democracy there must be some method for choosing the governors. Periodic elections provide both the method for choosing the governors and the method of ensuring accountability. From time to time, the governors have to submit themselves for re-election and, at least in theory, if they have not efficiently done that of which the majority of electors approve they are unseated. Clearly the story is not as simple as this, it may be that a particular representative has failed but is re-elected because their rivals are much less desirable still or there may be questions about the capacity or trustworthiness of a particular party to form and maintain a credible government which destroy otherwise strong candidates or strengthen weak ones.

It is also clear that there are a variety of electoral methods available. Most elections in Britain are held in single member constituencies on a first-past-the-post method, but there are other electoral methods in use. Top-up party lists, transferable votes and other methods, including proportional representation, are or soon may be in use. It is noteworthy that the European Convention of Human Rights does not require adherence to any particular formal model of democracy or voting system. This point was made in *Mathieu-Mohn v Belgium*,[21] in which it was said that states have a wide *margin of appreciation* in implementing the right protected by the Article. This means that it is not for the Court to impose a particular electoral system, such as 'first past the post', 'proportional representation', 'single transferable vote,' or indeed, any other, upon a High Contracting Party.[22] However, that having been said, it remains for the European Court of Human Rights to determine whether the electoral system in a state conforms to the standards of the Convention. This point was also made in *Mathieu-Mohn* and acknowledged in the English Court of Appeal by Sedley LJ in *Knight v Nicholls*.[23]

However, it is clear that the formal model is not sufficient. We would not call a state a democracy if only a small proportion of the electorate bothered to vote. Neither would we say that a state was democratic if people habitually voted for the party they had selected at the roll of a dice (for example, 1 or 4 – Conservative; 2 or 5 – Liberal Democrat; 3 or 6 – Labour). We would certainly not call an election democratic, if it was characterised by widespread intimidation or bribery of the electorate. Clearly these examples are somewhat fanciful, but only *somewhat*; what do we think when the turnout in a general election falls below an *acceptable* figure? This begs the question – *what is an acceptable turnout*? Similarly, what if a significant proportion of the electorate does not consider their vote *sufficiently carefully – what is sufficiently carefully*? What if the electoral procedures fall short of the ideal of perfection?

We could (more or less) meet the requirements of the formal model of democracy by having a low turnout of insouciant voters in a poorly designed electoral system. In fact, if most of the voters did not really care about the result, a faulty electoral system is all that is required because no one would bother to complain unless the errors were egregious.

From the outset let it be said that the aspiration is for a 100% turnout of electors, all of whom have considered their vote fully and carefully; and that the electoral system ought to be perfect. Clearly this ideal will never be met; but it is argued that we should have the highest aspirations. Let's start by looking at some aspects of the reality.

---

21 10 EHRR 1, see especially para 54.

22 This is the term used by the Council of Europe for its members; it is analogous to the use of the term 'Member States' when referring to members of the European Union.

23 [2004] EWCA Civ 68, paras 37–39.

Turnout, party membership and political engagement

Participation in the electoral process has fallen.[24] The percentage turnout in the June 2001 general election was, at 59.4%, the lowest recorded for a parliamentary election since the extension of suffrage to all women by s 2 of the Representation of the People (Equal Franchise) Act 1928. Indeed it could be argued that the percentage turnout of actual voters in 1918, during which election only women over 30 were entitled to vote was, in fact, higher in real terms than the 2001 turnout because the 1918 election was conducted on the basis of electoral registers which were at least 11 months old. Many registered male voters remained in France, some never to return. In any event, the mean turnout in general elections over the period 1834 –1998 was 72.62% (standard deviation = 7.74%),[25] and a turnout some 18% lower than this mean is, by any measure, exceptional. This may be a temporary phenomenon because the turnout in other countries has recovered after a slump. In both the 2004 Spanish general election and the 2004 US presidential election rises in participation seemed to reverse long-run declines in turnout.

The turnout in the 2005 UK general election requires some comment. Whilst the turnout was approximately 2% higher than the nadir recorded in 2001 at 61.3%, an analysis of the share of the votes cast is revealing. Labour obtained 9.56 million votes (35.2% of votes cast, supported by 21.6% of the total electorate), the Conservatives 8.77 million (32.3% votes cast, 19.8% of the total electorate), the Liberal Democrats 5.98 million (22% votes cast, 13.5% of the total electorate). The remaining 10.5% of the votes (6.4% of the total electorate) were split between a variety of regional or minor parties. The election of a government with the support of only just over one fifth of the total electorate is of grave concern when considered from the perspective of representative democracy – ie just how representative is the government in any case? The fact that such a government, with a parliamentary majority of 66 (or, counting the Speaker, of 67) has the ability radically to alter electoral law is of even greater import. However, at this stage of the argument the figures are simply used to demonstrate the gap between the government and the people.

If one looks at the 2001 UK general election one is struck by young people's reluctance to vote. It has been reported that three out of four people young people (aged between 18 and 24 years) did not vote.[26] The

---

24 For a complete account and some useful analysis, see Curtice, J and Seyd, B, 2004, pp 93–107.

25 Raw data taken from Rallings and Thrasher, 2000.

26 *Elections in the 21st Century: from paper ballot to e-voting. Report of the Independent Commission on Alternative Voting Methods*, 2002, London: Electoral Reform Society, See Dr Stephen Coleman's 'Foreword' p 5.

Electoral Commission has recommended, in *Age of Electoral Majority: Report and Recommendations*,[27] that the age of electoral majority be left unchanged for at least a period of five to seven years because many young people do not feel sufficiently politically mature or well informed to vote. One of the Commission's conclusions was that reducing the voting age now would further depress the percentage turnout in elections.

Political parties themselves seem to be in decline. In 1964 some 3.26 million people were members of the three main British political parties; by 1992 this had fallen to 0.88 million, whilst it is currently believed to be in the region of 0.7 million. The Electoral Commission/Hansard Society audit determined that only 5% of its respondents had attended a political party meeting, donated money or paid a membership fee to a political party in the last year. It may be that some of the enthusiasm within the political parties for 'electronic democracy', telephone canvassing and the like is motivated by their lack of party workers willing to foot slog, for the same study discovered that a mere 1% of respondents to the survey had taken part in a general or local election campaign.

There may well be an increase in other forms of political activity, in particular those associated with protests against the recent wars in Iraq and elsewhere, and in anti-capitalist protest.[28] In reaching this conclusion, Curtice and Seyd have commented upon their empirical data that:

> ... electoral participation may have fallen, but it has been accompanied by an increase in non-electoral participation [such as, taking part in demonstrations, signing petitions, writing to an MP], an increase that cannot itself be regarded as the cause of the decline in turnout. So the participation crisis in Britain is confined to the ballot box, and it is not part of a wider decline in the willingness of citizens to engage with the political system.

One might then turn to matters of political consciousness measured by means of the broadcast and print media visibility of political issues. The amount of serious political coverage in the press seems to be decreasing. Calvert[29] takes the view that, in the USA, press reports about potentially significant political events and about politically significant personalities (for example, the President) stress the personal or 'human interest story' at the expense of the political or public interest story. Calvert emphasises

---

27 London; The Electoral Commission 2004. But see, in the USA, Plan to lower California vote age (9 March 2004) http://news.bbc.co.uk/1/hi/education/3545933.stm.

28 See, for example, Curtice and Seyd, 2004, p 104.

29 Calvert, 2000, p 273.

the 'narcotyzing dysfunction' that such stories have, especially when coupled with consumption of the output of the mass communication media 'that substitutes passive observation and spectacle for active (political) participation'.[30] British evidence of this effect is revealed in the Electoral Commission/Hansard Society audit, *An audit of political engagement*,[31] in which it was estimated that only 38% of its respondents had discussed politics or political news in the past two to three years.

Furthermore, political parties are often themselves enthusiastic contributors to the trivialisation of complex political issues. For example, in 2003 when party political broadcasting was being debated,[32] the political parties themselves were keen to reduce the minimum length of a party political broadcast below two minutes and 40 seconds because they believed that they could make their points more powerfully using shorter, more frequent broadcasts. After making the point that even a two minute and 40 second party political broadcast is five times as long as the typical television advertisement, the Electoral Commission report goes on to say that it believes that it is possible to present a serious political message in less than that time. The Electoral Commission observes that:

> [m]any political news reports or political party press releases are short in length, with journalists and politicians alike recognising that in mass communication it is often more effective to make one clear point than attempting a lengthy, more detailed argument.[33]

This contradicts the Commission's earlier assertion that many political parties and broadcasters are opposed to substantial shortening of party election broadcasts. These respondents apparently argue that party political broadcasts should contain substantive political messages and that shortening the length would dilute the presentation and discussion of serious policy issues and thus 'encourage over-simplification, sloganeering and spin'.[34]

The suggestion is that people are becoming disengaged from the political process and that politics is becoming more like entertainment or a 'shopping experience'. Can any examples of this sort of disengagement or the conversion of politics into a commercial or entertainment enterprise be found? Amongst the most far-reaching development in this area is the promotion by Independent Television of a 'reality television

---

30 Calvert, 2000, p 279.
31 (London: Electoral Commission/Hansard Society, 2004) ISBN: 1-904363-38-5.
32 Party Political Broadcasts: Report and Recommendations Electoral Commission, 2003; see, especially, p 31.
33 Quotations in this paragraph all come from p 31 of the Electoral Commission, 2003.
34 *Ibid.*

show', inspired by the popular 'Pop Idol' format, in which contestants will be able to seek on-screen selection to stand as an independent candidate in the next general election. The idea is that ten potential candidates will be selected from amongst a pool of volunteers attracted by newspaper, television and website advertisements and, according to John Plunkett writing in the *Guardian* Media section on 20 April 2004, over 1,400 people have already applied to be considered as a candidate. The television show, 'Vote for me!', has already attracted unfavourable comment from at least two of the main political parties, which claim that it tends to trivialise the political process.[35]

Furthermore, Patrick Barrett writes that Conservative Party advertising strategists are 'abandoning overtly negative attacks' on Labour, such as the infamous red-eyed picture of Mr Blair (dubbed 'devil eyes') and replacing it with 'consumer style advertising humour, they say, will be a key weapon in their bid to unseat Tony Blair in the next year's expected general election'.[36]

Barrett goes on to report that the Conservative Party marketing director, Will Harris, who created the 'devil eyes' advertisement together with the Tory co-chairman, Lord Saatchi, said:

> There is a new appetite for a different type of political message. Very personal attacks don't seem to work these days. This approach is an oblique negative; it's amusing rather than an out-and-out negative attack. We want to do this as part of a general approach. We are looking at voters as consumers; they are the same people who buy sofas or cans of fizzy drink. We are trying to inject a bit of humanity into what we do.[37]

Harris's apparently 'throw-away' comment is telling. He makes an explicit link between voters and consumers.[38] It will be argued below that this connection is profoundly anti-democratic, but, despite this unfavourable view of the Conservative Party's campaign, it should not be taken as a criticism of the Conservative Party itself. It is beyond any serious doubt that the other political parties are engaged in very much the same sort of venture. For example, the Labour Party published a poster in 2005 depicting the Conservative leader and Shadow Chancellor as flying pigs. It is a criticism of modern political parties and modern politics.

---

35 See Leonard, 16 April 2004; and Plunkett, 20 April 2004. This series, entitled 'Vote for me!', started on Monday 10 January 2005 at 11pm. It is difficult to imagine that this, in the author's opinion, ludicrous series will have a positive effect on the political process.

36 Barrett, P, the *Guardian*, 23 March 2004 'Tories swap vitriol for humour in bid to unseat Blair'.

37 Will Harris quoted in Barrett, 2004.

38 He was not the first Conservative so to do. Patrick Minford, 1988, observed that political parties sell their wares in the marketplace of politics.

Before we can proceed further down this path of analysing the commercialisation of politics, it is necessary to draw a fundamental distinction – that between a 'constitutional citizen' and a 'market citizen' – the two conceptions of citizenship suggested by, amongst others, Mark Freedland. In distinguishing them he writes that a constitutional citizen is one who has a claim to participate in the processes of democracy and who is entitled to the protections afforded by constitutional and administrative law. That is to say, a person who has the right to be treated as a free and equal citizen with the right to fair treatment from the state in the handling of their affairs. A market citizen (or consumer citizen) is one whose primary role or position is one of a discriminating purchaser of goods and services, and the maker and enforcer of economically sound and rational consumer contracts.[39]

We can build upon this distinction by suggesting that a *democratic* polity is one in which the relationship between the representative government and the electorate is based upon an active participation in the processes of democracy, and the relationship between citizens and the state is actively governed by constitutional and administrative law. In a democratic polity the courts should be ready to step in to ensure that the electoral system is being operated fairly. On the other hand, a *market* system is one in which each citizen's involvement is limited to periodically choosing between the political parties on offer – in much the way as consumers choose between (to use the words of Will Harris) 'sofas or cans of fizzy drink'.

The suggestion is that, as shown by the kind of evidence marshalled above, citizens were transformed from being the more-or-less politically active constitutional citizens of the immediate post-Second World War period into more-or-less politically inactive market citizens sometime in the 1990s. It may be wrong to think of the 1997 election as the last 'political election' because, as Pippa Norris[40] describes, that campaign itself might well be described as consumer-orientated; indeed, she characterises it as 'postmodern' – centrally managed, tailored towards the media and designed to project the relevant party (as distinct from its policies) in the most favourable light, but it seems that 'consumer-orientated' is a more accurate description. She observes, furthermore, that the change in the style of election campaigning was gradual rather than sudden and took place over a number of elections. The evidence set out above demonstrates a drop in electoral participation and a rise in that which may well be called 'glitz'.

---

39 Freedland, 1998.
40 Norris, 1998, Chapter 5.

A political market?

Some might argue that the political process is correctly conceived as a marketplace of ideas. For example, in *R v Secretary of State for the Home Dept, ex p Simms*,[41] Lord Steyn said:

> Secondly, in the famous words of Holmes J (echoing John Stuart Mill), 'the best test of truth is the power of the thought to get itself accepted in the competition of the market': *Abrams v US* (1919) 250 US 616 at 630 per Holmes J (dissent). Thirdly, freedom of speech is the lifeblood of democracy. The free flow of information and ideas informs political debate. It is a safety valve: people are more ready to accept decisions that go against them if they can in principle seek to influence them. It acts as a brake on the abuse of power by public officials. It facilitates the exposure of errors in the governance and administration of justice of the country: see Stone, Seidman, Sunstein and Tushnett *Constitutional Law* (3rd edn, 1996) pp 1078–1086.

This seems to be correct; it cannot be doubted that a democracy is a marketplace of ideas, whilst in a totalitarian system one idea has triumphed over all others and its position is maintained ultimately by force. There is no necessary connection between the use of modern marketing methods and the continuation of a democratic way of life. Political parties may put their policies before the public in such a way that the ideas may be soberly considered and debated, rather than being packaged in such a way as to obscure the substance. However, there are two points to be made here and care must be taken not to elide them.

The first point goes to style and the more important second point goes to substance. The words 'the marketplace of ideas' are, at least for some, linked to the 19th century thought of John Stuart Mill or, further back, to the Athenian *agora*. This immediately brings to mind an image of serious-minded citizens engaged in the debate of weighty matters. The words are also linked to a more homely idea; they conjure up a collection of stalls from which prudent, rational and engaged consumers can pick the best of the wholesome products on offer. If we were instead to use the phrase 'the shopping mall of ideas', we would have a radically different image.

The shopping mall is well described by Jean Baudrillard in his book *The Consumer Society*.[42] Baudrillard describes '*Parly2 – the biggest shopping centre in Europe*' in a somewhat florid and exotic blend of his own text and the centre's self-description.[43] Having described the artificiality of

---

41 [2000] 2 AC 115 at 126.
42 Baudrillard, 1998.
43 See pp 29–31.

the environment, which is controlled so as to produce the effect of 'a permanent springtime', and the payment methods available (such as credit cards), which break the link between the pleasure of acquisition and the pain of payment, Baudrillard goes on to describe the effect of this lifestyle upon the consumers. Once again Baudrillard's style may be found rather ornate, but his sense is clear. His analysis is that the modern market ideology has emptied our lives; all contradictions and difficulties have been resolved into – in his words – 'an eternal combinatory of ambience in a perpetual springtime'.[44]

Baudrillard's proposal is that modern marketing techniques have transformed the marketplace into the shopping mall. Consumers of goods have been seduced, perhaps neither unwillingly nor unwittingly, into environments where they spend their money irrespective of the consequences because they focus only upon the pleasure of acquisition and consumption. One wonders whether political advertising and marketing has reached the same levels of hyperbole. Successive party manifestos seem to offer increasingly attractive policies at lower and lower rates of taxation, all to be funded by some form of efficiency gain. Modern voting techniques, a matter discussed in detail in Chapter 3, offer the convenience of the 'voting mall' or 'on-line voting – and the similarity with on-line shopping is inescapable.

Shifting the focus to the substantive problems of the market model, it is important to note that it has many advocates, including some who believe that the market approach is more democratic. The most highly articulated argument to this effect has been set out by Jennifer Lees-Marshment in _Political Marketing and British Political Parties: The Party's Just Begun_.[45] Lees-Marshment argues that marketing theory should be rigorously applied to the competition of political parties for votes, and she applies a typology familiar to marketing practitioners in order to develop her case. She divides marketing, whether of an orthodox good or of a political party, into three types of orientation. First, she describes a _product-oriented_ market strategy. A party following this strategy would design its policies according to its own ideologies and lay them before the electorate. If the electorate declined to elect the party to government, that party would simply conclude that 'the customer is ignorant and lacks appreciation of how good the product is'.[46] By way of illustration Lees-Marshment claims that this type of political marketing was exemplified by the Labour Party in the 1983 general election. She presents strong evidence to the effect that 'Labour was a Product-

---

44 See p 30.
45 Lees-Marshment, 2001.
46 At p 23.

Oriented Party, holding the view that politics is (and should be) about standing up for what you believe in', and quotes Jim Mortimer (the party general secretary) as saying, '[i]t is not the Party's policy, but public opinion which needs to be changed'.[47]

The second strategy that Lees-Marshment describes is the *sales-oriented* approach. Here again the party develops its policy internally in accordance with its own ideological commitments, but 'puts more effort into selling the good. The focus is on employing sales techniques such as advertising and direct mail to persuade buyers that they want the good the firm is offering. It tries to create the demand rather than respond to it.'[48] Lees-Marshment argues, again convincingly, that the Labour party in the 1987 and 1992 general elections adopted a sales-oriented approach; she demonstrates how the party used all the available techniques of market research to find out how potential Labour voters viewed the party, and then tailored the campaign toward wooing these voters.[49] Lees-Marshment is highly critical of these two strategies; she appears to believe that they are undemocratic in that they privilege party activists and members in the design of party policies and manifestos. She believes that a third approach to political marketing is both necessary and more democratic – the *market-oriented* approach. Here the political party would incorporate market information into the design of its policies, so as to 'deliver a product that reflects (the) needs and wants' of voters.[50] Lees-Marshment suggests, and backs her claim with an impressive array of evidence, that the Labour (or rather, the New Labour)[51] victory in 1997 should be ascribed to the party adopting a market-oriented approach.[52] Whilst she acknowledges that there were faults in the marketing process which could, she thinks, have been avoided, she concludes that the 1997–2001 Labour government succeeded because of its market orientation.

Her most telling two paragraphs, encapsulating her idea, begin her sixth chapter. The chapter is entitled 'The party's just begun' and the two paragraphs should be quoted in full; they summarise her entire argument and it is my intention to refute her case.

> British political parties use political marketing to win elections. Specifically they become Market-Oriented Parties. They conduct market intelligence to identify and understand people's demands; both their needs and wants.

47 Quotations from p 131.
48 Quotation from p 24.
49 See Chapter 4 of Lees-Marshment, 2001.
50 See p 24.
51 See p 186.
52 See Lees-Marshment, 2001, Chapter 5, 'Blair and the New Labour design: a classic market-oriented party'.

They then design a product, including leader, policy and organisation that responds to these demands, but is also one that they can deliver in government, is believable and is adjusted to suit internal views within the organisation. They also take into account the nature of the competition and the support they have or need to win an election. The product design is then implemented throughout the party and then communicated to voters on a daily basis over a number of years leading up to an election. The actual election campaign is then almost superfluous to requirements but provides the last chance to convey to voters what is on offer. If the party is the most market-oriented of its main competitors, it then wins the election.

At other times parties may move towards traditional politics and become more product-oriented; simply arguing for what they think is right. This does not win a general election, however. Similarly, Sales-Oriented Parties, the type most commonly associated with political marketing can produce well-organised and professional election campaigns. But a Sales-Oriented Party can never get to the heart of the British people. As Britain's electoral market will no longer vote for a party simply because their family supported them in the past, it will also not warm to snappy advertising and clever slogans, or sound-bites and spin-doctors. This is not enough for the British electorate. If politics is to do anything for the people of this country, it must deliver what they need and want, not just discuss political ideologies remote from their everyday lives.[53]

On the face of it, Lees-Marshment seems to be correct; politics must connect with the people, and the government must 'deliver the goods', but, as I shall seek to show, she simply misses the point about democracy by confusing it with the market.

It has already been argued that a democratic society is one in which all members of society have a stake in deciding upon the common goods of society. A polity in which each person individually takes delivery of what they 'need and want' is not a democratic society – it is a collection of atomised individuals. Markets are mechanisms for aggregating individual demands and facilitating the fulfilment of individual goods, whilst democracies are mechanisms for ensuring the collective good. An example might help to elucidate the point. It might well be in the individual interests of voters that the government pursue policies that lead to a steady and sustained increase in the price of houses. The average cost of a house in Britain was £178,796 on 14 March 2005, an annual rate of increase of 10%.[54] Individuals have profited from the economic system that drives house prices and it would be unrealistic to expect them to wish to see their gains evaporate; however it may well be in the interests of society more generally for house prices to fall very

53 Lees-Marshment, 2001, p 211.
54 http://news.bbc.co.uk/1/hi/business/4346847.stm.

sharply so as to promote wider property ownership.[55] Democracy is about more than the reflection of the majority interest. Indeed, it could be argued that the root of democracy is in a society which affords the opportunities to make meaningful choices to all of its members.[56]

Furthermore, Lees-Marshment misses a seemingly obvious point. Suppose that no party adopts a market-oriented approach in a general election, but all parties simply use product-oriented approaches. One might argue that all the general elections between 1834 and 1974 were fought between product-oriented parties; despite that fact a party won each election. The point is that one of the candidates *must* always win an election whether or not they utilise techniques of political marketing of whatever variety. Treating democratic elections as if they were akin to purchases, the culmination of a marketing exercise, mistakes the function and purpose of elections. Elections are designed to provide the country with a government to represent the public will for a period of up to five years.[57] Not many commercial transactions are designed to last for that length of time in the face of changing circumstances and it may well be that a government which starts out with one set of political priorities is obliged to change them in the face of ensuing events. Where local authorities are involved it would seem that there is judicial support for the proposition that a party's election manifesto should not be taken seriously at all,[58] but should be reconsidered in the light of developing circumstances.

In the field of contract law, Ian MacNeil draws a distinction between *spot* and *relational* contracts.[59] The paradigm of a spot contract is a one-off consumer contract for a discrete consumer good, such as a sofa or a can of fizzy drink; it is a discrete transaction that does not represent or signify any intention by the parties to repeat the deal. No relationship is formed between the parties beyond that necessary to complete the single bargain. On the other hand, a relational contract is one which represents the framework within which a number of exchanges can and do take place; a contract of employment or a long-term contract for the supply of goods over a number of years are good examples. Within such a framework the parties build a relationship and adapt one to the other. It

---

55 The arguments in favour of property ownership, as supported by a mortgage, are helpfully summarised in Gray, K, 1993, pp 931–96; and in the later edition, Gray, K, and Gray, SF, 2001, pp 1361–363. The sources cited range from Otto Kahn-Freund's introduction to the works of Karl Renner, to a speech delivered by Michael Heseltine, so it would seem that there is a broad political consensus.

56 See, generally, Raz, 1986.

57 Section 5 Parliament Act 1911.

58 See *Bromley LBC v GLC* [1983] 1AC 768 – this is generally known as the *Fares Fair* case.

59 MacNeil and Campbell, 2001.

is suggested that the relationship between the government and the citizens of a state ought to be closer to the relational model than the spot model. A state needs to be administered as an ongoing concern. It needs long-term planning and sometimes governments need to take unpopular measures in order to deal with some structural problem – environmental degradation and global warming or economic restructuring provide ready examples. The government may well have to adopt unpopular and painful policies to deal with these problems. Lees-Marshment's model seems to be more applicable to a spot contract model of government in which successive governments leap from one set of popular policies to another.

Finally, it should be observed that Lees-Marshment is providing, under cover of political neutrality, a recipe for governments that cater for the majority's desires rather than for the common good. It seems apposite to sum up her view in a reversal of the slogan contained in President John F Kennedy's inaugural address[60] – 'Ask not what you can do for your country – ask what your country can do for you.' Just as Kennedy's original slogan[61] was, of course, politically charged, so Lees-Marshment buys into an ideology that favours the market. This ideology favours the choice by individuals of their own *personal* selection of goods. This is the stuff of which political platforms are made and it is clear that it is one that many political parties and voters find attractive. However it is submitted that it is inappropriate for an electoral system to be designed in a way that determines, at least in part, the options available to the voters.

This discussion has focused, so far, upon political discussion at the expense of legal discussion. Where and how does the law come into play?

Electoral law

First, we need to examine the orthodox position of constitutional law prior to 1998. The standard, and undoubtedly correct, view was that an Act of Parliament (known as primary legislation) could not be challenged in the courts; this was recognised as an aspect or consequence of parliamentary sovereignty. No one could claim that, for example, the RPA 1983 was not valid law. The courts were limited to interpreting the law. Two examples will make the point. In Chapter 2 we will discuss the case of *Hipperson v ERO Newbury*;[62] here the courts were asked to

60 Delivered in Washington, DC, 20 January 1961.
61 'And so, my fellow Americans: ask not what your country can do for you – ask what you can do for your country.'
62 [1984] 1QB 1060.

determine whether a person unlawfully living upon property in an unconventional dwelling could register to vote under the provisions of Pt I of the RPA 1983. In Chapter 6 we will consider the case of *R v Rowe, ex p Mainwaring and others*,[63] in which the courts were asked to consider whether a tactic employed by the Liberal Democrats in a local government election was a 'fraudulent device or contrivance' within the meaning of s 115 of the RPA 1983 and therefore unlawful.

The courts could always consider whether a piece of *secondary* legislation (such as a statutory instrument), designed to amplify and bring into effect the framework established by an Act, was, in fact, consistent with the parent Act. Again an example would be helpful. Section 36 of the RPA 1983 provides that elections of councillors for local government areas in England and Wales shall be conducted in accordance with rules made by the Secretary of State. These rules apply the parliamentary election rules, contained in Sched 1 of the RPA 1983, to local elections, but those rules will be subject to such adaptations, alterations and exceptions as seem appropriate to the Secretary of State in order to make them appropriate to the circumstances of local government elections. Using this power the Secretary of State made the Local Elections (Principal Areas) Rules 1986 and the Local Elections (Parishes and Communities) Rules 1986. Whilst there do not seem to be any reported challenges to any of the rules or regulations made by ministers under their delegated powers[64] the possibility still remains.

However the Human Rights Act 1998 gave the higher courts a new range of powers to question primary legislation. Under s 4 of the Human Rights Act 1998 the courts have been given the power to declare that primary legislation (that is, an Act of Parliament) is incompatible with Britain's obligations under the European Convention of Human Rights. The most notable exercise of this jurisdiction was in the recent case of *A(FC) and others (FC) v Secretary of State for the Home Department, X (FC) and another (FC) v Secretary of State for the Home Department*.[65] This is the case involving the detention of a number of foreign nationals suspected of involvement in terrorism and detained without charge or trial in Belmarsh prison. The courts were called upon to determine whether s 23 of the Anti-terrorism, Crime and Security Act 2001 was compatible with Britain's obligations under Arts 5 and 14 of the European Convention of Human Rights. The House of Lords, sitting as a panel of nine Law Lords, determined (by a majority of eight to one) that the section was

---

63 [1992] 4 All ER 821.
64 As we can see, the parent Act (eg, the RPA 1983) gave a government minister power to act. This is often described as a delegated power.
65 [2004] UKHL 56.

incompatible with those rights guaranteed under the Convention and issued a Declaration of Incompatibility. This does not annul the section of the Act, which remains on the statute book, but represents the strongest of signals to the government that it is acting contrary to the convention by continuing to detain the suspects. However there was also some secondary legislation involved – the Human Rights Act (Designated Derogation) Order 2001 – and the House of Lords quashed that piece of delegated legislation.[66]

Clearly this does not exhaust the analysis of electoral law – so far we have only examined the jurisdictional points; courts have now have a jurisdiction to examine the fundamental statutory bases of election law. What if it is not the legislation that is under scrutiny? As we have seen above, questions of interpretation also arise, together with challenges to the behaviour of electoral administrators, political parties, candidates and their agents, and voters. These questions and challenges rarely raise questions as to the validity of statutes. How strictly should the statutes governing elections be interpreted? Should the statutes be strictly interpreted such that elections should be overturned for the smallest irregularity? Alternatively, should the judges take the view that, provided the law was more rather than less well followed, elections should be left undisturbed? Judges could, for example, take the view that they ought to defer to the will of the people as expressed in an election, provided that the people's will was clearly expressed through a sufficient majority even though there were faults in the election. This is not only a matter of statutory interpretation; it is also a matter of discretion. Many statutes provide for a margin of discretion within which decision makers may decide.

The traditional rule used in English administrative law has been the *Wednesbury* test. It is argued that a rule similar to the *Wednesbury* test has hitherto been used in election cases. The *Wednesbury* test derives from the leading case of *Associated Provincial Picture Houses Ltd v Wednesbury Corporation*,[67] and the classical statement of the doctrine, made by Lord Greene MR:

> Lawyers familiar with the phraseology commonly used in relation to the exercise of statutory discretions often use the word 'unreasonable' in a rather comprehensive sense. It is frequently used as a general description of the things that must not be done. For instance, a person entrusted with a discretion must direct himself properly in law. He must call his own attention to the matters which he is bound to consider. He must exclude from his

---

66 See, for example, para 73 of the report where Lord Bingham sets out his Opinion as to the law.

67 [1948] 1 KB 223.

consideration matters which are irrelevant to the matter that he has to consider. If he does not obey those rules, he may truly be said, and often is said, to be acting 'unreasonably'. Similarly, you may have something so absurd that no sensible person could ever dream that it lay within the powers of the authority. Warrington, LJ, I think it was, gave the example of the red-haired teacher, dismissed because she had red hair. That is unreasonable in one sense. In another sense it is taking into consideration extraneous matters. It is so unreasonable that it might almost be described as being done in bad faith. In fact, all those things largely fall under one head.

Clearly this doctrine requires judges to accord considerable deference to decision makers. Unless a decision maker takes a decision outside the range that would be encompassed by a reasonable decision maker taking the relevant facts properly into account and disregarding irrelevant matters, the decision will be allowed to stand. It is argued that the election cases that will be considered in Chapters 4, 5 and 6 show a similar phenomenon. It is argued that, at least prior to 2000 and the coming into force of the Human Rights Act 1998, judges were deferential to electoral administrators (for example, presiding officers) when they made questionable decisions. Somewhat more surprisingly they were also deferential to the interests of candidates and voters, although these people are not public officials and therefore, it might be thought, not entitled to the protection of the *Wednesbury* doctrine.

It would not be appropriate to give a further example of deferential treatment of candidate, voters or of administrators at this stage because the matter will be discussed in detail throughout the remainder of the book. However it is appropriate to give an indication of the alternatives to *Wednesbury* that have been developed since 2000. There are two leading cases. First, in *R (Pro-Life Alliance) v British Broadcasting Corporation*,[68] the House of Lords took the view that the *Wednesbury* test ought to be abandoned in favour of a more interventionist approach. Secondly, in *Ghaidan v Mendoza*,[69] the House of Lords provided a new interpretive doctrine for deciding the meaning of statutes which both raise matters encompassed by the European Convention of Human Rights (ECHR) and predate the coming into force of the Human Rights Act 1998. The House of Lords held that such statutes (and the RPA 1983 must obviously be numbered amongst these) should be interpreted so as to be consistent with the core value protected by the appropriate Article of the ECHR.

The scene is now set for the remainder of the book.

---

68 [2004] 1 AC 185.
69 [2004] UKHL 30; [2004] 3 All ER 411.

Chapters 2–8

Chapter 2

This chapter contains an analysis of the 'right to vote'. The analysis starts with a consideration of Holt CJ's dissenting judgment in *Ashby v White*. Whilst the judgment is a dissent from the majority of the Court of Common Pleas, his decision was subsequently upheld in the House of Lords and then reversed by resolution of the House of Commons. The development of the right to vote will be traced and it will be questioned whether the classification of the franchise as 'a right' is helpful to the nurture of a democratic polity. The nature of such a right will be considered in the context of both the English law and international human rights law. This examination will contain a consideration of the *Lorenzo* views of John Stuart Mill who, it is submitted, produced the most valuable analysis of the right to vote.

Chapter 3

This chapter develops some of the themes that were introduced in Chapter 2. The mechanism of voting will be examined and it will be argued that, whilst the present system of voting may have contributed to a fall in electoral turnout, the alternative voting methods (all postal ballots, e-voting etc) supported by the main political parties are designed to remedy weaknesses in their own party organisations caused by their steeply declining membership, rather than provide assistance to voters. The phenomenon of vote-bartering, which some see as disruptive to party hegemony, will be examined and its disruptive character called into question.

Chapters 2 and 3 also contain the first articulation of the main positive thesis of this book: that, whilst there may well be a 'right to vote', there are good reasons to conceive of voting not in terms of a right, but in terms of a duty. This duty, which rests equally upon all citizens, is to take part in their own self-government.

Chapter 4

The 1980s and 90s saw a number of cases in which candidates stood for election under names, both personal and party, that were designed to introduce confusion amongst voters. The Government's response, which was supported by the opposition parties, was to introduce the Registration of Political Parties Act 1998 which prevented candidates standing under confusing descriptions. It will be argued that this was not the best means by which to accomplish the intended end. Furthermore, the true effect of this Act and the PPERA 2000 is, it will be argued, to concentrate power in the centres of political parties, to stifle dissent and to ensure that all political parties conform to a single model. It will be argued that the effect of the legislation has been to put the main political parties into the position of clearly identifiable brands in a market order to the detriment of the democratic process.

Chapter 5

At first sight, the UK political landscape appears to be a battleground between parties in vigorous competition, and it may be that this is true at the policy level. It is often argued that vigorous competition between political parties provides the most effective safeguard for democracy. It will be shown, by reference to the leading case of *R v Jones*; *R v Whicher*, that the situation may be one in which, at least during election campaigns, there is a much higher degree of collusion between political parties than should be the case. It will be argued that this is characteristic of a market, rather than a democratic, electoral system. Furthermore, it will be argued that, despite the elaborate legal machinery governing the expenditure of money on election campaigns, the legal structure facilitates abuse because the independent regulators focus upon the collection of funds by political parties rather than the expenditure of funds. In so far as there is attention to expenditure, this is upon central expenditure, which further encourages the maintenance of monolithic party machines.

Chapter 6

In this chapter it will be argued that the current system of election petitions, as the main method of challenge to election results, is almost wholly in the hands of the political parties despite the legal provision stating that challenges to elections must be brought by an elector. Furthermore, the case law reveals that there is judicial deference which operates, at best, in favour of the electoral bureaucracy and, at worst, to protect incumbents even where the fairness of their election may be seriously doubted.

Chapter 7

In Chapter 7 the chains of argument that have been developed in the preceding chapters will be brought together in an attempt to develop a general theory of the standards that the people, Parliament and the courts ought to bring to bear in matters of electoral law. It is argued that Parliament ought not to have control over electoral law, but that the drafting ought to be given to a strengthened electoral commission. A new Elections Bill ought then to be submitted to the courts, which should scrutinise it in accordance with the standards laid down in Art 3 of the 1st Protocol to the ECHR. It should only then be submitted to Parliament and finally subjected to ratification in a referendum.

Chapter 8

The final chapter contains an analysis of the important decision in the Birmingham election petitions delivered in April 2005. The decision by Commissioner Mawrey QC in *In the matter of a Local Government Election for the Bordesley Green Ward of the Birmingham City Council held on 10th June 2004 and in the matter of a Local Government Election for the Aston Ward of the Birmingham City Council held on 10th June 2004*[70] is important for it reveals the extent to which the postal voting system is susceptible to corruption and provides, furthermore, some useful background to the Electoral Commission's foundation model of elections which was published in late May 2005. The Electoral Commission's paper 'Securing the Vote' is examined in some detail in this final chapter and it is hoped that this discussion, when taken together with the discussion in Chapter 7, will be a useful contribution to the debate surrounding the forthcoming Electoral Administration Bill.

---

70 Unreported, Election Court.

Chapter 2:
The Right to Vote

Voting rights lie at the root of parliamentary democracy. Indeed, many would regard them as a basic human right. Nevertheless they are not like the air we breathe. They do not just happen. They have to be conferred, or at least defined and the categories of citizen who enjoy them have also to be defined. Thus no one would expect a new-born baby to have voting rights or that citizens could vote in all constituencies or in that of their unfettered choice.[1]

This chapter examines the law relating to the right to vote; the law controlling the method of voting will be examined in the next chapter. Much of the discussion will be historical: it is only through an examination of the development of the so-called 'right to vote' and the way in which those votes are cast that we can see how the law fails to protect a democratic conception of the polity and instead promotes a market conception of citizenship. The right to vote seemed to start its development as a form of property right. Its development took it to the position of a fully-fledged fundamental human right protected by a legally enforceable national (and indeed regional) human rights instrument – Article 3 of the 1st Protocol of the European Convention of Human Rights (ECHR); it will be argued throughout this chapter and the next chapter that the formal developments obscure a deeper reality, namely the rise of the market conception of citizenship.

Some matters under discussion, such as the phenomenon of 'vote swapping' will appear in both this chapter and the next. Clearly in the United Kingdom, voting is fundamentally based on a franchise exercisable within a region, constituency, ward or other electoral division – if one has a right to vote, it is exercisable in that division and in no other. Vote swapping, the scheme facilitated by the internet whereby a person in one constituency agrees to vote for a candidate chosen by a partner in another constituency provided that the favour is reciprocated, by its very nature facilitates the avoidance of constituency boundaries. As the examples drawn from the Dorset constituencies demonstrate,

---

1 Opening statement of Sir John Donaldson MR in *Hipperson and others v Electoral Registration Officer for the District of Newbury and another* [1985] 1 QB 1060.

vote swapping works with any voting system, but it can only be truly effective when there are reliable, general means of communication, such as a website. Vote swapping is facilitated by remote voting, which is to say voting at home or in the workplace free from the supervision of electoral officials. The discussions in the two chapters will, when placed together, reveal definite features of electoral law. There are other areas of overlap, or at least close contact, between the second and third chapters of this book even though they deal with conceptually separate matters.

Who may register to vote?

The right to vote is possessed by (a) citizens, who are (b) of age, who are neither subject to (c) a general disqualification, nor (d) personally disqualified.

Citizens

In order to be registered to vote and subsequently to vote, a person must be defined by one of the following categories. They must be (i) a British citizen, or (ii) a Commonwealth citizen, or (iii) a citizen of the Republic of Ireland, or (iv) a citizen of another European Union state for local government and European parliamentary elections only. They must usually be resident within the United Kingdom, but there are exceptions to this rule.

Under s 14 of the Representation of the People Act 1983, and the following sections,[2] citizens living overseas for the purpose of Crown employment are entitled to be registered to vote by virtue of the service qualification. It is important to note that the service qualification extends beyond full-time members of the armed forces of the Crown to cover a wide range of persons who have to be overseas for reason of Crown service, and their married partners. This is in addition to those citizens resident overseas who choose to register as electors under the provisions introduced in the Representation of the People Act (RPA) 1985.

The law relating to unconventionally housed or homeless persons will be discussed below.

Age

A person who will attain the age of 18 years during the 12 months following publication of an electoral register is entitled to be registered to vote, but they may not vote until their eighteenth birthday. Subject to the following disqualifications, all persons over the age of 18 may vote.

---

2 For guidance and commentary, see *Schofield* section 4.07.

General disqualifications

There are three general categories of citizens who are disqualified. First, certain people suffering from severe mental illness and who are detained in a mental hospital, or who are unlawfully at large, are disenfranchised by s 3A of the RPA 1983. This section was inserted by s 2 of the Representation of the People Act 2000. All other patients in mental hospitals are taken to be resident in a mental hospital for electoral registration purposes, although they may register at home or some other address by means of a declaration of local connection. Secondly, convicted prisoners may not vote in any parliamentary or local government election during their detention in prison or if they are unlawfully at large when they would otherwise be so detained. This remains the law at the time of writing, although it must be observed that the European Court of Human Rights has ruled that the United Kingdom violates the rights of prisoners, in relation to voting, under Art 3 of the 1st Protocol of the ECHR because the ban affects all convicted prisoners, irrespective of the seriousness of their offence, and has been imposed without detailed parliamentary scrutiny. This decision was made in *Hirst (No 2) v UK*.[3] Prisoners who have not been convicted, but who are on remand in prison, are entitled both to be registered and to have absent voting facilities. Thirdly, sitting members of the House of Lords, whether as hereditary or life peers, have no right to vote in a parliamentary election, even though their names are on the register of electors; they may vote in local government elections.

Personal disqualification

Persons reported by an election court[4] as personally guilty or convicted of an election offence are disenfranchised for certain periods. A report or conviction for a corrupt practice under s 60 of the RPA 1983 involves a five-year period of disenfranchisement. A candidate or other person reported by an election court personally guilty of an illegal practice or convicted of an illegal practice under s 61 of the 1983 Act, is disenfranchised for three years from the date of the report or conviction. These incapacities may in certain circumstances be mitigated or remitted.

---

3 See *Hirst v UK (No. 2)* Application no. 74025/01, 30 March 2004. The law is set out most clearly in para 51 of the judgment. Following the decision of the Chamber of the ECtHR in *Hirst (No 2)* the UK government addressed an appeal to the Grand Chamber of the Court in April 2005. On 6 October the Grand Chamber announced by a vote of 12 ti five that the UK's blanket disenfranchisement of convicted prisoners was indeed a breech of Art 3 1st Protocol ECHR and awarded Mr Hirst damages and costs. The Grand Chamber followed the reasoning of the original Chamber. The UK government is considering its response.

4 See ss 158–160 of the Representation of the People Act 1983. The 'reporting' procedure is the element of the election petition procedure that punishes personal wrongdoing.

These criteria represent the current state of evolution of the right to vote. It is clear, from *Hirst (No 2)*, that the right may be further extended. It is, in the main, unnecessary to examine the content of these categories further since it is clear that they extend to cover the overwhelming majority of the adult population.

The right to vote: an introduction

There has been comparatively little discussion of the evolution of the right to vote in English law.[5] While concentrating on the comparatively recent case of *Hipperson and others v Electoral Registration Officer for the District of Newbury and another*,[6] – quoted at the very start of the chapter – it will also prove necessary to investigate some much older sources.

Having seen that the domestic situation has developed such that the overwhelming majority of citizens indeed possess a right to vote and that this right seems to be that guaranteed by the relevant major human rights instruments, the discussion in the final part of the chapter will turn to the question whether such a situation is characteristic of a democratic or a market based system. Whilst our intuitions may suggest that the question must be promptly answered in favour of democracy, it will be argued that the situation is more accurately characterised as a market based system. An argument in favour of compulsory voting, without the option of a 'none of the above' choice, will be presented. This argument will be based upon the premise that it is wrong to regard the franchise as a right possessed by individual members of the polity; it is better to conceive it as a reflection of the duty of citizens to engage in and with their own governance.

The English root

In early times the right to vote was not seen as a 'human right'; it was seen as a right affixed to the ownership of property. According to Holt CJ in *Ashby v White* (1703),[7] it would seem that, before 1430 and the Statute of 8 Henry VI cap VII:

> Any man that had a freehold, though never so small, had a right of voting, but by that statute the right of election is confined to such persons as have lands or tenements to the yearly value of forty shillings at least, because as the statute says, of the tumults and disorders that happened at elections, by the excessive and outrageous number of electors; but still the right of election is as an original right, incident to, and inseparable from the freehold.

---

5 However, for a comprehensive and scholarly account of the development of the franchise between 1832 and 1885, see Seymour, 1915.

6 [1985] 1 QB 1060.

7 See Holt CJ in *Ashby v White* (1703) 2 Ld Raym 938, pp 950–51.

Holt CJ went on to say:

> As for citizens and burgesses, they depend on the same right as the knights of the shires, and differ only as to the tenure, but the right and manner of their election is on the same foundation.

The first extract points to the fact that 8 Henry VI cap VII restricted the vote in the county franchise for the two 'knights of the shire' to men who owned a freehold worth at least 40 shillings (£2) per annum; it also provided that they had to be resident to vote. The term 'knights of the shire' is an archaism, dating from before 1430, for the two members elected to represent the county in parliament. This restriction of the vote, which brought the franchise into line with the qualification for jury service, appears to remain generous,[8] for yeomen,[9] at least the middling prosperous amongst them, continued to enjoy the county franchise. The qualifying value of 40 shillings remained in place until 1832 by which time the shilling had become greatly devalued by inflation and so the county franchise was enjoyed by a large number of electors. The distribution of seats was grossly unequal; for example, the two county members for Rutland were elected by a poll of the 600 voters, and the two county members for Yorkshire were elected by a poll of 15,000.[10] Furthermore, as Thomson points out, the political reality was that many elections to parliament were uncontested, the great men of the shire having arranged the nominations, and so the election was rather more of a sham than a reality.[11] This basic framework for the county franchise remained in place from 1430 until 1832 with some limited reforms.[12] On the eve of the reform of 1832 there were 94 English and Welsh knights of the shire seated in parliament

The other types of franchise, described by Holt CJ as those belonging to the citizens and burgesses, are more varied – as can be seen most vividly in their mature, overripe, or downright rotten form on the eve of the *Act to amend the Representation of the People in England and Wales*[13] of 1832, generally known as 'the Great Reform Act'. The forms of franchise require further explanation.

The most helpful description of the pre-1832 borough franchise is that set out by Holdsworth.[14] Holdsworth notes that the basis of the franchise fell into four classes, although he omits the four university

---

8 Thomson, 1983, p 115.
9 A yeoman is a freeholder of land. For a clear description of the complex social structure of England in the 15th and 16th centuries, see Harrison, 1984, pp 116–17.
10 Harrison, 1984, p 254.
11 Thomson, 1983, p 114.
12 For a full account see Holdsworth, W, 1966, pp 554–59.
13 2 Geo. IV ch 45.
14 Holdsworth, 1966, pp 560–63.

seats from this classification. (The university seats were filled through election by the members of the universities of Oxford and Cambridge.)

Otherwise the seats were known as the 'borough seats'; there were 415 members filling these in the pre-1832 parliament. First, there were the 'scot and lot and pot-walloper boroughs' in which men obtained the vote if they paid the poor or church rate or had attained the status of a 'pot-walloper', which peculiar term signified that the man in question could provide his own food and had his own hearth on which to cook it. Like the counties, these boroughs varied greatly in size, from Gatton with its six houses, which lost its seat in 1832, to Westminster, which had 9000 voters in 1761. Secondly, there were the 'burgage boroughs' in which the owners of certain, but not all, estates in land enjoyed the right to vote. Sometimes this depended upon actual residence on the tenement and sometimes, as in the notorious case of Old Sarum, which also lost its member in 1832, there was no need for the tenant to live on the land, but the requirement was merely to plough the fields. The six persons entitled to vote for the MP for Old Sarum did not live there, but simply owned and worked the farmland that made up the constituency. Thirdly, there were the 'corporation boroughs' in which the vote was restricted to members of the town corporation, sometimes with and sometimes without an additional property qualification. Membership of the corporation was itself a property qualification because the corporation owned property on behalf of the inhabitants of a town. Finally, there were the 'freemen boroughs' in which the vote was restricted to members of the trade guilds. Again it should be noted that this is a property qualification in all but name because the full members of the trade guilds were the owners of property in the sense that they each owned elements of the means of production.

This brings us back to the fundamental point emphasised by Holt CJ in *Ashby v White*; prior to 1832 the basis of the franchise in English law was a property qualification. This was controversial as early as 1647,[15] as reports of the Putney debates show. The Putney debates were debates of the General Council of the New Model Army – perhaps best described as the 17th century English equivalent of a soldiers' soviet – held in Putney church in 1647. Here, one Maximilian Petty, described as a civilian and a Leveller, said: 'We judge that all inhabitants that have not lost their birthright should have an equal right in elections.' He was answered by Lieutenant General Henry Ireton, the second in command of the New Model Army and Oliver Cromwell's son-in-law, who said:

---

15 Although Harrison draws links between the radical egalitarianism advanced by the Lilburne and his followers in the Civil War, and John Ball's preaching in the Peasants' Revolt of 1381. See Harrison, 1984, pp 87–109.

I think that no person has a right to an interest or share in the disposing of the affairs of the kingdom, and in determining or choosing those that shall determine what laws we shall be ruled by here – no person has a right to this, that hath not a permanent fixed interest in this kingdom. ... All the main thing that I speak for, is because I would have an eye to property.[16]

Harrison comments that the clash between two opposing ideologies could not be clearer. He posits the soldiers claiming a right to vote for every free Englishman against the Roundhead leaders whose claim was that the right to vote was based upon property.[17] As we have seen in *Ashby v White*, the leadership prevailed. It may be that the explanation for Sir John Holt's affirmation that the right to vote is affixed to the possession of property rather than an independent right of itself is that, whilst he was renowned as an independent thinker and was involved in controversy on a number of occasions, he took, according to Plucknett, 'a prominent part in finding a formula which would express the (Glorious) revolution in terms of constitutional law'.[18] It is therefore unsurprising that Holt CJ echoed the dominant parliamentarian view that voting is a species of property right.

So, from 1430, through the victory of parliament in the Civil War and its consolidation in the Glorious Revolution of 1689, until 1832, the country was ruled by a parliament elected by propertied men, supplemented in part by the members of the universities of Oxford and Cambridge. This meant that, on the eve of the 1832 reform, out of a population of approximately 14 million people, there were some 435,000 enfranchised citizens.[19] This sounds wildly undemocratic and yet the unreformed (pre-1832) House of Commons retained its supporters until well into the 20th century despite the fact that the supporters of the pre-reform Commons fully acknowledged that the propertied classes controlled the outcome of the elections by a system of rigged nominations and corruptions of the open poll. Holdsworth[20] commented that the unreformed franchise attained the two greatest ends of a system of representative government: first it resulted in the election of the ablest

---

16 The quotations from Petty and Ireton are taken from Harrison, 1984, pp 195–97, which he references to the Thomasen collection in the British Library. For extensive extracts from the debates of the General Council of the Army of 29 October 1647, see Sharp, A, 1998, pp 102–30. The extracts are worthy of a full reading and it should be noted that both Thomas Rainborough (who took a Leveller position in many matters and appeared in the debate to be more thoroughgoing than Petty) and Oliver Cromwell (for whom Ireton appeared to be acting as a spokesman) were active contributors to the debate.

17 See Harrison, 1984, p 197.

18 See, generally, Plucknett, TFT, 1956, pp 245–48; the quotation is from p 246.

19 Harrison, 1984, p 259.

20 Holdsworth, 1966, pp 565–69.

men from all important spheres of national life to parliament and, secondly, it gave 'adequate expression to the educated public opinion of the day'. His views are expressed in a forthright manner for he goes on to say that because it gave 'greater influence to the intellectual few than to the ignorant many' it produced a House of Commons 'which was intellectually the equal to any which has succeeded to it, and far superior to any which a completely democratic franchise can produce'. Citing Walter Bagehot as authority, Holdsworth then wrote as follows:

> It is the greatest of the blots upon the system introduced in 1832 that it substituted uniformity for variety, and threw away the greatest of the safeguards against the gradual introduction of a democratic representation which, in effect, disenfranchises the most enlightened classes, and thus introduces a vulgarity of tone into the discussions of public business, which tends to lower the political ability of the nation.[21]

Again referring to Bagehot's *Essays on Parliamentary Reform*,[22] Holdsworth repeats Bagehot's claim that the possession of property is not only an indication of a general mind, but has a peculiar tendency to generate a 'political mind'. The sceptic or cynic might well then reply that, if politics is the science of organising the distribution of scarce goods, the members of the pre-reform parliament certainly did a good job of ensuring that these goods remained in their own hands.

William Cobbett, writing in the *Political Register* of 2 April 1831, seems to have shared the view that there was a tight connection between the possession of political power and the ownership of wealth. Cobbett was an enthusiastic supporter of parliamentary reform:

> Will a reform of the Parliament give the labouring man a cow or a pig; will it put bread and cheese into his satchel instead of infernal cold potatoes; will it give him a bottle of beer to carry to the field instead of making him lie down upon his belly to drink out of the brook; will it put upon his back a Sunday coat and send him to church, instead of leaving him to stand lounging about shivering with an unshaven face and a carcase half covered with a ragged smock frock, with filthy cotton shirt beneath it as yellow as a kite's foot? Will parliamentary reform put an end to the harnessing of men and women by a hired overseer to draw carts like beasts of burden; ... will it put an end to the system which caused the honest labourer to be fed worse than the felons in the jails; ... will parliamentary reform put an end to ... the basest acts which the Roman tyrants committed towards their slaves? The enemies of reform jeeringly ask us, whether reform would do all these things for us; and I answer distinctly that IT WOULD DO THEM ALL.[23]

---

21 Holdsworth, 1966, pp 565–66.
22 London, *The Economist*, 1965–78.
23 Quoted in Harrison, 1984, pp 258–59.

However the 1832 Reform Act was much less radical in its immediate effect than the reformers – principally the Political Associations based in the major cities – wished. In the words of Seymour, the Act was:

> ... revolutionary only in so far as it began the series of organic changes in the English representative system. Designed to break down the electoral power vested in a small coterie of plutocrats, it was not intended to inaugurate a truly democratic regime. The measure abolished many of the old complex and restricted franchises and introduced a new general qualification upon what the ministers called 'the respectable mass of the nation.' But although the new qualification was more liberal in character than some of the earlier franchises, it was not such as to provide for a very material increase in the number of voters. More extensive was the rearrangement of seats, according to which the privilege of sending members to Westminster was taken from numerous small boroughs and granted to communities of greater importance. The act [sic] of 1832 also introduced a system of registration, having for its object the compilation of electoral lists, which was later to affect the practical exercise of the franchise in a very high degree.[24]

The three relevant demands of the city political associations, who were the ultimate moving force behind the 1832 reform, were general manhood suffrage, equal electoral districts, (that is, similar numbers of electors in each constituency) and the secret ballot. Clearly, the 1832 Reform Act did not accomplish even these aims. First, in consideration of the demand for a general manhood suffrage rather than a property based suffrage, the property based franchise was extended to include certain copy-holders and tenants in the counties who either possessed long leases worth more than £10 or shorter leases worth more than £50. The most important extension of the franchise was, however, in the boroughs where borough leaseholders, liable to an annual rent equal to or in excess of £10, were granted the vote. These provisions increased the electorate to approximately 652,000 out of a population of 14 million. Secondly, there was a reform of electoral boundaries. Constituencies were reformed to the extent that the 'rotten boroughs', which consisted mainly of land grazed by absentee owners' (and voters') sheep, were deprived of their representation, whilst the representation of many of the county constituencies was increased to as many as six 'knights of the shire' and the vote was extended to a number of the newer borough constituencies. However, it left intact the ancient distinctions between the county and the borough franchises, and left some of the antique forms of borough qualification ('potwalloper', 'scot and lot', etc) undisturbed. No concession was made to the demand for a secret ballot; it would

24 Seymour, 1915, p 9.

therefore seem that Holdsworth's comments were somewhat intemperate and hyperbolic.

The 1832 Reform Act was also seen as a failure by the extra-parliamentary reformers who banded together in the late 1830s to form a movement known as the Chartists, on account of their adoption of the People's Charter drawn up in 1838 by William Lovett. The Charter contained six principal demands that were developments of those advanced by the earlier political associations. The main demands were: votes for all men; equal electoral districts (as explained above); abolition of the property requirement for MPs; payment for MPs for their service in parliament; annual general elections; and, elections conducted by means of a secret ballot.

The Chartists obtained one and a quarter million signatures in support of the Charter and presented it to the House of Commons where it was rejected, but there began a series of attempts further to reform the 1832 Act. First, and immediately after 1832, the parliamentary Radicals (joined by some Liberals) campaigned for the reduction of the qualifying value for the borough franchise to £7, whilst arguing that the county franchise should be brought up to that value. Whilst the political parties and the middle classes were more interested in reforming the existing (1832) qualifications in order to maintain and enhance the middle-class domination of the political sphere, the working-class Chartists maintained their demand for a universal manhood suffrage. These divisions in the campaign to widen the basis of suffrage allowed the ruling parties in parliament to maintain the settlement of 1832. In 1839 an attempt was made in parliament to reduce the county tenancy qualification to £10, but this was unsuccessful. It was followed in 1843 and 1845 by unsuccessful attempts to introduce universal manhood suffrage. Between 1852 and 1860 three further attempts were made by Lord John Russell to reform the franchise. The intention was that the borough franchise should be reduced to £6 and the county franchise given to all occupiers of property worth more than £10 *per annum*. These Bills, some of which contained attempts to introduce novel kinds of qualification, based variously upon education, the receipt of dividends and the like (somewhat rudely termed the 'fancy franchises'), all failed. Clearly the 'fancy franchises' favoured the middle class. The Conservative Bill of 1859 also sought to enact some 'fancy franchises', usually in favour of those thought likely to be Conservatives (for example, those in receipt of a military or civil service pension of £20 *per annum*); it maintained the borough qualification of £10, but sought to reduce the county qualification. This Bill also failed because of dissent in the Conservative cabinet.[25]

---

25 This description relies upon Seymour, 1915, pp 235–45.

The 1832 Act was amended in 1867 and 1884. The genesis of the 1867 Act was in a Bill introduced by the Liberals in 1866. This Bill proposed that the qualifying value of property for the borough franchise be reduced to £7; the figure of £7 being set by a cynical method intended to increase the franchise of the middle-class, rather than working-class, voters.[26] The county franchise level would be reduced to £14. There would also be a number of 'fancy franchises' introduced, together with ratepayer and lodger clauses. These were radical measures that would have increased the total electoral body by about four hundred thousand voters or about 40%.[27] This Bill proved so controversial both outside and, more importantly, within the Liberal government that it provoked the resignation of the cabinet in 1866 and caused a general election. The incoming Conservative administration then brought forward a Bill that complicated the voting system to an almost unbelievable extent and precipitated lengthy and acrimonious debates in parliament. The details are unimportant for the present discussion, save that they would have introduced, had the original Bill been passed without amendment, a whole raft of 'fancy franchises' entitling some electors to dual voting rights. The Bill was steadily whittled down, no doubt because the Conservatives wished to avoid the fate of the previous Liberal administration, to a set of proposals that extended the franchise along the lines proposed in the Bills put forward in the early 1850s – no 'fancy franchises', but an extension of the vote downwards through the strata of wealth, and a partial assimilation of the borough and county franchises. The real practical effect of the 1867 Act, which Seymour comments 'led to an increase in the total electorate of far greater importance, relatively and absolutely, than that of 1832',[28] was to move the suffrage in England far closer to a 'household vote' than could have been envisaged in 1832. The property qualification still existed because the vote was restricted to those who had at least a lease on the property, but the value of the actual property needed to qualify was reduced. The further amending Act in 1884 extended the franchise to two-thirds of the adult male population. Indeed, it would seem that the franchise was based upon a property qualification throughout the period 1430 to 1918.

On 6 February 1918 the entire basis of the franchise was altered. By virtue of s 1 of the Representation of the People Act 1918:

> A man shall be entitled to be registered for a constituency (other than a university constituency) if he is of full age and not subject to any legal

26 Seymour, 1915, pp 247–48.
27 Seymour, 1915, p 250.
28 Seymour, 1915, p 281.

incapacity and (a) has the requisite residence qualification; or (b) has the requisite business premises qualification.

It is clear that the Act does not impose, by this section or otherwise, any form of property qualification upon voters; however, it did maintain, in principle, the six-month period of residence qualification, which was introduced in 1786[29] to prevent elections being corrupted by supporters of candidates moving into the constituency shortly before the an election. AJP Taylor summarises the effect of the Act rather neatly, as follows:

> The act [sic], which became law in June 1918, marked the victory of the Radical principle 'one man, one vote', except for the University seats and a second vote for business premises, both of which survived until 1948. The act [sic] added more voters to the register than all its predecessors put together. It settled in principle the question of votes for women (who, by virtue of s 4 of the Act, were granted the vote if they had attained the age of 30 years) which had caused so much turmoil before the war. Yet it went through almost without fuss. War smoothed the way for democracy – one of the few things to be said in its favour.[30]

This remark is interesting because it may usefully be compared with the remarks made in the Putney debates of 1647, and quoted above. It would seem that there was a deep-rooted feeling within the political and economic elites that the vote was only to be given to the ordinary person when he, or latterly she, had either acquired a financial stake in the country or, alternatively, had rendered, as a class, some extraordinary service.[31] This view can only be strengthened by recalling the statement of the former Prime Minister Asquith, who, in 1918 as he reversed his long-standing opposition to granting the franchise to women, said: 'Some years ago I ventured to use the expression, "Let the women work out their own salvation." Well, Sir, they have worked it out during this war.'[32]

Women gained the vote, at least to a limited degree and in limited numbers, in 1918 and this initial enfranchisement was of the first importance. Whilst it would have been possible for women to have held the franchise on the property qualification before 1918 if they were single or, following the Married Women's Property Act 1882,[33] married, but, for

---

29 26 Geo. III, ch 100.

30 Taylor, 1965, p 132.

31 For a pithy summary, see Fredman, 1997, pp 117–19.

32 Quoted in Taylor, 1965, p 133.

33 See Fredman, 1997, pp 44–49, for an account of the development of married women's property rights.

their gender, the success of the Suffragette[34] movement rendered an important legal development inevitable. Granting the vote to women secured the severance of the connection between the ownership of property and the vote. Allowing some women the vote whilst denying it to some men would, no doubt, have been politically unacceptable. The introduction of the women's vote marked the death of the property-based franchise; however, as we shall see below, it needed a further 60 years and the intervention of the women of the Greenham Common peace camp to (as it were) make the property-based franchise lie down. Secondly, the cumulative effect of the changes initiated by the 1918 concession of the vote to women aged 30 and over was that today women make up half of the electorate. Thirdly, the ultimately successful women's suffrage movement marked the end of popular agitation for reform of the voting system. In contrast, as we shall see in the next chapter, the reforms to the method of voting introduced over the years since 1997 have been instigated by either the government or the Electoral Commission with little popular involvement.

The wider significance of the debate over suffrage is that it illustrates that there are a number of competing bases for the possession of the right to vote in play. Petty, quoted above, and the Chartists provide an illustration of the view that the right to vote is natural to those who live in a democracy. There is some scholarship[35] that traces the 'natural rights' of British freemen and women to before the Norman Conquest and into the mists of antiquity; but, more importantly, this myth[36] of the ancient rights of the 'free-born Englishman'[37] was powerful in working-class and radical thought during the late 18th and early 19th centuries and seems to have been instrumental in mobilising mass pressure for reform. Holt CJ, Ireton and the politicians of the 19th century saw the right as being affixed to the ownership of property; Asquith (but surprisingly, not Ireton) saw the right to vote as something to be earned. It will become clear that the modern legal provision, entrenched in Art 3 of the 1st Protocol to the ECHR, is one in which the right is seen to be natural, absolute and to belong to citizens as of right.

---

34 For a complete history, see Pankhurst, ES, 1977. The history of the women's suffrage movement is, like all histories, deeply riven by ideological disputes; for a short account, see Stanley Holton, 2000.

35 For the influence of this thinking upon the movement for women's suffrage, see Stanley Holton, 2000, pp 13–15, and the works cited therein.

36 For a wider consideration of the influence of the myth of the 'Free-Born Englishman' upon working class thought, see Belchem, 1996; and Belchem, 1985; and Fox, 1985.

37 See Fox, 1985, p 41.

It is also useful to contrast Holdsworth's view with that of, for example, Coleman as reported in the first chapter. Many people believe that political life is weakened and the authority of politicians undermined if insufficient people vote. Clearly Holdsworth would disagree with this view and, if he were writing today, might display some perverse sort of optimism in the decline in turnout. He might even be moved to write that modern electoral arrangements are such that only those who have truly considered the issues are sufficiently motivated to vote. Clearly there are profound weaknesses in this thesis because it may be that the people who actually vote are those who have considered the issues least, because they are actuated by political passion rather than by reason. However the point is valuable because it demonstrates that not all writers believe that we should do all we can to boost electoral turnout.[38]

The victory of the Radical principle was consolidated by some final steps so that it became the right with which we are familiar today; three of these steps having been completed, the fourth being undertaken at the time of writing. In 1928, the age at which the franchise was obtained was equalised between women and men.[39] Secondly, by the provisions of s 1 and Sched 1 of the Family Law Reform Act 1969, the age of majority and thus the voting age was reduced to 18 years on 1 January 1970. Thirdly, the judgment of the Court of Appeal, in *Hipperson v ERO Newbury*,[40] made it plain that the links between the right to vote and the possession of property had been completely broken. It should be noted that it is the linkage between the right to vote and the *possession* of property which has been broken, rather than the link between the right to vote and the *occupation* of property. The fact that the franchise depends and, it will be argued, ought to depend, upon the recognisable occupation of some form of property, even be it so restricted as 'one's own space' (a novel concept, which will be explained and defended in the next chapter in the context of the discussion of vote swapping), was recognised by Sir John Donaldson MR in *Hipperson* where he said, in speaking of the RPA 1983, that:

> It should be noticed that whilst the current Act moves further towards universal suffrage than some of its predecessors, there is no sex disqualification or age differential, no property owning qualification and

38 A point maintained on different grounds by Dowd, 1999. Dowd looks forward to the withering away of the political state; see, especially, pp 42–43.

39 By virtue of 18&19 Geo. V. ch 12; the Representation of the People (Equal Franchise) Act 1928. According to s 8 of the Act it may be cited together with the various Representation of the People Acts from 1918 to 1926 with which it forms a harmonious code.

40 [1985] 1 QB 1060.

no requirement for residence over a specified period, and it still approaches the matter from the point of view of an entitlement to vote in, and in respect of the representation of the residents of, a particular area.

The facts of *Hipperson* are as follows: in the early 1980s, when the Cold War threatened to heat up, a number of women, often known as the Greenham Common 'womyn',[41] were protesting against the installation of nuclear-armed Cruise missiles at a USAF airbase outside Newbury in Berkshire. They were encamped in tents, under tarpaulins supported by bent saplings ('benders') and in a variety of more or less roadworthy vehicles on land, which was partly owned by the Department of Transport and partly common land subject to byelaws prohibiting, *inter alia*, camping or driving of vehicles on the land. They lived in this fashion for a number of years. In 1983 Newbury District Council, the local authority in which the common land was vested, obtained an injunction in the High Court requiring the protestors to vacate its land and in 1984 the Department of Transport obtained a similar order. Ms Hipperson and her friends, who were among the occupying protestors, sought to register their names on the local electoral register, in accordance with ss 1 and 2 of the RPA 1983 that, at the time, was the applicable law. The 'womyn' claimed to be persons eligible to vote in parliamentary and local elections by virtue of being resident at the qualifying date in the relevant (Newbury) constituency. Newbury District Council was, of course, the authority employing the Electoral Registration Officer (ERO), Mr Turner, who was (as his successor remains) responsible for maintaining the Register of Electors. One Mr Meyer objected, in accordance with s 10(c) of the 1983 Act, to the registration of the appellants as electors, on two grounds. First, that the 'womyn' could not be counted as 'resident' within the meaning of ss 1(1) and 5 of the Act since their vehicles, tents and benders did not qualify as 'residences' because they lacked the necessary degree of permanence. The second, alternative, ground of attack was that the 'womyn's' occupation was tainted by their general and specifically unlawful acts in breaching the byelaws and the court order, and in causing an obstruction of the highway.

At a hearing of the objection, the Electoral Registration Officer found that the appellants were resident within the electoral area on the qualifying date, but held that their residence was unlawful and

---

41 The neologism 'womyn' was chosen by the Greenham Common protestors to emphasise their separation from men whom many of the womyn saw as collectively responsible for the invention and accumulation of weapons of mass destruction. Sir John Donaldson's insistence upon calling them 'the Greenham ladies' surely cannot be seen as wholly a product of his undoubted charm and politeness.

accordingly removed their names from the register. The 'womyn' appealed to the county court, which allowed their appeal. Mr Meyer, the original objector, and Mr Turner, the ERO, appealed to the Court of Appeal. Sir John Donaldson MR dealt with the first ground of appeal quite quickly, holding that the earlier decision of the Court of Appeal, in *Fox v Stirk*,[42] was authority for the propositions that: (1) the words 'reside' and 'resident' are to be given their everyday or dictionary meanings of dwelling permanently or for a considerable time, or, having one's settled or usual abode, or, living in or at a particular place; (2) the purpose and other circumstances of the aspiring elector's presence at, or absence from, the address; (3) neither presence at nor absence from the address on the qualifying date is conclusive; and (4) a voter can, in principle, have more than one residence He therefore held that whether or not a person is resident in a particular place is a question of fact and degree to be determined by a tribunal of fact. He therefore decided that, whilst the 'womyn's' occupation was unusual and more than normally precarious, it should be regarded as amounting to residence.

The court considered that the question of the lawfulness of a person's occupation of a space required more analysis. Sir John Donaldson MR held that the mere fact that a person's occupation of property was, in general, unlawful was not enough to deprive them of the vote. This must be correct for the reasons which he gave when he adopted the reasoning of the judge in the county court below.[43] It is plain that, if it were otherwise, citizens would lose their vote for any number of technical breaches of the housing regulations or for the commission of certain crimes – such as those relating to the possession or consumption of controlled drugs or for some offences relating to, for example, prostitution. It would also be the case that squatters who had not been served with a specific injunction requiring them to quit would be automatically disenfranchised.[44] However, he then ruled that where somebody is present on premises in breach of a specific injunction, this would prevent their registration as an elector in respect of that address. He held, on the facts, that it had not been shown that the 'womyn' were living on land from which they had been expelled and prevented from entering by injunction and, accordingly, that they were eligible for registration as electors.

This requirement for the specifically lawful occupation of premises within the constituency or other electoral division was finally swept

---

42 [1970] 2 QB 463.

43 [1985] 1 QB 1060 at 1074 B-H.

44 See *Beal v Ford* (1877) 42 JP 119, which holds that residence as a trespasser would, provided that the other qualifying conditions for the franchise are met, meet the conditions for registration.

away, together with the last vestiges of a qualifying period of residency, by the provisions of the Representation of the People Act 2000, which amended the RPA 1983 in two respects, which are important for the present discussion. The requirement to be resident on the date for electoral registration – 15th October in the year preceding the coming into force of the electoral register in February – was abandoned and a system of 'rolling registration' introduced. This provides that voters may join or leave the electoral register at any stage throughout the year. There is, of course, a time lag in making the amendment to the electoral register and there are rules which prevent a person from joining an electoral register in the immediate run up to an election. The rules which are to be found in s 13A of the RPA 1983 are complex, and the Electoral Commission's proposed reforms to the Representation of the People Acts seem to envisage some simplification of the rules for the Commission has promised that the final date for registration will be much closer to election day.[45]

The second important change was to introduce clear statutory rules under which homeless people are entitled to register to vote. The editors of *Schofield*[46] refer to an unreported case in March 1996, in the Penzance County Court, in which a Mr Lippiatt successfully challenged the refusal of the Penwith ERO to place his name on the register. Mr Lippiatt was a homeless man who used the facilities of, and spent some time at a day centre, which he used as his postal address although he did not sleep there. It is believed that other registration officers were willing to grant the vote in such circumstances, and the 1996 Home Office Circular RPA 409, which contained valuable guidance, probably extended the practice of allowing unconventionally housed or apparently homeless persons countrywide the right to vote. In 2000 the practice was given statutory footing. Section 6 of the Representation of the People Act 2000 introduced a provision whereby a homeless person is able to make a statutory, 'Declaration of Local Connection', and thus apply for registration. This provision also allows patients in mental hospitals, provided that they are not detained for an offence, and prisoners on remand to register.

It is quite plain that there are further changes in the pipeline. In *Voting for Change*, the Electoral Commission have proposed that a new method of electoral registration be introduced. They propose the change in the following way:[47]

---

45 Electoral Commission, *Voting for Change*, p 4.
46 *Op cit*, at section 4.06.
47 Electoral Commission, *Voting for Change*, p 3.

> A central issue identified by voters and other stakeholders in relation to the electoral process – and particularly new methods of voting – is security. In our view the key to providing the appropriate level of security lies in reform of voter registration. Critically, we recommend a move from household registration to individual registration, backed by individual voter identifiers.

First, it is doubted that individual registration will, of itself, ensure the security of voting that the Electoral Commission envisage because, whilst it will ensure that voters who vote at the polling station will be obliged (as presently required in Northern Ireland)[48] to present some form of individual voter identification, it will not and cannot eliminate fraud in remote voting outside the supervision of electoral officials. However, these developments will make it clear, at least in the popular mind, that the possession of the vote has many of the characteristics of an individual legal right.

The focus of this discussion must now move. We now need to examine the status of the right to vote in international human rights law. This is because, as Sir John Donaldson made clear in the extract set out at the beginning of the chapter, the status of the right to vote remains unclear. The law set out so far in this book has made it plain that the right is 'not like the air we breathe, it is one which must be conferred'.

The international and 'human rights' root

There seems to be little more to be said than to set out the main international human rights instruments.[49] The important point to note is that many of the international human rights instruments were written in circumstances around the end of the Second World War when, as the Preamble to the Charter of the United Nations[50] makes clear, the nations of the world, led by the victorious powers,[51] were 'determined to save succeeding generations from the scourge of war … and to reaffirm faith in fundamental human rights'. Article 55 of the Charter pledged the UN to promote (at s 55(c)) 'universal respect for, and observance of, human

---

48 See the discussion of the Electoral Fraud (Northern Ireland) Act 2002 in Chapter 3 below.

49 For a complete account see Goodwin-Gill, 1994, who also sets out a large number of the secondary instruments and provides a useful guide to the international law and practice.

50 Agreed in San Francisco on 26 June 1945 and brought into force on 24 October 1945.

51 For a short history of the establishment of the United Nations see Chapter 2 of Goodrich, 1959. Goodrich traces the genesis of the UN to the Atlantic meeting between Churchill and Roosevelt in 1941 from which the general plans came that were subsequently firmed up in the Moscow, Teheran and Dumbarton Oaks meetings, which were attended by delegations from the Republic of China, Soviet Union, the United Kingdom and the United States. See Goodrich, 1959, pp 21–23.

rights and fundamental freedoms', but it must be noted that whilst the Universal Declaration of Human Rights was adopted on 10 October 1948[52] it is not a binding legal instrument. The relevant portion of the Universal Declaration is Art 21, which provides that:

> (1) Everyone has the right to take part in the government of his country, directly or through freely chosen representatives ...
>
> ...
>
> (3) The will of the people shall be the basis of the authority of government; this will shall be expressed in periodic and genuine elections which shall be by universal and equal suffrage and shall be held by secret vote or by equivalent free voting procedures.

Goodrich, writing in 1959,[53] observes that, whilst the Commission on Human Rights had started drafting the legally binding Covenants designed to put the Declaration into legal effect before the Assembly had approved the text of the Declaration, 'the process has not yet been completed' because of political difficulties involving opposition from the United States and from other members of the UN. The International Covenant on Civil and Political Rights was adopted by the General Assembly of the UN at its 1496th Plenary Meeting on 16 December 1966 and entered into force on 23 March 1976, the draft having been under consideration since the end of June 1954. Article 25 provides that:

> Every citizen shall have the right and the opportunity, without any of the distinctions mentioned in Article 2 (ie, those such as race, colour, sex, language, religion, political or other opinion, national or social origin, property, birth or other status) and without unreasonable restrictions:
>
> (a) To take part in the conduct of public affairs, directly or through freely chosen representatives;
>
> (b) To vote and to be elected at genuine periodic elections which shall be by universal and equal suffrage and shall be held by secret ballot, guaranteeing the free expression of the will of the electors;

The other noteworthy child of the Universal Declaration of Human Rights,[54] although the period of gestation was mercifully much shorter,

---

52 UN Doc A/811.

53 See Goodrich, 1959, p 33.

54 See the Preamble to the Convention which states: ' ... Considering the Universal Declaration of Human Rights proclaimed by the General Assembly ... ; Considering that this Declaration aims at securing the universal and effective recognition and observance of the Rights therein declared; ...'

was and remains the European Convention on Human Rights.[55] This Convention, which binds all the member states of the Council of Europe (termed High Contracting Parties), provides in its First Protocol at Art 3 that:

> The High Contracting Parties undertake to hold free elections at reasonable intervals by secret ballot, under conditions which will ensure the free expression of the opinion of the people in the choice of the legislature.

This amounts to an enforceable legal right, although the path to enforcement may be long and tortuous. Before the Convention was incorporated into domestic law, UK citizens were obliged to take the matter all the way through the domestic courts so as to exhaust the available remedies, and then to apply to bring the matter before the European Court of Human Rights.[56] It is now directly enforceable in the courts throughout the UK, as it has been since the passage of the Human Rights Act 1998. Clearly the pressures within Europe differed from those upon the American and international stages, the continent having been torn apart by the atrocities the Convention was designed to prevent in the 1930s and 40s. The denial of the humanity of the Jews and other ethnic and social groups must have made the enforcement of a code of human rights attractive, emphasising, as it did, the application of the code to 'everyone'[57] with 'no one'[58] being excluded, and providing that no distinctions could be made upon the basis of, for example, sex, race, colour language, religion or political opinion.[59]

A clear explanation of the status of the rights contained in Art 3 of the 1st Protocol was set out by the ECHR in *Hirst v UK (No 2)*.[60]

> While Article 3 of Protocol No. 1 is phrased in terms of the obligation of the High Contracting Party to hold elections which ensure the free expression of the opinion of the people, the Court's case-law establishes that it guarantees individual rights, *including the right to vote* and to stand for election. Although those rights are central to democracy and the rule of law, they are not absolute and may be subject to limitations. The Contracting States have a wide margin of appreciation in this sphere, but it is for the Court to determine in the last resort whether the requirements of Article 3 of Protocol No. 1 have been complied with; it has to satisfy itself that the

---

55 Signed in Rome on 4 November 1950 and entered into force as a whole on 3 September 1953. The 1st Protocol entered into force on 18 May 1954.

56 Art 26 ECHR.

57 See ECHR Arts 2, 5, 6, 8, 9, 10, 11.

58 Similarly Arts 3, 4, 7.

59 See Art 14.

60 Application no. 74025/01, 30 March 2004.

conditions do not curtail the rights in question to such an extent as to impair their very essence and deprive them of their effectiveness; that they are imposed in pursuit of a legitimate aim; and that the means employed are not disproportionate (see *Mathieu-Mohin and Clerfayt v Belgium*, judgment of 2 March 1987, Series A no. 113, p 23, § 52; and more recently, *Matthews v United Kingdom* [GC], no. 24833/94, § 63, ECHR 1999-I; *Labita v Italy* [GC], no. 26772/95, § 201, ECHR 2000-IV, and *Podkolzina v Latvia*, no. 46726/99, § 33, ECHR 2002-II). (emphasis added)

The universality of the codes and their framing in terms of 'rights' that are explicitly enforceable in the courts is clearly attractive although, as we shall see below, there are drawbacks to the use of the language of rights. Not least amongst these drawbacks is the fact that the use of this language often fails to bring home the responsibilities of right holders.

Analysis

In the first chapter, the issues of falling electoral turnout and the trivialisation of the electoral process were raised. Whilst there would not seem to be a simple linear relationship, and the point has not been scientifically investigated, the trend seems to be that as the franchise has grown the turnout has dropped and the discussion of political issues has become less rigorous. As we have seen in this chapter, Holdsworth and the 19th century writers upon whom he relied would have argued that an inevitable consequence of increasing the franchise is that 'a vulgarity of tone' would be introduced into 'discussions of public business'. The county franchise was restricted to 40 shilling freeholders in 1430 because 'of the tumults and disorders which happened at elections, by the excessive and outrageous number of electors'.[61] The point being repeatedly and implicitly made over the centuries is that the possession of property has a calming and civilising effect upon the population. Furthermore, there is no doubt that fashion, policing, and public order legislation have controlled 'tumults and disorders', but they seem to have been replaced by political lethargy and indifference.

The Government's practical response to the decline in electoral turnout and the apparent indifference of young people has been to introduce a requirement for citizenship education into the National Curriculum[62] for schools. There is a requirement at Key Stage 3 for some teaching of 'the electoral system and the importance of voting', although no further details are given beyond a cross-reference to the history

---

61 Holt CJ in *Ashby v White* (1703) 2 Ld Raym 938 at 951.
62 See /www.nc.uk.net/index.html.

curriculum. The Electoral Commission has conducted a number of voter education campaigns. There are a number of non-governmental organisations, such as *Operation Black Vote* and *Rock the Vote*, dedicated to increasing the turnout of voters within particular communities.

However, despite the fall in turnout, it cannot be denied that the franchise has expanded enormously since its restriction in 1430 and that the entitlement to vote has become more general and has increasingly been expressed in terms of a right to vote; not least because the words of Art 21 of the Universal Declaration of Human Rights express the core conception of democracy in terms of a 'right to take part in the government of his country'. Furthermore, it is asserted that the majority of the debates from the earliest times to date were phrased in terms of the 'right to vote'. Evidence in support of this proposition has been set out above. The focus on the right to vote may be explained by the fact that most of the debates about the extension of the franchise took place in the context of the denial of the vote or other form of democratic involvement, whether in the immediate aftermath of the English civil war, the struggles of the Chartists or the suffragettes, or the foundation of the United Nations in the aftermath of the Second World War.

If we conceive of democracy in terms of the right of a person to take part in the governance of their country, it is plain that we could formulate a description of this development in terms of the triumph of the democratic idea. However this victory of democracy seems rather hollow when we recall that, at the 2001 general election, less than 60% of eligible voters bothered to turn out.

'A right to vote' logically (but not as a matter of universal fact[63]) implies 'a right not to vote,' and the law emphasises this by providing that it is a corrupt offence to bribe, treat or unduly influence a person to refrain from voting or to vote.[64] Thus the law provides that it should be a person's free choice to vote or refrain from voting. If we transpose this back into the provision of Art 21 of the Universal Declaration of Human Rights we get a much less democratically attractive proposition, ie 21(1) 'Everyone has the right to take part or refrain from taking part in the government of his country'. When we couple that 'right' with Art 21(3), we arrive at the even less comfortable position that a person may generally withhold their authority from the state. If an elected

---

63 Since 1924 (or 1984 for Aboriginal people) all Australian citizens over the age of 18 must enrol to vote and attend a polling place at election time. Other countries in which there is some form of compulsory voting are: Argentina, Austria, Belgium, Bolivia, Brazil, Cyprus, Dominican Republic, Egypt, Greece, Guatemala, Honduras, Liechtenstein, Luxembourg, Panama, Philippines, Singapore, Switzerland, Uruguay, and Venezuela.

64 See ss 113–115 of the RPA 1983.

government were to say that it was simply not prepared to govern, the citizenry would, no doubt, be outraged, but in the last general election 40% of the electorate failed to live up to their part of the bargain. It is proposed that such a situation is far from being democratic; it is much closer to a market situation where citizens have the choice to participate or to refrain from participation and may, if they choose, simply sit on the sidelines and allow others to assume the democratic burden. The act of voting is, in a small way, an act of participating in government.

It is clear that there must be, in some sense, a right to vote and it is submitted that the only proper way of understanding the 'right' is to say that the notion of a democracy implies, as a matter of logic, the right of all citizens to participate in the act or acts of the government of the society. In a representative, as opposed to a direct, democracy the right to vote stems directly from this right to take part in government; it is the mechanism of taking part in government and it is a derivative, rather than a primary, right. It is meaningless without the right to take part in government. It is a right in another, more technical, sense according to writers such as Wesley Hohfeld,[65] in that, if it is what Hohfeld called a 'claim right', it arises together with a corresponding duty – the duty upon electoral administrators and returning officers to, first, afford the mechanisms for voting, deliver up ballot papers when demanded and so forth. Secondly, the returning officer is under a duty to properly declare the actual result of the poll rather than some other result.[66] The problem with the declaration of something as a right, and *a fortiori* as an individual right or a human right, is that it leads people into the sort of thinking rightly criticised, it is submitted, by John Stuart Mill.[67]

Mill argued that by calling it a 'right to vote', certain beliefs are raised in the mind of the voter. As we shall see in the next chapter, the particular beliefs that surround the core belief in a right to vote are supported by the institution of the secret ballot. Mill argues that, by insisting that it is a right to vote and by the fact that this idea has taken root in the public mind, a 'moral mischief' has been done 'outweighing all the good that the ballot could do, at the highest possible estimate of it'.[68] This statement is surely hyperbolic because it cannot seriously be argued that a dictatorship is better than even a seriously flawed democracy. As we shall see below, Mill does not believe that even a 'good despot' can be recommended as a serious alternative to a representative democracy. Mill's argument is that if it is a right to vote, it

---

65 See, generally, Hohfeld, 1978.
66 See Rule 50 of the Parliamentary Election Rules, Sched 1 of the RPA 1983.
67 Mill, 1991, p 206.
68 Mill, 1991, p 206.

must belong to the voter for their own exclusive use and, therefore, we have no grounds for objecting when the voter uses it in an immoral or selfish way. This works at two levels. First, we can neither object when the voter sells it, or barters it or uses it to please another and advance his own cause by sycophancy. Secondly, and this is the more important point, correctly conceived a 'vote is not a thing in which (the voter) has an option; it has no more to do with his personal wishes than the verdict of a juryman. It is strictly a matter of duty; (the voter) is bound to give it according to his best and most conscientious opinion of the public good.'[69] Mill argues that where people vote in accordance with their own interests they are little better than despots or oppressors because they are acting on the same motivations that actuate tyrants. No doubt at least part of the objection to the limited franchise before the reforms, which started with the 1832 Act, was that many of the voters behaved tyrannically. However it does not seem right to reform voting merely by increasing the number of petty tyrants; thus it is submitted that, a universal adult franchise having been achieved, it has gone past the time to describe the exercise of the franchise in terms of a mere right to vote. There is no doubt that there is a right to vote in the narrow Hohfeldian senses described above, but it now seems more appropriate to express the exercise of the franchise in the terms which Mill might have preferred – the exercise of a power over a trust.[70] Clearly, Mill was not a trusts lawyer, so it is to be presumed that his intention was not to launch us into the important debate as to the precise and fundamental difference between a trust and a power.[71] Mill meant, and the following argument means, that citizens must exercise their public duty to vote.

The question, therefore, must be considered as to whether there ought to be an obligation to participate in government. If voting were to be made compulsory it would, of course, be necessary to amend the 1983 Act in order to effect such a change. Elsewhere, in *Considerations on Representative Government*, Mill drew our attention to the fact that the British people have always, perhaps when faced with some mistake of a democratic government, pronounced that 'if a good despot could be ensured, despotic monarchy would be the best form of government'.[72] Mill points out that the core supposition is that if absolute power were placed in the hands of some eminent individual it would ensure that all the tasks of government would be efficiently and effectively conducted.

---

69 Mill, 1991, pp 206–07.
70 Mill, 1991, uses the terminology of a trust on p 206.
71 Perhaps never more clearly stated than in Martin, JE, Hanbury and Maudsley, 1985, p 60: 'The distinction between trusts and powers is fundamental. Trusts are imperative; powers are discretionary. Trustees must exercise the duties connected with their trusts. A donee of a power may exercise it, or not, at his choice.'
72 Mill, 1991, pp 53–56.

For the sake of argument Mill is prepared to concede that such a thing would come about although he has very considerable reservations about whether such a person could exist. Let us use a familiar device to explore the character of such a monarch; Ronald Dworkin has provided us with such a person, whom he uses as the exemplar of a perfect common law judge and whom he called 'Hercules'.[73] We could invent such a model ruler, to be called, say, Achilles.[74] Mill points out that our Achilles would not only have to be supremely intelligent, but also informed correctly at all times in the exact detail of the running of the state in all its branches and capable of choosing his lieutenants with perfect skill.[75]

However, Mill does not make one highly significant point concerning the nature of our Achilles. Unlike the real Achilles, who was given to sulking in his tent after a quarrel with Agamemnon roused by the death of Patrocles, for whom he had considerable fondness, our Achilles must also be free from passion.[76] He must neither favour nor disfavour any individual or class because of some personal like or dislike. This seems to make the concession of the argument considerably more difficult than Mill would allow, but let us proceed nevertheless, although we shall revisit Achilles in the final chapter.

Mill then makes his most telling observation; government by superhero requires the passivity of the populace. As Mill says:

> Their passivity is implied in the very idea of absolute power. The nation as a whole and every individual composing it, are without any potential voice in their own destiny. They exercise no will in respect to their collective interests. All is decided for them by a will not their own, which it is legally a crime for them to disobey.[77]

Mill points out that such subjection is both intellectually and, more importantly, morally stultifying. He writes:

> Whenever the sphere of action of human beings is artificially circumscribed, their sentiments are narrowed and dwarfed in the same proportion ... Let a person have nothing to do for his country and he will feel nothing for it.[78]

Mill is surely correct in saying that where a person has no part to play in the running of the country, passivity and insouciance are nurtured. Such

---

73 Dworkin, 1986.
74 I am grateful to Elaine Watt for this suggestion. For a description of the 'real' Achilles see, generally, Homer's *Iliad* (trans Fitzgerald), 1992, London: Everyman.
75 See Mill, 1991, pp 55–56.
76 For the full story, see Graves, 1961.
77 Mill, 1991, pp 56–57.
78 Mill, 1991, p 58.

passivity also requires a certain predisposition toward, or a pre-existing habit of, carelessness regarding the running of the state. Further, Mill is persuasive in arguing that there is a positive connection between performing a service for someone or perhaps a more abstract something (such as a group, society or country) and developing an emotional attachment. However Mill does not consider, possibly it being no part of his project, the fact that people can and do form commitments because of their social and biological nature, perhaps in spite of themselves. As Joseph Raz comments, '(t)he ideal of the perfect existentialist with no fixed biological and social nature who creates himself as he goes along is an incoherent dream'.[79] People do form commitments to others and these commitments may be small in scale and personal – such as marriage, partnership or friendship – or larger in scale – such as commitments to a football or cricket team, a political party, a town or a country. Commitments may even be so wide as to be abstract – such as commitment to a political ideal. The struggles for the right to vote conducted by the Levellers, the Chartists or the Suffragettes may thus be seen as struggles to make a commitment.

It is not inconsistent with Mill's insight that giving a person a right to vote is not to be seen as giving a person some form of reward or honour, to argue that the vote should be regarded as a partial fulfilment of that person's humanity. Given the human propensity to form commitments, a person not afforded the franchise may well, rather than forming such commitments as will advance the collective welfare, turn in upon themselves and form less virtuous associations and relationships dedicated, at best, to the fulfilment of their own selfish desires. It seems that there is something to be said for using the law to coerce people into engagement with political life even though it would *prima facie* offend against John Stuart Mill's well known 'harm principle'; an argument in favour of such coercion is set out below.

The use of coercion in a free society is often seen as problematic,[80] but Raz demonstrates that it is relatively unproblematic in a liberal society where the individuals are guaranteed 'adequate rights of political participation in the liberal state'. He argues that some forms of coercion can be 'genuinely for the good of the coerced'.[81]

The argument is that obliging people to vote is imposing an obligation upon them to contribute to their own self-governance. It is calling upon them to contribute to society and thus to fulfil their own good by being part of society. This is not to impose any particular model

---

79 Raz, 1986, p 155. References in this book are to the paperback edition.
80 See, for example, the discussion in Raz, 1986, Chapter 6, 'The exclusion of ideals'.
81 See Raz, 1986, pp 155–57, and section 4 of Chapter 6.

upon the society that the citizens are called upon to form. It may be that the majority believe that the good of all would be furthered by a nightwatchman state, in which the public authority does no more than secure the population against internal and external enemies and leaves the private sector free to provide a range of goods and services. Alternatively, it may be that the majority decide that the common good would be advanced by the provision of a more or less socialist welfare state. The argument is simply that it is for the people as governors to decide. In a slogan, which sounds contradictory, they should be forced to be free.

This legal coercion to vote does not seem to violate the principle of autonomy as advanced by Joseph Raz; indeed it seems to fulfil some of its conditions. Raz notes that coercion is 'normally an insult to the person's autonomy. He is being treated as a non-autonomous agent, an animal, a baby or an imbecile.'[82] The treatment that is being afforded by obliging a citizen to vote is exactly the opposite of this affront or insult; it is obliging the citizen to behave as a responsible agent who bears responsibility, in perhaps a very small part, for guiding the state.

This is not to say that Raz's argument is to be endorsed in its entirety. This is because Raz believes that '(t)he principles of representative government guarantee some measure of control by the population over those in authority'[83] and that the proper concern of the state 'is with the provision of adequate means for individuals to pursue their own ideals of the good'.[84] With regard to the first statement it is argued that the implied distinction and distance between the citizen and those in authority is false. It is argued that 'those in authority' derive their political authority from the people and thus the population has, or should have, a full measure of control over them. Secondly, Raz seems to imply a consumer conception of the state in which the citizen goes, as it were, to the market stall set out by the state and buys a set of goods from a range made available.[85] This implies a static view of the individual and a monolithic and unchanging view of the state. Yet, since the state is, or should be, the creature of the population it should properly reflect both the changing interests and the changing composition of the population.

If we accept that citizens have a duty to vote, and thus a duty which the law should enforce, the question remains as to whether voters ought to have the option of selecting 'none of the above' in addition to the choice between the candidates on offer. If the elector was obliged to vote

82 Raz, 1986, p 156.
83 Raz, 1986, p 139.
84 Raz, 1986, p 144.
85 This view has been criticised elsewhere; see Watt, 2001.

under the threat of a legal sanction, they might well say, 'But none of
these people represent my views at all, I can't vote for any of them.' This
purported answer is, in fact, an answer to a question that the ballot box
was not designed to answer. The ballot box is designed to receive the
voters' choices as to who is to sit in the legislature in their stead because
the Houses of Parliament are simply not large enough to admit all
citizens. For the voter to say 'none of the above' is certainly to say that
they decline to buy any of the goods on display on the stall, but they
cannot legitimately be permitted to say that they will not take the
allotted proxy place in the legislature. Furthermore, the voter is not being
asked for their unfettered choice as to which candidate will best satisfy
all, or most of, their preferences; they *are* being asked which of the
candidates, or the parties the candidates represent, will provide the best
set of policies to advance the common good. For the voter to say that
'none of the above' will best advance the common good is incredible,
since that would require the contenders, or more strictly their parties for
it is political parties which form governments, to be so alike in the lack of
credible policies, competence, and trustworthiness as to defy belief. It is
submitted that giving the voter the explicit opportunity to vote for 'none
of the above' is to invite the voter to behave with at least a measure of
laziness or to jump to the conclusion that there is nothing to compel a
choice between the candidates or parties. It remains open to the voter to
leave the paper blank or to spoil the ballot paper, but the state should not
encourage citizens to avoid their public duty.

In a parliamentary election, and the rules are only slightly different
in a local government election,[86] the ballot paper may be rendered void,
and thus subject to rejection under r 47 of Sched 1 of the RPA 1983, by the
voter voting for more than one candidate, or by writing something upon
the paper by which the voter can be identified, or by leaving it
unmarked, or by making a mark such that no clear intention of the voter
to select a particular candidate can be discerned. It is submitted that
obliging a voter to deliberately act wrongly – although the wrongdoing
does not bear a sanction – is a deterrent to all but the most committed
non-voter.

However, the argument in favour of compulsory voting set out
above only holds if voting is conceptualised as an act of engagement
with the process of governance rather than an act of choosing between
'parties as products'. If a voter is forced to choose between 'parties as
products', by being obliged to ask the question: 'which one of these
parties best fulfils my own individual needs and desires?', it is clear that

---

86 See, eg, Rule 41 of the Local Elections (Principal Areas) Rules SI 1986/2241. The
difference between the rules is caused because it is sometimes necessary to vote for
more than one candidate in a local government election.

they may well say, 'none of them'. To force the voter to vote in such circumstances would surely amount to a minor act of oppression, and even a minor act of oppression is unacceptable in the context of electing representatives to government.

The argument that the voter is, in a democratic polity, being asked to take part in government rather than exercise a choice between political parties as consumer products, will be set out at greater length in the next chapter. This argument depends upon further points to be discussed in the following chapter. John Stuart Mill argues that the secrecy of the ballot predisposes voters to treat their vote as their personal property. Whilst his view is ultimately rejected the discussion in the following chapter will reveal some important factors of the right to vote.

It must also be observed, in passing, that it is now clear that there are alternative robust moral theories[87] that do not depend upon the existence of individual human rights to provide a condemnation of tyranny; perhaps these may be further articulated to provide a moral theory of voting, but this is beyond the scope of this book.

---

87 See, eg, Parfit, 1984; or Glover, 1999.

Chapter 3:
The Mechanism
of Voting

Introduction

This chapter examines the mechanisms which facilitate the casting of ballots by UK voters. The focus is, of course, upon the election of representatives rather than the conduct of, for example, referendums, because the UK is a representative democracy and the number of elections far outweighs the number of referendums. Are ballots to be cast in person in a ballot box situated in a polling station or elsewhere, or should we be able to vote by post or by some digital means, such as via the internet, telephone or even by text message? The method remains far more controversial than it might, at first sight, appear. The discussion in Chapter 2 showed that the evolution of the 'right to vote' took place in circumstances of political turmoil. The restriction of the franchise in 1430 was occasioned by tumult at the polls because too many people (men) had gained the right to vote. After the civil war there were furious debates over the question whether the franchise should be based upon property or should become available to all men. The political associations and the Chartists fought for the extension of the franchise throughout the reigns of William IV and Queen Victoria. The final major extension of the franchise – namely, to women – was brought about by an almost unprecedented campaign of civil disobedience by the suffragettes. Even the clarification that the franchise was based upon a somewhat inchoate and ill-defined human right, rather than the occupation of a house, had, as its backdrop, the campaign against cruise missiles led by the 'womyn' at Greenham Common. Whilst the emergence of the secret ballot in 1872 was accompanied by civil disturbances and a vigorous public debate, the recent moves away from the secret ballot conducted in the tightly supervised polling place have occurred in a more muted and peaceful political atmosphere. The move from the public poll to the secret ballot came about in 1872 by positive public demand; the retreat from the supervised polling place to the home vote was brought about by the government and the Electoral Commission without the exertion of notable public pressure. That is not to say that there has been silence over the introduction of new voting mechanisms in the UK. Furthermore, elsewhere in the world the introduction of electromechanical voting machines and the use of remote voting (voting from home) have been highly controversial.

The mechanisms of voting remain far more controversial than might, at first, appear. True, there have not been civil disturbances in the UK brought about by disputes over the method of voting. In the Ukraine the situation was quite different. Following the elections of November 2004 thousands of citizens took to the streets claiming that the election was not fully free and fair. Prominent amongst their complaints, which were echoed by international election observers from the Organisation for Co-operation and Security in Europe, the European Union and NATO, were claims that public employees were coerced into handing over their absentee voting papers so that they could be filled in by their superiors, presumably in favour of the officially supported candidate. In the US Presidential election of November 2000 there were difficulties with the electromechanical voting machines used in Florida, which led to huge numbers of ballot papers being rendered unreadable. The questions of whether these ballots should be counted and the calendar for the counting of these disputed votes were litigated in the Florida courts and thence to the US Supreme Court.[1]

It will be argued that, whilst the present system of voting may (or may not) have contributed to the fall in electoral turnout in the UK, as is frequently claimed, the alternative voting methods supported by the main political parties (such as all-postal ballots, e-voting etc) are not only antithetical to the democratic model of voting – in effect, extensions of the market model – but are, in fact, primarily designed to remedy weaknesses in their own party organisations caused by steeply declining membership. The phenomenon of 'vote bartering' or 'vote swapping' – which must be sharply distinguished from the related practice of 'tactical voting' – will also be examined. Tactical voting will be considered as a matter of principle and as a matter of political tactics. Whilst some commentators have suggested that tactical voting disrupts party hegemony, it will be argued that the opposite is the case.

What underlies all these disputes about the method of voting is a deeper question of principle about how to understand the relation between the voter and 'their' vote. The main argument presented in this chapter is that, rather than the vote being seen as the personal or individual property of the voter to be disposed of in whatever way they think best (including not using it all), the vote should be seen, at least in one important sense, as a species of communal property. This means, in turn, that the act of voting has to be, in a sense, separated from the

---

1   See *Bush v Gore* 531 US 98 (2000).

content of the vote: whilst the content of the vote must remain secret (private, personal and 'individual') for reasons that will become all too obvious, *the act of voting* itself is a public or citizenly act.

Mechanisms of voting: the history

The original method of voting in England was by public show of hands, but there is a 17th century judgment[2] establishing that it is unlawful for the official conducting the election to deny the candidates a poll in circumstances where the result could not readily be seen. Furthermore, in the 18th century secret ballots were conducted from time to time in situations where there was a danger that the person elected might subsequently favour his supporters or disfavour his opponents, if these were made known through the voting process.[3] Lord Denning MR, in *Morgan v Simpson*,[4] referred to the large number of contested election results between 1848 and 1858, as reported in Power, Rodwell and Dew's Election Cases; he also drew attention to Charles Dickens' fictional account of the Eatanswill election in Chapter 13 of *The Pickwick Papers*. The problem with an open vote is that voters can easily and verifiably be bribed, treated (the technical term for bribery with food or drink) or intimidated. Today the principle of the secret ballot in elections would seem almost incontestable, so 'self-evident' that it would be unimaginable to return to any system where it is readily visible how the individual voter has chosen.

However, there are respectable arguments in favour of open, that is, publicly visible voting and it may well be that some of these arguments supported the survival of the open poll into the 19th century, albeit at that moment in a way that was linked to the argument (propounded by Bagehot and supported by Holdsworth – see Chapter 2) against widening the franchise. So the question is how could a property-based franchise be connected with open voting? Laying aside the cynical view that a propertied class would in any case be adept at maintaining its own privileges, there was also a strong expectation that these property-entitled voters could view themselves as having obligations, social, religious and moral, to act for the common good in the conduct of public affairs and that whether they lived up to these expectations would be appropriately represented and tested in open voting. With an open and public poll it might well be that the selfish voter would subsequently find themselves disfavoured by their colleagues. Thus in *Starling v*

2 *Starling v Turner* (1684) 2 Lev 50.
3 See the discussion in *Anthony v Seger* (1789) 1 Hag Con 9.
4 [1975] QB 151; [1974] 3 All ER 722.

Turner,[5] the mayor who refused the voters a poll, and presumably appointed his own favoured candidate, was spared further punishment by the courts because he was then deprived of his mayoralty by the voters.

However, the arguments for open voting have been made, most persuasively by John Stuart Mill in *Considerations on Representative Government*.[6] He argues for open voting to take place even where there is a universal adult franchise. He argues, in Chapter X *'Of the Mode of Voting'*, that the impression misleadingly presented to the voter 'is that the suffrage is given to him for himself – for his particular use and benefit and not as a trust for the public'.[7] Mill's views on the 'right to vote' have already been discussed in Chapter 2 above, but in Chapter X he makes clear his views on the connection between the method of voting and the right to vote, specifically on the connection between secret ballot voting and the misperception that the vote is a species of personal property. For Mill, voting ought to be open and public because this method would promote decisions in the public good; voters would be obliged to justify their choices to their fellows and might therefore be less willing to behave in a wholly selfish manner.

This argument was revived in the 20th century by Geoffrey Brennan and Philip Pettit, whose argument will be considered in detail below.[8]

It would seem that John Stuart Mill's argument was rejected because of the prevalence of corruption in 19th century elections. It had been hoped that bribery treating and intimidation would be brought to an end by the passage of the Ballot Act 1872,[9] which amended the law relating to procedure at parliamentary and municipal elections. Section 2 of the Act still serves as a description of the present state of the law and the first two paragraphs may, with advantage, be quoted in full.

> In the case of a poll at an election the votes shall be given by ballot. The ballot of each voter shall consist of a paper (in this Act called a ballot paper) showing the names and description of the candidates. Each ballot paper shall have a number printed on the back and shall have attached a counterfoil with the same number printed on the face. At the time of voting, the ballot paper shall be marked on both sides with an official mark, and delivered to the voter within the polling station, and the number of such voter on the register of voters shall be marked on the counterfoil, and the voter having secretly marked his vote on the paper, and folded it up so

---

5   See *Starling v Turner* (1684) 2 Lev 50.
6   References are to the 1991, New York: Prometheus Books edition.
7   Mill, 1991, p 205.
8   For a trenchant argument in support of public voting see Brennan and Pettit, 1990, pp 311–33.
9   35&36 Vict. ch 33.

as to conceal his vote, shall place it in a closed box in the presence of the officer presiding at the polling station (in this Act called 'the presiding officer') after having shown to him the official mark at the back.

Any ballot paper which has not on its back the official mark, or on which votes are given to more candidates than the voter is entitled to vote for, or on which anything, except the said number on the back, is written or marked by which the voter can be identified, shall be void and not counted.

The principle of secrecy set out in s 2 of the Act was buttressed by s 4, which provided that all those present at a polling station or at the count 'shall maintain and aid in maintaining the secrecy of the voting' under penalty of up to six months' imprisonment with or without hard labour. The same penalty was available to punish those who induced voters to show them their marked ballot.

A comparison of the 1872 Act, including its first Schedule, the Rules for Parliamentary Elections, with the Representation of the People Act (RPA) 1983 will, not surprisingly, reveal a high degree of congruence because the 1983 Act is little more than a consolidation of the 19th and early 20th century Acts. Unfortunately the 19th century reforms were not immediately effective in curtailing the abuses, for it took until the beginning of the First World War for the flood of claims of abuse to subside to the trickle that finally dried up in the 1920s. Few of the cases in the period 1872 to 1914 need detailed analysis. They mainly serve to illustrate the various types of bribery and corruption to which those desirous of obtaining the election of their candidate would resort.

Some examples of 19th century electoral corruption will, no doubt, help to make the point. If we look at the first five cases reported in Volume 3 of O'Malley and Hardcastle's Reports, which relate to election petitions brought in 1874 and 1875, we find that they each begin with sentences containing the words '(t)he petition (or petitions) contained the usual allegation (or allegations) of corrupt practices'. The third case, *Borough of Stroud*,[10] shows that a large number of voters were bribed (that is, paid money) to vote for a particular candidate or to emigrate so that they would not vote. Further electors were *treated* (that is, given food or drink) at a hotel in order to secure their vote. In the following case, *St Ives*,[11] there was such general treating proved that the election was declared void at common law. Finally, in the *Borough of Norwich*[12] case, the successful candidate was shown to have given employment (though the duties were purely nominal) to a number of men in order to secure

---

10 (1875) 3 O'M & H 7.
11 (1875) 3 O'M & H 13.
12 (1875) 3 O'M & H 15.

their support. If we were to look back to the cases in the first volume of O'Malley and Hardcastle's Reports, which predate the 1872 Act, we would see that the situation was even worse. Bribery, treating and the issuance of threats and blandishments were so common as to be almost *de rigueur*.

Perhaps the most important feature of the 1872 Act in regard to the method of voting was the fact that the Act only provided for voting at the polling station. There was no provision for postal or any other form of absentee voting. Even those voters who could not personally vote, by reason of their blindness or other physical cause, or who could not read or, if the poll was on a Saturday, would not vote because it would breach the Jewish Sabbath, were obliged to ask the presiding officer to complete a ballot paper on their behalf in the presence of the agents of the candidates.[13] Over the years between 1872 and 1945 there was a slow and gradual move to allow the casting of votes by proxies where the voter himself (or, latterly, herself) could not attend the polling station. The rules for allowing a proxy vote or even a postal vote for an absent voter were substantially relaxed in 1945, no doubt as a consequence of the absence of many men fighting in the armed services – and a man absent on military service or working away from home[14] clearly provided the model behind these new rules, which were intended to be temporary, but were then consolidated into the Representation of the People Act 1948.

These provisions were in turn consolidated into the RPA 1983 with the basic scheme remaining that the concession of a proxy or a postal ballot was extraordinary and was only to be granted where the voter was unable to attend at the polling station. A small extension was introduced to the law in 1985 whereby British citizens living overseas became eligible to vote and a number of technical amendments were made to the law on postal and proxy voting. The provisions contained in the 1983 Act were repealed and replaced by those of the Representation of the People Act 1985, but it seems that the only issue of principle introduced was the extension of suffrage to overseas voters.

However, the most far-reaching amendments to the law relating to methods of voting were made in 2000. First, the Representation of the People Act (RPA) 2000, by s 12 and Sched 4, superseded the provisions of

---

13 See Rule 27 of the Rules for Parliamentary Elections contained in the First Sched to the 1872 Act.

14 See Pt 4 of the RPA 1945; 8&9 Geo. VI, ch 5 of 15 February 1945. The folklore is that the Service vote was instrumental in electing the 1945 Attlee government and that the result was a 'popular Labour landslide', but the figures do not bear this out. For a discussion of the timetable, the catalogue of events, and a breakdown of the figures, see Calder, 1969, pp 660–73. Calder's approach bears comparison with the understandable elation and hyperbole to be found in Williams, F, 1950, pp 355–58.

ss 5–9 of the 1985 Act and provided that any person could apply for and be granted a postal vote for an indefinite time without having to fulfil any of the restrictions contained in the earlier Acts. It would be true to say that the current law provides for postal votes on demand. Secondly, ss 10–11 of the 2000 Act provide that the Secretary of State shall have power to approve pilot schemes to try out new methods of voting in local government elections. These pilot schemes have included tests of a wide range of ideas, such as extended polling hours and weekend voting, all-postal balloting and remote electronic voting using a variety of digital technologies in a variety of environments including the voters' own homes.[15] The most radical extension of these schemes was during the combined local government and European polls in June 2004 when, by virtue of the provisions of the European Parliamentary and Local Elections (Pilots) Act 2004, all-postal ballots were held in a number of areas. Section 10 of the 2000 Act provides that the operation and outcome of all pilot schemes will be subject to scrutiny by the Electoral Commission. The Electoral Commission has reported, in *Delivering Democracy?*, that it is unable to support the principle of further trials of all postal ballots.[16]

Why should the government, and (in so far as they do) the other political parties, want all-postal voting or remote voting by electronic means? Ostensibly this is because home-based voting will boost turnout.[17] However, there are two major drawbacks to this scheme. The first drawback is that there are very good reasons for believing that an election of representatives to the legislature, conducted under conditions which did not guarantee the secrecy of the ballot, would be held to be outside of the provisions set down in Art 3 of the 1st Protocol to the European Convention of Human Rights (ECHR). The argument may be summarised in the following way. Secrecy of the ballot is a fundamental principle of democracy and has been guaranteed under English law since the 19th century; it has also been enshrined in a number of international human rights instruments, notably Art 21(3) of the Universal Declaration of Human Rights, Art 25 of the 1966 International Covenant on Civil and Political Rights and, most importantly, in Art 3 of the 1st Protocol of the European Convention of Human Rights. This

---

15 See the Electoral Commission's Circular EC29/2002, which is a much more accurate and balanced summary of the research underlying the Pratchett Report, 2002 than the report itself. For the legal report, the emphasis of which was somewhat muted by Dr Pratchett, see Watt, B, 2002 'Legal issues concerning the implementation of electronic voting' http://www.local.regions.odpm.gov.uk/egov/e-voting/01/index.htm.

16 This point is subject to further comment in Chapters 7 and 8 of this book.

17 See, Birch and Watt, 2004, pp 60–72.

instrument has been incorporated into English law by the Human Rights Act 1998. The relevant provision of the Protocol states:

> The High Contracting Parties undertake to hold free elections at reasonable intervals by secret ballot, under conditions which will ensure the free expression of the opinion of the people in the choice of the legislature.

The precise legal meaning of the term 'secret ballot' has not been defined and there have been no cases in the European Court of Human Rights. However, some national decisions do point towards its meaning, especially the leading Irish case of *McMahon v The Attorney General*.[18] This case contains a number of challenges to Irish electoral law; the focus is upon the challenges to those provisions of the law that allowed for derogations from the principle of absolute secrecy.

The Irish Supreme Court held, affirming the ruling of Pringle J below, that the words 'secret ballot' in Art 16.1.4 of the Constitution of Ireland 1937 mean a ballot in which there is complete and inviolable secrecy. The wording is very similar to the words of Art 3 of the 1st Protocol ECHR. The Court held that that any provisions of the 1923 Ballot Act that enable a voter's completed ballot paper to be identified are inconsistent with the provisions of the 1937 Constitution. The Supreme Court held that there were circumstances in which secrecy could be restricted in order to assist the disabled voter. Ó Dálaigh CJ held that the Irish Constitution regarded the use of a companion's services, as required by the circumstances of the voter, as a minimal derogation from the strict secrecy of the ballot required by the Constitution, and that the Constitutional provision guaranteeing secrecy of the ballot remained intact. The words of the judgment are unambiguous. Referring to the fact that the limited secrecy enjoyed by disabled voters is not secrecy Ó Dálaigh CJ said:

> A law which contained provisions which enabled (a disabled person) to vote with the maximum degree of secrecy compatible with his incapacity would not only be desirable but would be necessary to implement the right to vote conferred on such person by the Constitution. I do not look upon the exercise, with less than full secrecy, of the incapacitated voter's franchise as being based on the principle of waiver by the voter; willy-nilly and of necessity his vote cannot be cast otherwise.

The plain words of Ó Dálaigh CJ in *McMahon* seem particularly apposite:

> (The Constitution) speaks of voting by secret ballot. The fundamental question is: secret to whom? In my opinion there can only be one plain and logical answer to that question. The answer is: secret to the voter. It is the

---

18 [1972] IR 69, p 105.

voter's secret. It is an unshared secret. It ceases to be a secret if it is disclosed.

In summary, the *McMahon* judgment provides that under the Irish Constitution any interference with the secrecy of the ballot has to be necessary in order to allow the voter to cast the ballot and must not be construed as a waiver by the citizen of the constitutional right.

It is clear, from the judgment of Sedley LJ in *Knight v Nicholls*,[19] that any substantive challenge to national voting practice under Art 3 of the 1st Protocol ECHR would need to be made before the European Court of Human Rights. Since the European Court of Human Rights has not yet tried to define 'secrecy', it must be the case that the meaning proposed by the Irish Supreme Court will be laid before the Court of Human Rights. The author has made this proposal in published work on a number of occasions and it appears to have received substantial endorsement from the Parliamentary Joint Committee on Human Rights.[20]

Secondly, there are clear dangers that postal voting and, *a fortiori*, remote voting by electronic means will increase the opportunities for bribery, treating, and the exercise of undue influence to corrupt the ballot and will improve the efficiency of vote bartering schemes (see below).[21] The argument may be summarised by saying that if people are able to associate into groups – such as in the home, the workplace, or friendship associations – whilst voting, they are likely to vote for reasons dictated by kinship and affection (or their opposites – dislike and fear) rather than in accordance with their judgment. This is a controversial view and in direct opposition to that put forward by John Stuart Mill and Geoffrey Brennan and Philip Pettit.

Mill (joined by Brennan and Pettit) believed that if and when we vote in a group we are more likely to vote in accordance with our balanced political judgment as to the best interests of society because, they argue, voting in a group opens each of us up to the democratic challenge of our

---

19 [2004] EWCA Civ 68; see, especially, paras 37–39.
20 See the Eighth Report of the 2003–04 Session of the Select Committee on Human Rights. http://www.publications.parliament.uk/pa/jt200304/jtselect/jtrights/49/4906.htm Paragraph 3.3 draws attention to the present author's work: '3.3 We have also received from the author copies of several published articles arguing that all forms of remote voting from home, including both electronic voting and postal voting, are intrinsically incompatible with the right to a secret ballot under Article 3 of Protocol No. 1 to the ECHR and the right to be free of discrimination in the enjoyment of Convention rights under ECHR Article 14. We understand that some people have also suggested that the amendments to clause 2 outlined in paragraph 3.17 below might be incompatible with the right to respect for private life under ECHR Article 8. We now report our view of the human rights implications of the Bill in the light of these various submissions and suggestions.'
21 These arguments are set out in full in Birch and Watt, 2004.

fellow citizens. An example would clarify the point. Suppose that a voter was known by their fellows to be a lifelong supporter of the Labour Party and yet, in an open poll, they voter for the Conservative Party candidate. Their fellows might then say, 'You have always been a Labour voter, why the change?' If our voter were to say that they had experienced a change of heart and now considered that the Conservative Party's policies were better for the country as a whole and mounted a spirited defence of that view, the Mill-Brennan-Pettit position would be vindicated. Our voter has stood up to the democratic challenge. However there is an obvious difficulty with this view. Supposing our voter puts their hand up for the Conservative candidate, whilst they are standing in the middle of a Labour group, they might well, in certain circumstances, be persuaded by hostile stares to lower their hand before it is counted. How can the 'circle be squared' and our voter be permitted to vote in accordance with their judgement?

The answer to this question can be found in a detailed examination of the arguments put forward by the 'public choice theorists', most notably Geoffrey Brennan and Philip Pettit, James Buchanan, and Geoffrey Brennan and Loren Lomasky. Each of these writers (or pairs of writers) has made a significant contribution to the literature.[22] The arguments that are most germane to the themes set out in this book are best articulated by Brennan and Pettit (1990) and Brennan and Lomasky (1997). Brennan and Lomasky write from within the 'public choice' camp although they see their theory as being both 'an application of public choice theory' and 'also a critique of it'.[23] It therefore seems fair to characterise their theory as a *mature* statement of public choice theory.

'Preference voting' and 'democratic voting'

John Stuart Mill argued that the secret ballot, as provided for in the 1872 Act, led voters to believe that the franchise was something which a voter possessed 'for himself – for his particular use and benefit and not as a trust for the public'. In 1872 the vote had to be exercised personally in a strictly regulated polling station. In 2004, as a result of the legal changes over 132 years, which we have tracked, we can see that the suffrage may be exercisable in the home, in the shopping mall or in a variety of places without any supervision of a public official. It is easy to imagine John Stuart Mill's reaction. Clearly if the suffrage was rendered individual

---

22 For an assessment of their respective contributions, see the preface to Brennan and Lomasky, 1993, Cambridge. Page references are to the 1997 paperback edition and are rendered as 'Brennan and Lomasky, 1997, p x'.

23 Brennan and Lomasky, 1997, p 2.

and personal in 1872, it is now much more strongly atomised, without even the vestiges of public supervision at public sites. We must now expect the voter to think that the vote is for their individual use.

Brennan and Lomasky point out that there is a complex and obscure relationship between policies and electoral candidates,[24] and this cannot seriously be doubted. They present their arguments without troubling to unpack the distinctions between 'candidates' and 'policies', and this seems to be an acceptable way forward. It seems that it may most easily be rationalised by saying that candidates are representatives of, or champions for, policies.

John Stuart Mill championed that which might be called the 'democratic vote'; we can use the language of Brennan and Pettit to express this in terms of the 'judgement ideal'.

> The judgement ideal holds that a person's vote ought … to express his ranking of … candidates in the light only of matters which are of public interest. The ranking orders candidates' policies or persons by consideration of what is best for all, with no special weighting of what is best for the voter or for his immediate associates.[25]

Brennan and Pettit argue, along with Mill, that public voting promotes and fosters the 'judgment ideal' because if persons are liable to be called to account for their vote they are more likely to consider much more carefully the reasons for voting for a particular candidate. This is doubtful because if people are in small groups – such as family, workplace or friendship groups – they are likely to adopt, or at least incorporate, the social norms or opinions prevalent in the group and these may well have 'special weighting for what is best for the voter *or his immediate associates*' (emphasis added). Public voting in a 'town meeting' is judged less likely to suffer from this problem because voters in a 'town meeting' are more likely to be part of a large anonymous crowd. Accordingly, whilst truly public voting may further the judgment or democratic ideal, group voting is likely to inhibit truly reflective or democratic voting.

If we turn to Brennan and Pettit's alternative model, 'the preference ideal', we will see that the problems are even greater.

> The preference ideal claims that a person's vote … reflect[s] how he orders the alternative outcomes in his overall ranking of them. The outcomes on offer are the candidate policies or persons which compete for his support. His overall ranking of those candidates is that which he makes in the light

---

24 Brennan and Lomasky, 1997, p 22.
25 Brennan and Pettit, 1990, p 313.

of all relevant aspects of the outcomes, those of private concern as well as those of public.[26]

In their mature development of the work Brennan and Lomasky fully articulate the preference ideal. They believe that it explains actual voter behaviour. Necessarily, at least at the time of their writing, this was in the context of fully secret ballots; Brennan and Pettit explained in 1990 that the secret ballot promoted the ideal of preference voting. A preference voter is one who votes not only in accordance with their economic interests – as a personal wealth maximiser[27] – but also in accordance with 'various kinds of ethical and ideological principles that are suppressed in the market setting'.[28] Brennan and Lomasky describe the behaviour of voters (which we must understand as voters in secret) in terms of *expressive behaviour*. Voters behave not only in accordance with their own economic self-interest, but also in accordance with the way in which they see themselves as reflecting or living out a set of ethical self-images. Compare the two contrasting value sets set out below.

(1) I believe the people should be big, and the state should be small. I believe that personal happiness and economic success alike flourish when individuals and families are free to seize opportunities in their own way. I believe in the great national institutions – monarchy, parliament, courts of law – which enshrine our country's values and guard its identity.

(2) I believe that by the strength of our common endeavour we achieve more than we achieve alone, so as to create for each of us the means to realise our true potential and for all of us a community in which power, wealth and opportunity are in the hands of the many, not the few. I believe that the rights we enjoy reflect the duties we owe.[29]

The person who holds the first value set is pre-disposed to vote for the Conservative party, whilst the second voter tends towards the Labour party. Clearly, and this is the point made by Brennan and Lomasky,[30] neither set of ideological commitments is determinative of the actual vote cast. All political parties, including those mentioned by way of

---

26 Brennan and Pettit, 1990, p 313.

27 Brennan and Lomasky, 1997, p 10.

28 Brennan and Lomasky, 1997, p 16.

29 These two statements are adaptations of material on the Conservative Party (www.conservatives.com) and the Labour Party (www.labour.org.uk) websites respectively.

30 Brennan and Lomasky, 1997, appear to prioritise the economic interests of voters above their ideological interests. They first describe the voter as a species of *homo economicus* (at pp 9–10) before going on to set out his ideological interests. It is suggested that this is purely artefactual because they wish to distinguish their argument from that of earlier public choice theorists, notably James Buchanan.

example, have their sets of ideological values and their sets of economic and social policies; one may quite plausibly think of a voter who, initially or *prima facie*, prefers (or leans towards) one party 'ideologically' and another 'economically'. The 'balance point' of these sets of initial preferences is, in the view of Brennan and Lomasky, the voter's' *preference* – the determinant of the way in which the voter casts their ballot.

Brennan and Pettit claim that the secret vote permits a person to vote in accordance with their preference whilst, as we have, seen public voting tilts the voter towards their judgement vote. This may indeed be the case where the choice is between 'pure secret voting' (where the voter is shut away from the world in a polling booth isolated from their fellows) and 'pure public voting' (where the voter stands in the town square subject to the interrogation of their fellow citizens); however it need not be the case where voting takes place by a variety of means.

Consider first the situation where the voters cast their ballot by means of a mobile telephone, voting by 'text' or by voting by internet or digital interactive television. This may conveniently be called 'semi-secret voting'. Apart from the difficulties with the secrecy of the ballot where voting takes place in a semi-secret way, there is another problem raised by the use of the technology.

First addressed are the difficulties of the semi-secret vote; despite the optimism expressed by Brennan and Pettit[31] that there would be no return to 19th century levels of bribery, corruption and intimidation if the secret ballot is abandoned, we have no reason to think that this would be the case. Brennan and Pettit do not give a convincing reason for their view. A modern public vote and *a fortiori* a home vote (or semi-secret vote) does or would take place in a microcosm of society, and in those circumstances it is very easy for bribery, corruption and intimidation – explicit or implicit – to take place. Mill, in giving his arguments for a public vote, was writing in a situation in which patterns of social and emotional interdependence between voters were very different to those that subsist today. Whilst it is undoubtedly true that voters would be able to influence one another by means of rational argument, corruption having been rendered generally unlawful at the time he was writing, by the Corrupt Practices Prevention Act 1854 or its amendment in 1868, it is highly unlikely that many voters would be able to exert personal or familial pressure upon another voter. It is suggested that now that the age of majority has been reduced to 18 and women have obtained the vote it is far more likely that voters in the same household will be able to

---

31 Brennan and Pettit, 1990, pp 329–30.

exert emotional pressure one over the other. It is suggested that patterns of emotional pressure are likely to be far more complex than the mere issue of instructions by some Victorian *paterfamilias*, but no less effective. Women and children are, at least, as capable of using emotional pressure as men. These reasons suggest that it would be, at the least, unwise to allow the rules on secrecy of the ballot to be relaxed.[32]

If, following Brennan and Pettit, a public vote is a judgement vote and a secret vote is a preference vote, one might reasonably expect a semi-secret vote to be rather more 'judgement' than 'preference'. This need not be the case, perhaps somewhat paradoxically; the semi-secret vote may be more 'preference' than 'judgement'. If people are randomly distributed in a town meeting, there openly to cast their votes, we can expect them to have to justify their vote to all comers. Electors would have both attackers and defenders. If a person advanced an illegitimate or irrelevant reason to try to persuade someone to vote for a particular candidate, that person may well be shouted down. For example, if someone proposed to vote for a candidate (say, Mr Smith) and another voter said, 'I wouldn't vote for Smith because he has a "geeky" haircut', we could reasonably expect the author of the silly remark to be ridiculed. Smith's hairstyle is, of itself, irrelevant to whether or not he is worthy of election. It could conceivably be a signal of his policies, but without further information it is wholly irrelevant. However, in the home or social group, the fact that Smith has a 'geeky' haircut may be common currency. If we couple that with the fact that the technology would then allow the ballot to be instantly cast, we could have a number of votes being recorded against Smith on the basis of his questionable barbering. This seems to be a preference outside the sphere envisaged by Brennan and Lomasky, but we can easily conceive of other (un)ethical preferences in a social group, which would be closer to Brennan and Lomasky's thoughts. Whilst membership of a social group can tend against, for example, racism – because few people would voice racist opinions in a public forum – it may be that they would be willing so to do in a small group. Group leaders may speak or act against racist sentiments, but they could, equally well, encourage them. Again the immediacy of the technology allows for unfortunate results. It is conceded that within some social groups and families high level political discussions are the norm and the judgment view may prevail, but, even amongst those who discuss politics for a living, everyone needs a rest.

Secondly, the technological factors are important. The digital communication technologies are intimately connected with the market

---

32 Quite apart from the pre-emptive legal reason for supporting the secrecy of the ballot, ie, Art 3 of the 1st Protocol to the ECHR, there seem to be good policy reasons for retaining the secret ballot.

and consumerism. If one looks at the average television screen, advertising hoarding or high street shopping centre one cannot fail to notice the messages extolling the supposed virtues of this or that mobile telephone, computer or television. The communications networks and broadcast media are similarly promoted. If any goods are 'lifestyle goods', digital communications technologies must fit that description. It cannot be too speculative to suggest that the use of these technologies has an effect upon voting behaviour. If people identify with their mobile telephones, might they not also say that they are the kind of person who votes by means of their mobile telephone. This is not so far from the ideas set out by Brennan and Lomasky.[33] They suggest that much of human behaviour, including voting behaviour, can be described as *expressive* behaviour. For example, people buy expensive 'get well' cards to send to their friends who are unwell. Clearly, a card is no substitute for medical treatment and it can have no more than the narrowest marginal effect upon the patient's recovery. Nevertheless, people continue to buy such cards to send to their friends because cards of that nature express something of their own personalities. It is suggested that a voter may well say that voting by digital electronic means expresses some part of the voter's personality. It might say, for example, 'I am an up-to-the-minute person', 'I am a busy person', 'My time is simply too valuable to waste queuing in a polling station' or 'I can afford this technology'. These expressions of personality are central to Brennan and Lomasky's idea of preference voting and move us further away from the judgment ideal of democracy.

Clearly 'preferences' in the ordinary sense of the word are central to markets and, if we examine Brennan and Lomasky's idea just a little more closely, we can see that 'preference voting' is very close to a market idea. Preference voting involves the voter in making a decision on the basis of a wide range of factors, economic and social. People participate in a consumer market on grounds other than the purely economic. If people were pure economic actors they would simply buy the cheapest goods that fulfilled the function. They do not, because they take into account such concepts as 'style' and 'luxury'. People do not buy 'prestige cars' simply because they are more mechanically efficient than other vehicles; they buy them because of the reflections of self worth and social esteem they cast on the owner.

These ideas are not expressed in a final form because empirical research will be needed to test them out. The central claim is that the new voting technologies and, to a lesser extent, the general availability of postal voting increase the tendency of people to 'vote their preferences'

33 Brennan and Lomasky, 1997, p 33.

rather than 'vote their judgment'. This is more compatible with a market model of voting law rather than a democratic (or judgment) model of electoral law.

Before suggesting that there is available an alternative model of voting reform that is more compatible with the democratic ideal, we need to examine two further serious disadvantages of elections based upon digital electronic technology. The first of these disadvantages arises from the application of the internet as a vote-bartering technology. If people can vote on the internet it seems that they will be only a few keystrokes away from bartering their vote on the internet.

Vote bartering

Vote bartering or vote swapping is the process whereby one voter, whose favoured party (Party A) has little chance of success in their own constituency, makes contact with a voter in another constituency, whose own party (Party B) is similarly situated, and says: 'If I vote for Party B in my constituency, there is a good chance that Party B will win the election over Party C whom we both detest; whilst in your constituency my Party A candidate has a good chance of beating Party C. If you vote Party A (which is your second choice) instead of Party B, and I vote Party B (which is my second choice) instead of Party A, we stand a good chance of getting a Party B MP in my constituency and a Party A MP in your constituency. That way we both get our second choices rather than our third choices; furthermore it means that there is a Party A and a Party B member in the House rather than two Party C members. This may determine the party of government.'

This is, in effect, what is involved in tactical voting. However, vote bartering must be sharply distinguished from tactical voting although the proponents of both schemes, or to use the pejorative (which seems preferable) 'scams', confuse the terms. Vote bartering is that process described above; it depends critically upon direct contact between voters. Tactical voting is much less structured. It does not depend upon direct contact between voters, but instead relies upon the publication of lists of seats in which tactical voting can make a difference and the impassioned pleas for people to vote tactically.[34]

There are two mechanisms whereby vote bartering can be effected. The first, which will be described as 'high-trust vote bartering', involves two people from different constituencies simply agreeing to vote for each other's choice of candidate. The second, which will be described as 'low-trust vote bartering', involves these two people swapping voter

---

34 See, eg, Toynbee, 2001; McDonald, 2001.

identifiers in order to vote in each other's place. For example: I live in the North-East Essex parliamentary constituency; if I wish to vote in Colchester in order to help secure the election of my preferred candidate and my vote bartering partner wishes to vote in North-East Essex to secure the election of their preferred candidate, we simply swap our electronic voter identities and vote in accordance with our own choices. If we vote by text, for example, this simply means that I give my vote bartering partner my electoral roll number and any authorisation code and they text the number appropriate for their choice. They would then give me their identifiers and I would act similarly. It is suggested that the 'low-trust' model will soon overwhelm the high-trust model if vote bartering is permitted to thrive.

The effect of vote bartering has, to date, been rather small, and it is not possible to determine the effect of ordinary tactical voting. If we look at vote bartering in the 2001 general election we can only see two constituencies in which it plainly had an effect. The votedorset.net website makes the claim that 'tactical voting [for which read 'vote bartering'] by Labour and Lib Dem [Liberal Democrat] supporters across the country kept Tory gains to the barest of minimums'[35] – one seat.[36] The organisers of votedorset.net claim that the results of the polls were, at least in part, determined by Liberal Democrats voting for their second preference in South Dorset, which Labour won by a majority of 153 votes against a small national trend, and Labour supporters voting their second preference in Mid-Dorset, which was captured by the Liberal Democrats by a margin of 384 votes.

Is vote bartering lawful? The provision which comes closest to outlawing such activity is s 115 of the RPA 1983:

> 115 (1) A person shall be guilty of a corrupt practice if he is guilty of undue influence.
>
> ...
>
> (2)(b) if, by abduction, duress or any fraudulent device or contrivance, he impedes or prevents the free exercise of the franchise of an elector or proxy for an elector, or so compels, induces or prevails upon an elector or proxy for an elector either to vote or to refrain from voting.

In fact, it is clear that in law, on the current reading of s 115 as set down in *R v Rowe ex p Mainwaring and others*[37] (discussed in Chapter 6), that it is unlikely that such a practice could amount to undue influence in the

---

35 www.votedorset.net.
36 This was the Newark seat that was lost by Fiona Jones. Ms Jones' case is discussed at length in Chapter 5.
37 [1992] 4 All ER 821; [1992] 1 WLR 1059.

form of impeding or preventing the free exercise of the franchise because it would not seem that the voters who were induced to change their vote were in any way defrauded. The current law, as we shall see, requires that an actual voter must in fact be deceived or impeded in their vote for the offence to be made out. In the case of these 'vote swappers', they were not cheated, they entered the scheme knowingly and willingly and voted for a party other than their first choice in order to gain what they saw as a greater good. They wished to keep out candidates of one political party at all costs. They did so without violating the letter of current electoral law. That having been said, it is argued that vote swappers are cheats of an egregious order. Representatives are sent to parliament to act as advocates for a particular and identifiable group of citizens. Nowadays the group of citizens is identified on the basis of geographical areas (such as parliamentary constituencies, district council wards etc) containing more or less equal numbers of citizens. In the recent past the Boundary Commissions took into account the existence of identifiable communities of citizens who might be taken to share a common interest.[38] In earlier centuries this could be seen in the multiplicity of franchises. Some authors have even advocated the adoption of a franchise based upon types of voters.[39] No matter how the franchise is constructed, there is clearly a need for an individual or collective function of advocacy for the resolution of individual or group problems. The phenomenon of vote bartering clearly degrades this function, for it may be that the local majority's choice of advocate is frustrated by the influence of voters from outside the constituency

Secondly, and this is a point of general application which will resurface throughout this book, we need to consider the potential significance of the notion of a 'fraudulent device or contrivance' in the context of what is being determined and who is being affected. The voters of a given area or constituency normally go to the polls in the expectation and belief that the choice (on whatever basis they make that choice) of their majority will be elected. They have every right to expect that the choice will be that of people in the area or constituency. In the case of low-trust vote bartering (described above) it is clear that the actual votes being cast are not the votes of people inside the constituency, but are, in fact, those of outsiders. If vote bartering takes place it is the honest voters within the constituency who are being defrauded by a device or contrivance.

---

38 For a full account of the work of the Boundary Commissions, see Rossiter, Johnston and Pattie, 1999; and McLean and Butler, 1996.

39 See the useful summary and critique of the ideal political constitution set out in von Hayek, 1989, pp 1–38, at p 14.

Is there a legal mechanism which might be used to prevent this sort of abuse? There are two candidates. The first potential mechanism comes from traditional English administrative law and involves a novel use of the rule against fettering one's discretion. The traditional use of this rule is to prevent a public administrator from binding himself to taking a decision in a particular way rather than using his unfettered discretion at the appropriate time. A useful example can be found in the *Fares Fair* case.[40] A detailed discussion of the facts of the case is unnecessary; suffice it to say that the members of the Labour group who had recently been elected as the controlling majority on the Greater London Council (GLC) considered themselves to be under an obligation to implement a commitment made in their joint election manifesto which had been drawn up by the London Labour Party. In the case when it came to the House of Lords, Lord Diplock declared that it was unlawful for the councillors to bind themselves to such an obligation:

> A council member once elected is not the delegate of those who voted in his favour only; he is the representative of all the electors (ie, adult residents) in his ward. If he fought the election on the basis of policies for the future put forward in the election manifesto of a particular political party, he presumably himself considered that in the circumstances contemplated in the manifesto those policies were in the best interest of the electors in his ward, and, if the democratic system as at present practised in local government is to survive, the fact that he received a majority of votes of those electors who took enough interest in the future policies to be adopted by the GLC to cause them to cast their votes, is a factor to which considerable weight ought to be given by him when participating in the collective duty of the GLC to decide whether to implement those policies in the circumstances that exist at the time that the decision falls to be made. That this may properly be regarded as a weighty factor is implicit in the speeches in this House in *Secretary of State for Education and Science v Tameside Metropolitan Borough*,[41] although the issues dealt with in that case were very different from those arising in the present appeals. In this respect, I see no difference between those members of the GLC who are members of what as a result of the election becomes the majority party and those who are members of a minority party. In neither case when the time comes to play their part in performing the collective duty of the GLC to make choices of policy or action on particular matters, must members treat themselves as irrevocably bound to carry out pre-announced policies contained in election manifestos even though, by that time, changes of circumstances have occurred that were unforeseen when those policies

---

40 *Bromley LBC v GLC* [1983] 1 AC 768.
41 [1976] 3 All ER 665; [1977] AC 1014.

were announced and would add significantly to the disadvantages that would result from carrying them out.[42]

The important features of Lord Diplock's judgment are, first, that a councillor is not bound by their election manifesto, which represents no more than a loose commitment to their own supporters. Once councillors are elected they become subject to a duty to consider the interests of all their constituents. They must consider the situation that meets them upon attaining office, and that situation may mean breaking manifesto commitments. This may sound counter-intuitive because it is certain that the majority of voters expect their councillors to carry forward the manifesto, but it is nevertheless the law. Secondly, it must be noted that Lord Diplock's formulation places the power to decide policy back where it belongs – in the hands of the public official. Could this second principle be used to prevent vote bartering? It can if we take the view, and this position is urged upon the reader throughout this book, that the vote is not the property of the elector, but is held by the elector in the interests of the polity as a whole. Just as the Labour councillors were obliged by the law (as stated by Lord Diplock) to consider the interests of the electorate as a whole, a voter ought to consider the interests of the polity as a whole. Clearly, voters might not do this, but at the very least they ought to be obliged by the law (in accordance with the second principle) to use their own judgment in voting on the choices before them. They ought not to be permitted to have another person dictate their vote.

This is an extension of the rule against fettering discretion and, it is conceded, be a step too far. It clearly involves treating individual voters as a species of public official. However, and in answer to that point, it has been argued that the responsibility upon a citizen is to use his or her own judgement to choose the best government in the interests of all citizens. Obliging citizens to use their own judgement does not seem to be an unduly onerous obligation.

Before moving to consider a mechanism for enforcement, it is useful to set out a second potential legal mechanism for enforcing a rule against vote bartering. The discussion of s 115(2)(b) of the RPA 1983 in Chapter 6 below makes it plain that, for the election offence to be made out, the attempt to deceive an elector (or electors) must succeed in actually deceiving an elector and thus impede the free exercise of the franchise of an elector. The rule established in *R v Rowe ex p Mainwaring* is criticised in Chapter 6 and, towards the end of the chapter, a legal mechanism is proposed for the general control of electoral malpractice. This involves using the radical teleological, or purposive, approach to the jurisprudence of the European Convention of Human Rights set out by

---

42 At p 829.

the House of Lords in *Ghaidan v Mendoza*.[43] In *Ghaidan*, the House considered whether the provisions of an Act of Parliament (the Rent Act 1977) that predated the Human Rights Act 1998, but which contained an issue addressed by the European Convention of Human Rights (the right to respect for a person's home), should be interpreted in a manner consistent with the European Convention. The House of Lords decided that the 1977 Act should be given an interpretation consistent with the core meaning of the Convention right. The question thus becomes: 'should s 115(2)(b) of the RPA 1983 be given a meaning consistent with the right contained in Art 3 of the 1st Protocol ECHR?' The only permissible answer to that *general* question must be 'yes', and that *general* answer must extend to the whole of the 1983 Act. This answer to the general question does not amount to an answer to any specific question raised under the RPA 1983. The specific question now becomes: 'does an agreement between a number of electors to engage in vote bartering amount to a fraudulent device which is an impediment to a free and fair election?' This question can only be answered by a court, but the proposed answer is that such an agreement is indeed a fraudulent device.

Support for this proposition can be constructed in the following way. We can postulate that the expectation of voters in any given constituency is that the wishes of the majority of *bona fide* electors expressed in the ballot box will (not may) lead to the election of the MP. Electoral law would not permit voters from outside the constituency to vote within it; neither would it permit people from outside the constituency to appoint proxies to vote within it in accordance with the wishes of the external electors. To use the example of Colchester and North-East Essex set out above – if an elector were to present themselves at the ballot box in Colchester saying that they were a proxy for a North-East Essex elector, they would be turned away.

Accordingly, by either of these theories, vote bartering is legally a highly dubious practice and it is hoped that it will be challenged through the courts if it is used in the forthcoming (perhaps 2005) general election. Should newspaper encouragements to vote tactically be similarly treated? The only answer consistent with the theory set out in this book is positive. How might this be accomplished? The best answer would be by the creation of a specific electoral offence, but there may be a, perhaps rather weak, common law alternative. The House of Lords held, in *DPP v Shaw*,[44] that the publication of details of prostitutes, so that they could be contacted by prospective clients, amounted to the novel common law

---

43 [2004] UKHL 30; [2004] 3 All ER 411.
44 [1962] AC 220.

offence of a conspiracy to corrupt public morals. This sounds, at least *prima facie*, to be a very long way from election law, but there are a number of similarities, at least in principle, between the offence of conspiring to corrupt public morality and the proposed offence of conspiring to corrupt an election. Not least one could argue that the damage to the body politic is greater in the second case.

The 'Daily Me'

There is a further political argument against the introduction of remote electronic voting.[45] This argument is a development of that set out by Cass Sunstein in his book *Republic.com*.[46]

Sunstein's argument is that the observed pattern of internet use is that users, instead of stretching their intellectual horizons by means of the internet, soon become consumers of the 'Daily Me' which is to say that by the use of collaborative filtering software[47] internet users are able to build up, or have built up for them, a personalised or individualised menu of web sources. They obtain their goods, information and ideas from a relatively small pool of sources, which they revisit frequently. The practice of obtaining goods and services via the internet inhibits them from browsing amongst a wider range of goods and ideas and thus making chance discoveries. This leads to the citizens becoming highly individualised consumers of goods and ultimately of political and social ideas and *mores*. Sunstein argues that the motivating force behind the political culture of the USA – the 1st Amendment to the Constitution – which guarantees freedom of speech, is being weakened because the ideas of citizens are not being challenged in public *fora*. Accordingly, the reflective or deliberative nature of republican democracy is being undermined by the soundbite and the ready opportunities for polling provided by the internet. To put this argument into the terms suggested in the first chapter of this book, the internet cannot be conceived of as a 'marketplace of ideas'; it is much more like 'home shopping' in which, quite unlike the real marketplace, one cannot be tempted by the unfamiliar or chance item seen on the stall, one is limited to one's original choice of good.

It must be observed that the contrast between the delivery of political information by internet and the physical delivery of a full range of paper

---

45 This is not to resile from the other arguments I have advanced. The argument was deployed at the Association of Electoral Administrators' Annual Seminar and Conference, Blackpool, February 2004. I am grateful for the feedback from members of the Association.

46 Sunstein, 2001. Page references are to the 2002 revised paperback edition.

47 Sunstein, 2001, p 25.

literature from all the political parties and candidates offering themselves for election could not be clearer.[48] Whilst people cannot be forced to read political leaflets it is much more likely that they will at least glance at a wider range of ideas when faced with 'hardcopy' than if they are simply faced with the opportunity to press the 'Del' key.

It could plausibly be argued that one of the main reasons the political parties are so interested in moving over to 'electronic campaigning' is that membership of political parties is falling, so there are fewer people to campaign on the doorstep. The real problem with the internet as a source of political information, as opposed to the party worker, is that the internet is simply a source of information; it is easy to argue with a canvasser, difficult to argue with a computer.

A practical suggestion

It is now time to try to 'cash-in' some of the ideas set out above in this chapter, by means of a practical suggestion. As we have seen from the work of Brennan and Lomasky, electoral behaviour is expressive behaviour. People try to 'say' something about themselves as they vote. It is proposed that people be given a better opportunity to express themselves whilst voting as citizens of a democracy. The five elements which make up this proposal are set out below, together with some argument in favour of each one of the elements.

As explained above, s 10 of the RPA 2000 allows local authorities, with the approval of the Secretary of State, and under the oversight of the Electoral Commission, to conduct pilot schemes to evaluate novel voting methods. It is proposed in this book that a particular pilot experiment be conducted. It might be that the running of individual pilot schemes in a few areas would not be an appropriate way of conducting this trial because other amendments to the law would be necessary. It could be that a nationwide trial is needed. The outline conditions for the pilot scheme would be quite familiar to those voting under the conditions imposed by the 1872 Act; the overwhelming majority of ballots would be cast in an ordinary polling station by the personal attendance of voters at the polling station.

Date of the ballot

First, the ballot should be conducted on the usual day for voting in district council or county council elections, in other words, on the first Thursday in May. There have been trials of voting on other days of the

---

48 As set out in s 71 of the RPA 1983, tested out in the Watford pilot discussed below and in the London Mayoral election in 2004.

week. One of these trials took place in Watford in May 2000. That trial was evaluated by Steven Lake on behalf of the Association of Electoral Administrators.[49] Mr Lake is a highly experienced election official. The turnout was low for a number of reasons and these reasons explain why the proposed trial should be held on the ordinary voting day. In the Watford trial there was the opportunity for early voting over an extended period (that is voting on the ordinary day for voting (Thursday) and over the following weekend, so that voting was completed before the usual polling day). Lake commented, in his evaluation of the Watford experiment, that this wider availability of dates may have confused voters about the proper day for voting. There were other elections, including some with high media profiles, taking place around the same time as the Watford election. Lake's study also showed that, whilst there was some support for weekend voting because people were grateful not to have to go out again after work on the Thursday, there were also a significant number of adverse factors. Some people objected to Sunday voting, presumably – it is not stated – on grounds of their religious observance. This is an important objection because those who attend church on Sunday are deeply committed to their faith and it is clearly important that they should not have conflicting pressures placed upon them. If they see church attendance as an important religious duty they should not be placed in a position where this would conflict with their civic duty to take part in government. By the same token, exactly the same considerations apply to Fridays and Saturdays because neither Muslim nor Jewish citizens should be faced with this conflict of loyalty between observance of their faith and observance of their public duty. Furthermore, Lake observes that the weekend was favoured with good weather and he believed that many people took the opportunity to leave the town for recreation, thus depressing the turnout. It is argued that since voting is a public, rather than a private, responsibility people ought not to be obliged to give up their leisure time in order to vote.

The final important reason for the ballot to be conducted on the same day as every other vote is to emphasise the fact that voters are participating in an act of civil solidarity.

This brings us to the most important element in the proposed pilot scheme. It has been argued over the course of this and the preceding chapter that voting is a civic duty. Democracy is government by the people and therefore the state promotes opportunities for the citizenry to take part in its own self-government. It should do this not only by ensuring that barriers are removed, such as the possibility of conflict

49 See Baston and Ritchie, 2004, pp 26–27.

between religious and civic observance or, for that matter, between recreation or family commitments and civic duty but by positively promoting the opportunity to vote.

Time off work to vote

It is accordingly proposed that all employees be given a half-day, or even a full day, free from work in order to vote. This could be done by the grant of an extra day (or half-day) of paid leave. This would be simple in the case of public employees and, in the case of private employees, by recompensing their employers by a rebate through the national insurance and PAYE tax system. If employers objected, 'What? Another day's holiday?', and attempted to prevent employees from taking the day off, this should be seen as both an automatically unfair employment wrong remediable through the Employment Tribunal system and as an electoral wrong under the provisions of s 115 RPA 1983. Employers are already used to granting employees two days of rest each week and annual holiday,[50] and the addition of a single day each year at the expense of the state is hardly to be seen as an intolerable imposition. Since it is normally possible to ascertain the time of local elections for some years ahead, it should be possible to plan for an extra day's closure. Clearly, there will be some essential workers, members of the emergency services, etc, for whom it will be much more difficult to make arrangements, but this could be accomplished by rostering a half-day and recompensing the workers concerned by giving them time off in lieu.

The establishment of a right to complain to an Employment Tribunal that a voter had been denied the right to time off work to vote would require an amendment to the provisions of Pt VI of the Employment Rights Act 1996. This would best be accomplished by means of the addition of a new s 50A to the Act. This would make it clear that voting is to be seen as a public duty in the same way that acting as a Justice of the Peace or a member of a statutory authority is a public duty. Whilst a person is not paid by the employer for acting as a member of a statutory authority, because out-of-pocket expenses and allowances are normally paid, it is argued that arranging for payment through the employer, with reimbursement as a tax or national insurance credit, is the least administratively onerous way of dealing with the matter. It is also submitted that it seems rather peculiar that parents and others should, and quite properly so, be given time off work so as to cope with their

---

50 See the Working Time Regulations 1998 SI 1998/1833 as amended by the 1999 Regulations SI 1999/3372.

dependents' needs under s 57A of the 1996 Act whilst they are not given time off work in order to fulfil their most basic duty as citizens.

The objection will be made that if people wish to vote that is surely a matter for them; it is a matter of their own individual choice; why should they be supported in this activity? John Stuart Mill has already shown us the path to an answer. Voting is not an individual private activity; it is a civic activity and for that reason ought to be publicly nurtured.

Polling station provision

Secondly, we should turn to the provision of polling stations. Sufficient polling stations should be provided with the capacity to cope with a 100% turnout and these polling stations should be readily accessible.

Mill took the view that: 'The polling places should be no numerous as to be within easy reach of every voter, and no expenses of conveyance, at the cost of the candidate, should be tolerated under any pretext. The infirm, and they only on medical certificate, should have the right of claiming suitable carriage conveyance at the cost of the state or the locality.'[51]

Under Rule 20 of both the Local Elections (Principal Areas) Rules 1986[52] and the Local Elections (Parishes and Communities) Rules 1986[53] and, for the sake of completeness, Rule 25 of the Parliamentary Election Rules 1983:[54]

> The returning officer shall provide a sufficient number of polling stations and, subject to the following provisions of this rule, shall allot the electors to the polling stations in such manner as he thinks most convenient.

Schools and other public buildings are freely available to the returning officer in order to site the polling stations under the relevant rules contained in the same legal instruments.[55] The returning officer should book sufficient school buildings and rooms to cope with a 100% turnout. Whilst there have been complaints in the recent past about schools being closed at election time and parents having to take time off work to care for their children, this should present no hardship under the present proposed scheme because the overwhelming majority of parents will have the day off in order to vote. The particular advantage to this proposal is that the use of buildings belonging to the public and maintained at public expense emphasises the public nature of the duty

---

51 Mill, 1991, p 221.
52 SI 1986 No. 2214.
53 SI 1986 No. 2215.
54 Contained in Sched I of the RPA 1983.
55 *Ibid*, Regs 53 and 54.

and may assist in bringing home to voters the fact that they are engaged in voting for representatives who may (depending upon the type of Council which is being elected) have some measure of stewardship over the building. Furthermore, the closure of schools, together with the routine use of school buildings, will work together with the Electoral Commission's welcome suggestion[56] that children accompanying a voting adult be admitted to polling stations to encourage the development of the habit of voting once they have reached 18 years.

We have seen that, even as early as 1872, some measure of support was afforded to voters living with disabilities, and Mill wished to extend the level of support at public expense. *Voting for Change* is much less positive on this point than it could have been, for the Electoral Commission's proposal is that in order to promote participation in elections *more* (cf all) polling stations should be made suitable for access by disabled people. This gives an additional reason for expecting school buildings to be used for voting because the provisions of s 14 of the Special Educational Needs and Disability Act 2001 require local education authorities and others responsible for schools to ensure that they are made accessible to disabled people. Once people living with disabilities have entered polling stations there is a range of help available to them in order to allow them to vote. Section 13 of the RPA 2000 makes a number of useful amendments to the Parliamentary Election Rules in that polling stations must now have available a large print version of the ballot paper so that partially sighted voters may inspect it, together with a Braille template to allow blind or partially sighted voters to exercise their franchise without assistance.[57] Rule 39 of the Parliamentary Election Rules is also amended in order to allow voters living with other forms of disability to have assistance with voting.

It is of fundamental importance that arrangements are made to allow voters living with disabilities full access to all polling stations and that proper arrangements are made to allow these citizens to vote on terms that are as close as possible to those enjoyed by citizens who are not disabled. This is because voting is the most important civic activity and to exclude those living with disabilities to some ghetto is to treat them as lesser citizens.

Strict application of the law

The third point which needs attention is the control of the act of casting the ballot. The law relating to the casting of the ballot should be strictly

---

56 See Electoral Commission *Voting for Change* at p 4.
57 See the amendments to Rule 29.

applied. Schedule 1 of the Ballot Act 1872 contained a detailed list of instructions for casting the ballot; this was designed to inform voters how they should vote in the reformed system. The rules laid down in the Schedule have been repeated in subsequent versions of the Parliamentary Election Rules, and the rules governing the conduct of local elections. We will see in the discussion of the leading case of *Morgan v Simpson*,[58] in Chapter 6, that the rules are often not followed by either voters or presiding officers, indeed even the Master of the Rolls admitted to treating the provisions of the law with contempt. This is wholly unacceptable. It is proposed that an essential feature of the pilot scheme be that the provisions of the election rules be rigorously followed. It is important to reintroduce due solemnity into the conduct of an election. This is not an appeal for empty ritual or for some form of quaintness, but is intended to emphasise the fact that elections, which are the method by which citizens take part in their own self-government, are a matter of the utmost seriousness. It is not that the particular provisions drawn ultimately from the 1872 Act are in themselves valuable, because as Lake points out in his evaluation of the Watford election pilot, it is difficult to see the value of the stamping instrument, which is used to deliver the Official Mark that validates individual ballot papers at the time of issue. It is obvious that just as the procedures for the issue of, for example, passports, road fund licences, and MOT certificates have, over recent years, been streamlined and modernised, the procedures for voting can equally be brought up to date. A useful model can be found in the Electoral Fraud (Northern Ireland) Act 2002, which extends the requirement that citizens wishing to vote in Northern Ireland produce one of a number of documents, which may include an electoral identity card, before they are issued with a ballot paper. However, and because successive governments have neglected to reform the law, we in the remainder of the UK are left with the 19th century law. This remains the law and it should be enforced. How can we expect the law of elections to be upheld in other respects if public officials do not follow it rigorously?

Distribution of election communications

One election communication from each candidate should be distributed free of charge. One of the useful innovations of the Watford pilot was the free distribution to voters by mail of one election communication from each of the candidates. This provision mirrored the benefit provided to candidates in parliamentary elections by s 91 RPA 1983, which allows them to send one election communication of a specified description to

---

58 [1975] QB 151; [1974] 3 All ER 722.

voters.[59] It would appear from Steven Lake's evaluation of the pilot that this innovation was unpopular with some of the political parties who said that the distribution of election communications should be the responsibility of the individual political parties. This comment is an example of market behaviour by the party(ies). One can certainly appreciate that, for example, supermarkets might expect both themselves and their rivals to produce their own publicity material; however political parties and candidates are engaged in quite a different enterprise. Political parties aim to provide representatives for the people in government; they are not suppliers of goods or services. Surely the citizenry ought to be provided with a basic level of information to facilitate their choice. The Electoral Commission has recognised this point in *Voting for Change* in which it is proposed that there should be a duty imposed upon the main television channels to provide information about political parties and their election platforms through election broadcasts. This must be welcomed. However the next step, which is to require the posting of such information on the internet, is to be deplored. It is undesirable because it is likely that once such a trend starts, increasing amounts of information will be posted on the internet and smaller amounts of information will be broadcast or distributed. Industry pressure, and perhaps pressure from some sectors of the public, may over time lead to the complete replacement of broadcast information with political websites. This is undesirable for the reasons set out above.[60]

Conclusion

This chapter has looked at a range of issues concerning the method of voting. Voting is, in the words of Brennan and Lomasky, expressive behaviour, and the central thrust of the argument here presented is that it should, first and foremost, express democratic (or judgement) norms rather than the norms of the market.

A range of objections has been raised against remote electronic voting and the use of digital technologies in voting more generally. These objections are narrowly legal, and address wider concerns in the law. The

---

59 See P2246D, Regulations of the Post Office under s 91 of the RPA 1983 of 5 April 1983.

60 I am here following Cass Sunstein in declining to discuss the 'digital divide' in terms of the differential access to the internet enjoyed by various groups of citizens. It is surmised that in the medium term that this divide will substantially disappear, at least amongst registered voters. However the argument herein does not depend upon the continuance or the disappearance of the divide. For a comprehensive treatment of the digital divide as differential access, see Norris, 2001.

internet is, it is argued, particularly applicable to voting abuse and the phenomenon of vote bartering has been raised as a particular concern.

Comparatively little has been said about postal voting,[61] although it is argued that all forms of semi-secret voting are inherently flawed.

It was proposed that an election pilot be conducted under conditions which, as far as possible, showed voting to be an exercise of a public duty. This would mean emphasising the fact that the franchise should be exercised in a public building in circumstances such that, for example, workers and citizens living with disabilities would be given ample opportunity to cast their ballots. Workers would be given time off work to vote and all polling stations would be made accessible to disabled people. The fact that people over 18 are voting should be made clear to children and young people. Election materials should be distributed on behalf of the candidates at public expense.

Voting should, it is argued, be conducted in an atmosphere of civic solemnity, not so as to make it an empty ritual, but so as to emphasise the public importance of voting. Rick Vallely, who appears to have written the first article critical of remote voting by electronic means, makes a powerful point when he argues that, whilst the act of voting is brief, it remains a civic ritual which makes us think about public issues in a way that emphasises their public nature. It is argued that the pilots to date 'far from enriching democracy ... [push] us towards political anomie'.[62]

---

61 For a wider discussion, see Birch and Watt, 2004, pp 60–72, especially at pp 69–70.
62 Valelly, 1999.

Chapter 4:
The Nomination
of a Candidate

The nomination of a candidate comes after the selection – or even, self-selection – of a candidate to fight an election. There is no legal requirement for a candidate to be selected by a particular, or indeed any, process; a person who desires to stand for election may simply declare their candidacy. The key focus of this chapter is the *so-called* abuse of the right of nomination. The epithet 'so-called' is justified because there is a dispute concerning the nature of the legal doctrines concerned. This will become clear later in the chapter. The chapter starts by introducing the problem of the 'spoiler candidate', that is, the candidate who stands for election in order to disrupt that election in one of a number of ways. Some spoiler candidates stand in order to draw attention to the (allegedly) farcical nature of the electoral process, others stand in order to damage the chances of another specific political party, whilst still others stand for complex political reasons in an attempt to influence the make-up of, for example, a local council. Whilst it might seem from a cursory glance at the '*Margaret Thatcher* case' (which is considered below) that the issue is minor, trivial (or, it has been suggested, even fun[1]), and the discussion is, perhaps, highly legal and technical, it is important in two different dimensions. First, it is important, for its own sake and for the issues it raises about the democratic process. Secondly, the problem of the spoiler candidate was the pretext used for introducing legislation in 1998, the Registration of Political Parties Act 1998 (RPPA 1998), allegedly to solve the perceived problem. This legislation was superseded by the Political Parties, Elections and Referendums Act 2000 (PPERA 2000), which *inter alia* extended, and re-enacted the RPPA 1998.[2] The legislation will be considered in its mature and complete form that is in the PPERA 2000 and in the amended Representation of the People Act 1983 (RPA

---

1   I am grateful to Beverley Brown for this suggestion. It is in disagreeing with her point that the argument is clarified.

2   In part, by adding additional sections to earlier legislation, such as the Representation of the People Act 1983 (RPA 1983).

1983).[3] It will be shown that the legislation does not, in fact, address the perceived problem and is instead addressed and was intended to solve another issue, that of party discipline, which is not, it will be argued, a proper subject for electoral law.

Next, a number of cases are examined in order to demonstrate that there is an alternative method for dealing with the problem of 'spoiler candidates' and that this method does properly address the democratic concerns raised when a person is prevented from standing as a candidate in an election. Following this examination of the law, the issue of party discipline within the Labour party will be discussed.

Finally, the chapter concludes with a drawing together of the threads of the argument. It will be demonstrated throughout the chapter that the present law is much more suited to dealing with 'brand competition' between parties than with fostering a democratic polity.

Before a person can be elected as a representative to sit in parliament or on a local authority they must be nominated to appear upon the ballot.[4] This process usually comes after the process for the selection of a person as a candidate; but recall that there is no need for the candidate to be selected. The method of selection of a candidate for election is a matter for each individual political party and is usually set out in its rules. There is little statutory material relating to the process of selection, save for the Sex Discrimination (Election Candidates) Act 2002, which, in amending the Sex Discrimination Act 1975, allows political parties to adopt procedures which discriminate on the grounds of sex in order to address the gender imbalance that pervades British representative democracy. There have been a small number of legal challenges, typically mounted by disappointed party members or candidates in the selection process, to the adoption of particular procedures in the selection process. Disappointed candidates have usually claimed that the party has been biased against them on the grounds of their race, whilst the party has pointed to policy disputes or to evidence of packing selection meetings with personal supporters of the unsuccessful candidates. One of these cases, *Triesman v Ali*, reached the Court of Appeal in a challenge to the membership of the panel from which candidates might be chosen for the Slough Unitary Authority, but this case is of greater relevance to the law of unlawful discrimination than electoral law as such.[5] In *Triesman v Ali*, the unsuccessful candidate claimed that he was barred from membership

---

3   In the view of the author the most helpful thing that the Electoral Commission could do is to draw up a single consolidated Elections Act split into a number of clear parts or chapters so that we could all see the law in one easily recognisable statute.

4   The process of nomination is helpfully set out is s 8.03 of Schofield.

5   See *Triesman v Ali and Anor* [2002] IRLR 489.

of the panel because of his race, whilst the Labour party successfully averred that his disbarment was due to irregularities in his party membership and the membership of his prominent and numerous supporters. This is not truly part of electoral law because it is silent as to the methods of selection.

However once a candidate has been selected, there is a complex procedure that must be followed in order to allow that candidate to use the name of a registered political party when standing for election. Any person may stand for election as an 'Independent', that is, with that single word description upon the ballot paper. Whilst this procedure has only been in place since 2000 and the passage of the Political Parties Elections and Referendums Act 2000, it may be that it will prove to be short lived because the Electoral Commission has proposed, in *Voting for Change* that the procedure be revised.

The problem of 'spoiler candidates'

Prior to 1998, from time to time candidates stood under descriptions calculated to confuse the electorate. This involved using personal names or descriptions that could easily be confused with the names or party descriptions of other candidates upon the ballot paper. Plainly, a genuine candidate would wish to be clearly distinguishable from other candidates so as to garner as many votes as possible because it is clear that confusion can operate both to gain votes and to lose them. People adopting such confusing tactics are thus assumed not to be seeking to win, but rather to spoil the chances of another candidate, and are consequently seen as 'spoiler candidates'. The purpose of their ruse was usually to attempt to prevent the *bona fide* candidate, representing the target party, taking the seat; the spoiler candidate knew that they had no real chance of taking the seat themselves. Often the spoiler candidate would claim membership of some fictional or purported political party by changing the spelling of a real party's name to sow confusion and doubt. Examples include the 'Conservatory Party', the 'Literal Democrat' or the 'Labor Party' candidate. The most important examples are found in the cases of *R v Returning Officer for the Parliamentary Constituency of Barnet and Finchley ex p Bennett v Thatcher*[6] and *Sanders v Chichester*.[7] Richard Huggett, the prime mover in *Sanders v Chichester*, who subsequently stood, or attempted to stand, in a number of Liberal

---

6   [1983] CA Bound transcript 237.

7   *Sanders and Another v Chichester and Another* QBD (Election Court), *The Times*, 2 December 1994, the *Independent*, 16 November 1994. The most convenient report is to be found in *Schofield* at E104–E123.

Democrat target seats as a 'Literal Democrat',[8] not only succeeded in annoying the party hierarchy and a considerable number of returning officers, but also can take almost sole credit, whether in the form of praise or blame, for the introduction of the Registration of Political Parties Act 1998.

At district council level as well, there were a number of elections where candidates stood under a variety of labels and sought to prevent opposition groups or alliances taking control from the previous ruling group. For example, in the Cherwell District Council elections of May 1998 a candidate, widely believed to be a Conservative, stood under the description 'Labor' in an attempt to take the vote away from a Liberal Democrat in a closely fought ward. The reasons for this candidacy were as follows: Cherwell District Council – a mainly rural district – had been controlled by the Conservatives for a number of years; they held the majority of rural seats. The Labour Party formed the opposition, supplying the majority of councillors in two of the district's urban or suburban areas. The Liberal Democrats were the smaller opposition party and held a small number of rural seats. The problem for the opposition parties was that, if they each fought all the seats in the District, they would simply divide the anti-Conservative vote and allow the Conservatives to win. Labour and the Liberal Democrats entered an informal pact. Labour would fight all the urban and suburban seats and the Liberal Democrats would fight all the rural seats. This would lead to a 'straight fight' between Conservatives and anti-Conservatives in all seats and give the opposition parties their best chance of taking control of the Council from the Conservatives. So, all nominations were duly submitted and the Conservatives saw that they were faced with a credible opposition alliance. The Conservatives identified one ward as a 'pivot' – if they won it they would keep control of the council, if they lost the ward they would lose control. The Conservatives were faced with a single Liberal Democrat candidate; so, it was widely believed, they found a sympathiser to stand in the 'Labor' interest to try to split the opposition vote. The ruse failed because the Labour Party and the Liberal Democrats publicised the attempt widely.

On other occasions in district council elections, such techniques were adopted by candidates genuinely attempting to secure election against a party's own nominated candidate because of some dispute within the party. They would often affix the epithet 'real' or 'independent' or 'true' to the name of the party (for example, 'Real Labour', 'Independent Liberal', 'True Conservative'), the most obvious example being the

---

8   See, eg, *Spencer v Huggett; Richards v Neal and Another; Oaten v Huggett, The Times,* 12 June 1997, (Transcript: Barnett, Lenton & Co).

attempt to stand as the 'Official Byron Ward Conservative'[9] in a district council election in Nottingham in 1988.[10]

The solution?

In an attempt to stop such machinations, the then recently elected Labour Government brought forward the Registration of Political Parties Act 1998. The purpose of the original Bill was well set out by the then Home Secretary (Jack Straw MP) when he moved its second reading as follows:

> The Bill is designed to improve the fairness of our democratic process.
>
> ...
>
> The Bill will help to prevent the use of misleading candidates' descriptions on ballot papers at elections, thus helping to protect the identity of political parties and, therefore, the integrity of the political process. In addition, the Bill will allow, for the first time, a registered party's emblem to be printed on the ballot paper as a way of helping to distinguish as clearly as possible between candidates from different parties.

The Bill introduces no criminal sanctions against non-registration. It does not make the registration of political parties compulsory, but it creates strong incentives for them to register. Any serious party that intends to put forward candidates at an election would be well advised to register so as to be allowed to do the following four things, which otherwise would not be permitted under the Bill.[11]

Thus the first claim made by Mr Straw is that *a party will be able to protect its name from misuse by others*. The degree to which this purpose has become submerged in the legislation and replaced by quite another principle will become clear within this chapter.

The main provisions of the legislation are (so far as it affects 'spoiler candidates'), first, to establish a register of political parties such that parties can be distinguished from one another by their names and registered symbols and, secondly, to provide, by virtue of a new Rule 6A of Sched 1 to the Representation of the People Act 1983 (the Parliamentary Election Rules),[12] that, in order to stand as a candidate under a particular party's description, any candidate would need to be certified by a nominated officer of the political party concerned. The central provision of the Rules is:

---

9 See *Patterson v Merrick and Hammond*, Court of Appeal 2 November 1988, unreported.

10 See the discussion of 'Walton Real Labour' in Chapter 5 below.

11 Hansard, House of Commons Debates Col 515, 4 June 1998.

12 A similar rule is to be found in Rule 4A of the Local Elections (Principal Areas) Rules 1986, SI 1986/2214.

6A (1) A nomination paper may not include a description of a candidate which is likely to lead voters to associate the candidate with a registered political party unless the description is authorised by a certificate – issued by or on behalf of the registered nominating officer of the party, and received by the returning officer at some time during the period for delivery of nomination papers ...

(2) A person shall be guilty of a corrupt practice if he fraudulently purports to be authorised to issue a certificate under paragraph (1) on behalf of a registered political party's nominating officer.

This apparently simple provision may be likened to the visible tip of an iceberg: it implies a set of regulations of titanic proportions upon political parties. Indeed it may be argued that the effect upon a democratic, as opposed to a market, system of representation is akin to the effect of the infamous iceberg upon the SS *Titanic*.

The 1998 legislation has now, in the main, been consolidated into Pt II of the Political Parties, Elections and Referendums Act 2000 (PPERA 2000), although (as demonstrated in the preceding paragraph) important measures have been inserted into the RPA 1983. First, s 22 of the PPERA 2000 provides that, in order for a person to stand nominated in the interest of a political party in an election, save at the level of a parish or community election, the political party must be registered in a register of political parties maintained by the Electoral Commission under s 23 of the PPERA 2000. Special, and less onerous provisions apply in the case of candidates who wish only to stand at parish or community level and there are special provisions under s 28(2)(d) and s 34 of the PPERA 2000 for political parties ('minor parties') who seek only to contest parish or community elections.

If a person decides to stand in any capacity other than those special limited capacities listed above (parish or community councils), they must do so under the description of 'Independent' or, in the one other relevant case, 'the Speaker seeking re-election', or without any description whatsoever. Furthermore, and here the link to s 6A of the RPA 1983 is apparent, in order to stand nominated they must present a certificate from the relevant officer of their political party endorsing their candidature.

Apart from the requirement that political parties are registered in order to field candidates in relevant elections, the 2000 Act also enacts detailed regulations for the structure of registered political parties. First, the office holders of a party must be registered under s 24 of the PPERA 2000. These registered officers include the leader, treasurer and the nominating officer. The treasurer is required to make detailed financial returns and the financial structure of the party must be reported under ss 26 and 27 of the 2000 Act.

Section 28 of the PPERA 2000 provides the details of that which must be included on the Register of Political Parties. The party must declare that it intends to field candidates, and there are divisions in the register according to geographical area and tier of government. However, and secondly, the most important information within this s 28 of the Act relates to the name of the party, in so far as its name must not lead to confusion with another party or contain certain words (such as 'royal') or obscenities, or non-Roman script. Section 29 of the PPERA 2000 provides similar rules with respect to the parties' emblems.

It is plain that all this is designed to provide a comprehensive code with two purposes. The first is, as Mr Straw noted, to allow a political party 'to protect its name from misuse by others'. The second purpose is to facilitate the maintenance of party discipline. It will be argued below that earlier provisions and the common law were and remain quite capable of protecting party names from misuse by others – while the maintenance of party discipline is not a fit subject for election law at all. Party discipline should be maintained by the rules of the party itself, supplemented, if necessary, by the provisions of private law.

Before considering these matters it is useful to consider the debate in parliament that led to the rejection of an earlier scheme designed to prevent spoiler candidates. This occurred in 1968 when the opposition Conservatives sought to introduce a scheme simpler in form, but identical in effect as an amendment to (Labour) government legislation updating the 1948 Representation of the People Act, but the government was adamantly opposed and had its way. The words of the Labour Home Secretary (and later Prime Minister) James Callaghan, used in rejecting the Conservative amendment are worthy of quotation in full because they also expose some of the difficulties with the current legislation:

> Every case put forward has some difficulties and objections. The objection to this is clear. It is the prospect that some candidate might use descriptions to mislead electors. This is something that we shall have to take into account. In considering it I have had regard to past history and future prospects. If I may put it on the most pompous plane, it would show a lack of proper respect for our Parliamentary procedures if we proceeded on the view that candidates who were advancing themselves for selection by their fellow citizens for elevation to this House or to local government were likely to so misuse the procedure as to endeavour to deceive the electors about themselves.

> I would hope that most people who stand for election would have a proper sense of responsibility. I agree that one cannot wholly rely on that. I do not think there is much in the argument that any political party will find a series of £150 deposits to put up so that they can nominate mischievous

candidates on the other side. That is not the way we normally conduct our affairs, but it is a risk we will have to take in adopting a procedure of this sort.

The greatest difficulty is likely to come when one has a candidate who is slightly off-centre from his party and wants to claim the right to call himself by that party name. I would answer that by saying he can do that at the moment on everything but the ballot paper. He can do it in his address to the electors, in his window bills, in any election literature including his 'election specials' that he cares to send round. So we are not removed from that danger at all, although obviously we are increasing it marginally by allowing such a misleading description, if it is misleading, to be included in the ballot paper.[13]

A consideration of the points made in Callaghan's speech makes it clear that the problem of spoiler candidates who might confuse the electorate remains just as unresolved by the current legislation. There is nothing in PPERA 2000 that prevents the candidates from describing themselves in any way they wish in every place, save on the ballot paper. However it is commonsensical that, as far as political parties are concerned, the really important point, as far as the identification of a candidate is concerned, is that their name and description should appear on the ballot paper in such a way as to unambiguously identify a candidate as being associated with a given political party. It is argued in this book that the voter should then cast their ballot in the best interests of the community as a whole, but this is not necessary for this part of the argument: it would suffice that the voter could simply distinguish between the candidates. Under the legislation as it stands, a really determined spoiler candidate may vigorously contest the entire election campaign using the chosen misleading name and description all the way, as it were, to the ballot paper. Their name may then appear on the ballot paper, albeit without a party name or party symbol, and yet the nefarious purpose may have been achieved – some portion of the electorate may well have been sufficiently confused.

Accordingly the legislation now contained in PPERA 2000 is pointless for the reasons set out by Callaghan. However, the legislation is pointless in another sense – it is just wholly unnecessary. The purpose of the legislation could be accomplished equally well by a rigorous application of the common law – indeed where really obvious or egregious spoiler candidates are concerned, the current common law could accomplish the purpose more securely. This is not necessarily to argue that a statute should not be enacted, for a well-designed statute may improve the common law, but it should not accomplish less. Let us therefore examine the common law position.

---

13 Hansard, Commons Vol 775, Col 1404, 18 December 1968.

Exclusion of spoiler candidates

The question here is, can a spoiler candidate be excluded without the use of the statutory provisions for registering political parties and certifying candidates?

The first case for consideration is the unreported case in the Court of Appeal of *R v Returning Officer for the Parliamentary Constituency of Barnet and Finchley ex p Bennett v Thatcher*, heard on 3 June 1983, shortly before the general election of 9 June that year. The relevant political context is that the then Conservative Prime Minister, Mrs Margaret Hilda Thatcher, who was defending her Barnet and Finchley seat, had called a snap general election following the party's success in the May 1983 district council elections. Unless the context allows otherwise, the Prime Minister will be given her full name in this chapter in order to avoid confusion, because she was challenged in her constituency by quite another Margaret Thatcher, who was a bearded man. Mrs Margaret Hilda Thatcher was confident about the election result because of the successful campaign led by her in 1982 to repel the Argentinian invaders from the Falkland Islands in the South Atlantic, which had brought her and her party popular acclaim. Furthermore the Labour party, led by Michael Foot, was seen to be split and lacking in popular esteem. Amongst the main issues before the electorate were the siting of cruise missiles at Greenham Common and at Molesworth, the Labour party's strong anti-nuclear stance and its perceived anti-Americanism. Most commentators judged that the close links between Michael Foot, the Labour leader, and the Campaign for Nuclear Disarmament would make the Labour party unelectable, whilst many on the Left were deeply suspicious of the close bond of political and personal friendship linking the British Prime Minister and the US president, Ronald Reagan. The *Hipperson* case, discussed in Chapter 2, forms another part of the political and legal background.

The general election was called on the Friday following the district council elections, in which the Conservative party had polled strongly. On 17 May 1983 the returning officer for the Barnet and Finchley constituency (along with all other returning officers), issued the statutory notice under Rule 5(1) of the Parliamentary Election Rules, to be found in Sched 1 of the Representation of the People Act 1983, requiring completed nomination papers to be delivered to the returning officer by 4.00 pm on 23 May. On 17 May, a Mr Colin Hanoman was living at 83 Northfield House, Peckham Park Road, London. This address is in the postal district SE15, in south London; Finchley – Mrs Margaret Hilda

Thatcher's constituency – being in the north of the city (N12). The point is that Hanoman had no discernible interest in the electors of Barnet and Finchley; he was attracted by the opportunity of standing against the Prime Minister. His reasons are made clear below. On 20 May Hanoman changed his name by deed poll to Margaret Thatcher, and his address to 'Downing Street Mansions at 83 Northfield House'. Clearly this Margaret Thatcher needed an election agent, so he persuaded his friend, a Mr Simon Stansfeld, of 37 Northfield House, Peckham Park Road to serve. Stansfeld changed his name to Ronald Regan [sic] and his address then became 'Whitehouse Mansions, 37 Northfield House'.

On 23 May the ex-Mr Colin Hanoman, having selected himself as a parliamentary candidate, personally submitted his nomination paper and the returning officer was thus faced with two papers in the name of 'Margaret Thatcher'; one from Mrs Margaret Hilda Thatcher, the Prime Minister, giving an address of '10 Downing Street' and describing her as 'The Conservative Party Candidate', and the other from Margaret Thatcher, Conservationist Party, Downing Street Mansions, 83 Northfield House. The returning officer challenged the particulars on the nomination paper, but Margaret Thatcher produced a deed poll confirming his then rightful name. Shortly after the close of nominations, Mrs Margaret Hilda Thatcher's election agent lodged an objection under Rule 11(3) of the Parliamentary Election Rules on the ground that Margaret (ex-Hanoman) Thatcher's[14] nomination paper was an abuse of the right of nomination.

On 24 May, the returning officer attempted to hand back to Margaret (ex-Hanoman) Thatcher his nomination paper, endorsed with a rejection, but he refused to take it, and so it had to be sent to him by registered post, which introduced a delay until 27 May. Margaret (ex-Hanoman) Thatcher then applied for judicial review of the returning officer's decision and he was granted leave by McCowan J on 31 May. The substantive hearing was held on the morning of 3 June, and at that hearing McCowan J refused (ex-Hanoman) Thatcher an order of mandamus[15] that would have compelled the returning officer to place his name on the statutory statement of persons nominated and hence on the ballot paper. The returning officer gave four grounds for rejecting

---

14 This style, although it may be thought inelegant, has been adopted to avoid further confusion between the two Thatchers.

15 In the words of Wade and Forsyth, 2000, p 604:

The ... remedy of mandamus has long provided the normal means of enforcing the performance of public duties by public authorities of all kinds. ... The commonest employment of mandamus is as a weapon in the hands of the ordinary citizen, when a public authority fails to do its duty by him. Certiorari and prohibition deal with wrongful action, mandamus deals with wrongful inaction.

Margaret (ex-Hanoman) Thatcher's nomination paper: first, that it was an 'abuse of the right of nomination'; secondly, that it was 'an obvious unreality'; thirdly, that his (that is, (ex-Hanoman) Thatcher's) Consent to Nomination form was not duly attested; and finally, that the particulars recorded in his statutory documents were 'not as required by law'. McCowan J upheld the returning officer's decision and, since Margaret (ex-Hanoman) Thatcher wished to proceed with his case, he appealed to the Court of Appeal. Clearly time was now very short – the election was timed for 9 June – and so the matter was allowed to proceed to the Court of Appeal that same afternoon, rather than on the usual timetable, which would have involved a delay of some months.

The decision of McCowan J to refuse (ex-Hanoman) Thatcher's application for judicial review and mandamus was appealed on three grounds: first, that McCowan J had misdirected himself in law in exercising his discretion against (ex-Hanoman) Thatcher in holding that an election petition under s 120 of the RPA 1983 was 'an equally convenient and effective remedy' (words quoted from the then current O 53 r 1 Supreme Court Practice). In other words, McCowan J had ruled that if the returning officer was wrong in refusing to accept his nomination (ex-Hanoman) Thatcher could, after the election was completed, have challenged the result on the grounds that he had been prevented from standing. (Ex-Hanoman) Thatcher argued in his appeal that a post-election challenge would be less effective in protecting his rights.

The second ground is of much greater interest and was left unresolved by the Court of Appeal. It was (to quote directly from the words of Stephenson LJ in the transcript):

> That the Learned Trial Judge misdirected himself in law in holding that there was jurisdiction for the Respondent to declare a nomination paper invalid on the grounds of its being 'a mere abuse of the right of nomination'.

The dispute is simple: in essence, McCowan J said that a returning officer may reject a nomination paper by saying that it constitutes 'a mere abuse of the right of nomination, (ex-Hanoman) Thatcher claimed that there is no legal foundation for such a rejection. This dispute will be considered in detail below.

The final ground of appeal was that McCowan J had misdirected himself in law in holding, as a matter of fact, that (ex-Hanoman) Thatcher's nomination paper was such an abuse. The dispute is again simple: in essence, the returning officer, having decided that he had the power, at least in principle, to decline to accept a nomination paper on the grounds that it was an abuse of the right of nomination, went on to decide that (ex-Hanoman) Thatcher's paper was such an abuse.

McCowan J agreed with the returning officer. (Ex-Hanoman) Thatcher alleged that this decision of fact was wrong.

(Ex-Hanoman) Thatcher succeeded on the first ground to the extent that the Court of Appeal, on the basis of the notes made by counsel, there being no transcript available, considered that McCowan J might have misdirected himself as to the proper place to apply a balance of convenience test and whose convenience ought to be considered. McCowan J had taken the view that it would be equally convenient to (ex-Hanoman) Thatcher to challenge the result of the election by means of an election petition as to mount a substantive legal challenge to the decision to disallow his nomination. Stephenson LJ, together with Eveleigh and May LJJ, though that McCowan J could have used the wrong test in determining this matter and thus considered that the court ought to hear the matter ab initio.

Stephenson LJ returned to the original grounds for the returning officer's refusal to accept (ex-Hanoman) Thatcher's nomination and was convinced that the returning officer had acted lawfully in refusing to accept the nomination paper on the grounds that (ex-Hanoman) Thatcher's particulars on the statutory documents were not as required by law. The court considered the effect on Margaret (ex-Hanoman) Thatcher's candidacy of such a ruling and, having decided that such a ruling was necessarily fatal to his nomination, went on to consider whether the ruling could be supported against a challenge that his nomination had been wrongfully struck out. Stephenson LJ held that the proper way of dealing with any question of the balance of convenience between the two available methods of challenge – judicial review of the returning officer's decision before the election and election petition after the election – was to consider the interests of all the electors of Barnet and Finchley. This does indeed seem the proper test: the essence of a democratic procedure is that the legitimate interests of all members of the community be taken into account, and here the court was careful to consider the facts of the matter including the way in which Margaret (ex-Hanoman) Thatcher had attempted to obstruct the electoral process, first by submitting his nomination paper shortly before the deadline and then refusing personally to accept the rejection. Furthermore the court was particularly impressed, in a wholly negative sense, with the bearded and otherwise colourful Margaret Thatcher's clear declaration in his application for judicial review that, amongst his reasons for standing as a candidate in the Prime Minister's constituency, and against Margaret Hilda Thatcher personally, was the statement that he wished '(t)o make the electoral process more farcical, we [presumably (ex-Hanoman) Thatcher and (Stansfeld) Regan] believe it is already a frightening farce.'

Having decided that his particulars on the nomination papers and the supporting statutory documents were 'not as required by law', and thus ending Margaret (ex-Hanoman) Thatcher's case, the court went on to consider the most important matter – the abuse of the right of nomination. The court considered McCowan J's ruling that Margaret (ex-Hanoman) Thatcher's nomination was an abuse of the right of nomination, whilst clearly acknowledging the fact that any such discussion would only be *obiter dicta*[16] because the case had already been decided. One case, which might have given rise to the right of a returning officer to strike out a particular nomination as an abuse, was that of *Harford v Linskey*,[17] where, at the end of Wright J's judgment he said, apparently with the approval of Bruce J:

> We do not understand it to be laid down in the *Bangor* case[18] that a nomination cannot ever be rejected except for informality in the form or presentation of it. If the nomination paper is, on the face of it, a mere abuse of the right of nomination or an obvious unreality, as, for instance, if it purported to nominate a woman or a deceased sovereign, there can be no doubt that it ought to be rejected, and no petition could be maintained in respect of its rejection.

The construction in *Harford v Linskey* is, of course, rather peculiar for, in the *Bangor* case, the House of Lords held that the grounds for striking out a nomination were those in the statute and they did not consider whether there were any other grounds. In *Harford v Linskey*, Wright J thus seems to have indulged in some judicial creativity in stating that there might be grounds for rejecting a nomination beyond the statutory grounds of informality in the form or presentation of it. Stephenson LJ was not minded to accept this view in any case, because he considered Wright J's remark to have been wholly *obiter* and superseded by later statutory developments. However, both Eveleigh and May LJJ seem to have been more sympathetic to Wright J's view and, had it been necessary to the disposal of the case, would have considered it in detail.

Had a consideration of the *Harford v Linskey* point taken place in the Court of Appeal in *R v Returning Officer for the Parliamentary Constituency of Barnet and Finchley ex p Bennett v Thatcher*, and the point been decided in favour of there being a discretionary power for the returning officer to strike out a nomination in the event of it being in their view 'a mere abuse of process', it may be that much of the subsequent law (which is to say both litigation and statutory reform) would have been obviated. In

---

16 *Obiter dicta* (trans. words by the way) are statements of law in a judgment, which do not contribute to the decision in the law relating to the case.

17 [1899] 1 QB 852.

18 *Pritchard v Bangor Corporation* (1888) 13 App Cas 241.

Sanders v Chichester (which is discussed below), the deputy returning officer would have been able to say that Huggett's candidacy was a sham and refused to accept his nomination paper; thus the 1998 government would have been deprived of a major reason for its legislation. No criticism can fairly be levelled at either counsel or judiciary in the Margaret Thatcher case because they were working under considerable pressure of time, and this was exacerbated by (ex-Hanoman) Thatcher himself trying to, or saying that he was trying to, make 'a farce' of the electoral system. It must be presumed, from the context of the election and the facts, that he was dedicated to the cause of nuclear disarmament.[19] It is argued in this book that matters of politics, such as the question of nuclear disarmament, cannot and should not be regarded as risible by either side of the debate. The maintenance of peace and security are central to a democratic world order, and should not be reduced to the level of farce in the manner proposed by (ex-Hanoman) Thatcher. Thus, the effect of the judgment in *R v Returning Officer for the Parliamentary Constituency of Barnet and Finchley ex p Bennett v Thatcher*, in that it stopped Margaret (ex-Hanoman) Thatcher standing against the Prime Minister seems wholly acceptable and indeed to be applauded. It would be quite otherwise if the returning officer had rejected a nomination correct in form for Colin Hanoman standing in the interest of a political party or single issue pressure group calling itself, for example, 'No cruise missiles in Britain; withdraw from NATO now'.

The argument that the spoiler candidate raises must be made explicit. In attempting to stand as 'Margaret Thatcher', Colin Hanoman set out to bewilder the electorate. He claimed that the electoral system was a farce and by standing as Margaret Thatcher he wanted to make it 'more of a farce'. Contrary to Hanoman, it is asserted that the electoral system is not a farce; it is surely in need of improvement – it may fail to represent some interests adequately, a 'first-past-the-post' election may mean that the winner takes all and other interests are ignored – but these are matters to be addressed in mature political debate rather than by attempts to *trash the system* (see the discussion of 'trashing' below). The interests of a democratic society are served in allowing candidates of the widest range of genuine political persuasions to stand for election, because having a wide range of candidates in the political process allows political ideas to be aired. Spoiler candidates cannot, it is argued, be allowed to abuse the political process. (Ex-Hanoman) Thatcher was not,

---

19 The election was dubbed 'the nuclear election' by many people within the Labour party and the Campaign for Nuclear Disarmament. It is noteworthy that Stansfeld, his election agent changed his name to 'Regan' (cf US President Ronald Reagan) rather than to, eg, (Norman) Tebbit or (Keith) Joseph – leading members of the cabinet.

in reality, abusing only the Prime Minister, Margaret Hilda Thatcher, he was attempting to abuse all the electors of Barnet and Finchley who wanted, in good faith, to take part in democratic governance.

The argument against (ex-Hanoman) Thatcher is not an argument against robust, or even rough, politics. It is perfectly possible to support robust, abrasive, rude and offensive political positions whilst condemning (ex-Hanoman) Thatcher. Consider the well-known US case of *Cohen v California*.[20] In April 1968 Cohen went into a courthouse in California wearing a jacket on which were painted the words 'fuck the draft' as a protest against the Vietnam War and conscription. He was convicted at first instance under a public order statute and appealed the case all the way to the US Supreme Court. There Cohen was acquitted on the basis that he was exercising a right to free speech protected by the First Amendment to the US Constitution. The reasons for acquittal, given by Harlan J, can be used to protect demonstrators, such as the Greenham Common women, but not, it is argued, people who interfere with the electoral process. Harlan J said as follows:

> The constitutional right of free expression is powerful medicine in a society as diverse and populous as ours. It is designed and intended to remove governmental restraints from the arena of public discussion, putting the decision as to what views shall be voiced largely into the hands of each of us, in the hope that use of such freedom will ultimately produce a more capable citizenry and more perfect polity and in the belief that no other approach would comport with the premise of individual dignity and choice upon which our political system rests. See *Whitney v California*, (274 U.S. 357, 375–377 (1927) (Brandeis J, concurring)).

> To many, the immediate consequence of this freedom may often appear to be only verbal tumult, discord, and even offensive utterance. These are, however, within established limits, in truth necessary side effects of the broader enduring values which the process of open debate permits us to achieve. That the air may at times seem filled with verbal cacophony is, in this sense, not a sign of weakness but of strength. We cannot lose sight of the fact that, in what otherwise might seem a trifling and annoying instance of individual distasteful abuse of a privilege, these fundamental societal values are truly implicated. That is why '[w]holly neutral futilities ... come under the protection of free speech as fully as do Keats' poems or Donne's sermons,' *Winters v New York*, (333 US 507, 528 (1948) (Frankfurter, J, dissenting)), and why, 'so long as the means are peaceful, the communication need not meet standards of acceptability', *Organization for a Better Austin v Keefe*, (402 US 415, 419 (1971)).

> Against this perception of the constitutional policies involved, we discern certain more particularized considerations that peculiarly call for reversal

---

20 403 US 15 (1971).

of this conviction. First, the principle contended for by the State seems inherently boundless. How is one to distinguish this from any other offensive word? Surely the State has no right to cleanse public debate to the point where it is grammatically palatable to the most squeamish among us. Yet no readily ascertainable general principle exists for stopping short of that result were we to affirm the judgment below. For, while the particular four-letter word being litigated here is perhaps more distasteful than most others of its genre, it is nevertheless often true that one man's vulgarity is another's lyric. Indeed, we think it is largely because governmental officials cannot make principled distinctions in this area that the Constitution leaves matters of taste and style so largely to the individual.

Additionally, we cannot overlook the fact, because it is well illustrated by the episode involved here, that much linguistic expression serves a dual communicative function: it conveys not only ideas capable of relatively precise, detached explication, but otherwise inexpressible emotions as well. In fact, words are often chosen as much for their emotive as their cognitive force. We cannot sanction the view that the Constitution, while solicitous of the cognitive content of individual speech, has little or no regard for that emotive function which, practically speaking, may often be the more important element of the overall message sought to be communicated. Indeed, as Mr. Justice Frankfurter has said, '[o]ne of the prerogatives of American citizenship is the right to criticize public men and measures – and that means not only informed and responsible criticism, but the freedom to speak foolishly and without moderation'. (*Baumgartner v United States*, 322 US 665, 673–674 (1944)).

The opinion is perfectly clear; robust and emotive expressions of political opinion are necessary in a democracy so that citizens may make up their minds about matters of public concern. It is argued in this book that it is likely that were an act similar to that in *Cohen* be performed and prosecuted in the UK, it would gain at least *prima facie* protection under the free speech law of the European Convention of Human Rights (that is, Art 10(1)).[21] However, it seems that no such protection ought to be given to those who set out to trash the political process. The word *trash* is deliberately chosen; it is used in two senses. If (ex-Hanoman) Thatcher was genuinely trying to expose the 'farcical' nature of the political and electoral systems, so as to replace it with something better, he might have been *trashing* the system in the sense used by, for example, Mark Kelman.[22] *Trashing* in this sense means to expose the contradictions in a system in order to allow it to be replaced by something better. However, since (ex-Hanoman) Thatcher does not give us any clues as to the

---

21 Article 10(2) lays down the conditions under which states may lawfully deny the principle of free speech to their citizens. There is no analogous provision in the 1st Amendment to the US Constitution.

22 See Kelman, Mark, 'Trashing' 36 *Stanford Law Review* 293 (1984).

difficulties with, or inconsistencies in, the electoral or political systems, it is assumed that he was seeking to trash them in the simpler sense of 'wantonly destroying'. It is argued that by refusing to accept (ex-Hanoman) Thatcher's nomination, both the returning officer and the courts were defending the democratic system against those who sought to abuse it.

Another variety of candidate whose *bona fides* might be called into question are those standing, for example, in the interests of the 'Monster Raving Loony Party' founded by David (Screaming Lord) Sutch whose main policy seemed to be to promote the concerts of his pop group and, following his death, to promote the pub which serves as party headquarters. The party now claims that it is dedicated to showing the stupidity of British politics, but it is difficult to ascertain why this is so and easy to see why they are rightly described as 'loonies'.[23] Neither does there seem to be anything on their website that illustrates what is, allegedly, wrong with the political process. This party's candidates cannot be called 'spoilers' as the party's candidates stood under the party's own name and fielded a variety of improbably named candidates whom no one could plausibly confuse with those of the other parties. Some people may consider that the policies of the British National Party today, or those advocating unilateral nuclear disarmament in the 1980s, are, or were, barely more credible than those advocated by the Monster Raving Loonies, but that is not the point. Genuine adherents of these latter policies ought to be free to stand so as to attract, if they can, the allegiance of the voters and thus gain the opportunity to progress policies in the best interests of the people. Provided the party stays within the law, the public has a right, indeed a duty, to consider whether society ought to be governed in the way which they propose and therefore every party's policies should, rightly, be put before the electorate. The point is that the mechanisms, first introduced by the Registration of Political Parties Act 1998, do nothing to control candidates who stand to disrupt the political process.

However, in practice it is beyond doubt that, were a returning officer maliciously to reject a nomination paper, his or her continued tenure of the office would be in question. Indeed, it will be argued below that a returning officer's rejection of a nomination paper is susceptible to judicial review. Hence these potential dangers attached to a returning officer's discretion to reject a nomination are more theoretical than practical unless the candidate is a 'genuine spoiler'. It may also be that a

---

23 See, at www.omrlp.com, the website of the Official Monster Raving Loony Party. The text starts with the words 'Welcome to the home of the Official Monster Raving Loony Party! You can make an arse of yourself in any political party, but we are a political party dedicated to being a real farse [*sic*] to be reckoned with.'

returning officer who deliberately and maliciously rejected a nomination paper would be in breach of his or her official duty under s 23(2) of the RPA 1983 and thus liable to conviction under s 63 of the Act. It should also be noted in passing that, in regard to the faults in Margaret (ex-Hanoman) Thatcher's nomination papers, judicial note has been taken of the fact that returning officers urge candidates to submit their nomination papers in good time so that candidates and their agents have the opportunity of rectifying any faults.[24] Indeed in many areas it is the practice that party agents make specific appointments with the returning officer or a senior member of the relevant election office staff so that nomination papers may be individually validated.

If some rule whereby nomination papers, otherwise good in form, were to be rejected at some point in the electoral system by a returning officer, how might any such rejection be challenged? The current law (leaving aside the unresolved point of whether the rule in *Harford v Linskey* is good law) is that, once a returning officer has accepted a nomination paper as valid, this decision may not be impugned by way of judicial review. This is evident in a brief preliminary consideration of the case of *Sanders and Younger-Ross v Chichester and Palmer*.[25] (The case will be discussed at greater length below.) The descriptions of the candidates, Adrian Mark Sanders as 'Liberal Democrat' and Richard John Huggett as 'Literal Democrat', are essential to the case. Sedley J refused Adrian Sanders, the Liberal Democrat candidate in the 1994 European Parliamentary election for the Devon and East Plymouth seat, leave to apply for judicial review of the deputy returning officer's decision to accept the nomination of Richard Huggett as Literal Democrat candidate for the seat. Sedley J held that the court's jurisdiction was ousted by r 12(5) of Sched 1 of the RPA 1983, that is, the Parliamentary Election Rules which were (at that particular time) applied to elections to the European Parliament by the European Parliamentary Election Regulations 1986.[26] This rule, and Sedley J's ruling on it, simply and unequivocally provide that nominations, once accepted by the returning officer, cannot be challenged. However, it would appear that the converse of the rule is not true. If a nomination is rejected by a returning officer, that rejection may be challenged by means of judicial review. Authority for this proposition is given in the judgment of Scott Baker J in *R (on the application of De Beer*

---

24 See *R (on the application of De Beer and others) v Balabanoff (Returning Officer for London Borough of Harrow)* [2002] EWHC 670 (Admin), CO/1670/2002.

25 *Sanders and Another v Chichester and Another* QBD (Election Court), *The Times*, 2 December 1994, *The Independent*, 16 November 1994.

26 This is set down in Dyson J's introduction in the report of *Sanders v Chichester*.

and others) v Balabanoff (Returning Officer for London Borough of Harrow).[27] Here the returning officer rejected the nomination papers for almost the entire Liberal Democrat field of candidates for the Harrow London Borough elections in 2002 because their description in their nomination papers did not accord with the description given in the certificate from the party, which authorised them to stand in the Liberal Democrat interest. The Liberal Democrat candidates in Harrow each gave their description as the 'Liberal Democrat Focus Team', whilst the registered description of the party is the 'Liberal Democrats' and was so set down in the authorising certificate. The law relating to these certificates stems from Rule 4A(1) of the Local Election (Principal Areas) Rules 1986, which provides that:

> (1) A nomination paper may not include a description of a candidate which is likely to lead voters to associate the candidate with a registered political party unless the party is a qualifying party in relation to the electoral area and the description is authorised by a certificate –
>
> (a) issued by or on behalf of the registered nominating officer of the party, and
>
> (b) received by the returning officer before the last time for the delivery of nomination papers.

Clearly this is similar in form to Rule 6A of the Parliamentary Elections Rules as set out above and stems from the same set of legislation (RPPA 1998 and PPERA 2000). Such a certificate is now necessary for a nomination to be accepted. In the *Balabanoff* case, the returning officer, having obtained the advice of leading counsel, determined that he should reject the nomination papers on the grounds that the description on the certificate did not match that on the nomination papers. His rejection was immediately challenged by De Beer (a Liberal Democrat candidate in Harrow) on behalf of the Liberal Democrats. Scott Baker J, having considered the effect of the decisions in *Sanders v Chichester* – which might have suggested that the jurisdiction was ousted – nevertheless decided that he had jurisdiction to hear an application for judicial review from De Beer. Scott Baker J observed that the relevant law in this case was Rule 7(6) of the Principal Areas Rules 1986, which provides that: 'The returning officer's decision that a nomination paper is valid shall be final and shall not be questioned in any proceeding whatsoever.' However, he then held – and this is the kernel of the judgment – that: 'The wording of that rule seems to me to leave open the converse situation where the returning officer has decided that a nomination paper for one reason or another is invalid.' He then held,

---

27 [2002] EWHC 670 (Admin), CO/1670/2002.

inevitably on the basis of this second ruling, that he could judicially review the returning officer's decision to reject the nomination. Although he then went on to reject the application on its merits, the rule seems clear. On the basis of these latter two cases (*Sanders* and *Balabanoff*), there is thus a strong argument in current law that, where a returning officer decides that a nomination paper is valid, the decision cannot be impugned, but, where the returning officer decides that the nomination is *defective* and rejects it, their decision may be questioned by the courts through judicial review.

Whilst we have not yet finally determined whether the supposed rule in *Harford v Linskey* is good law, this interim formulation of the law is invaluable. If a returning officer did have the power, under a *Harford v Linskey* rule, to determine that a nomination paper was void for abuse of process, the decision could be brought before the courts on an application for judicial review and thus challenged by the disadvantaged party. This provides, or at least may provide, an essential democratic safeguard because, at least in elections to legislatures, Art 3 of the 1st Protocol to the European Convention on Human rights must surely be engaged. In *Balabanoff*, Scott Baker J applied the *Wednesbury* test to the decision to reject the nomination papers and held, on the facts, that a reasonable returning officer properly exercising their discretion could have decided to reject the papers. The introduction of a more robust and searching test into such a judicial review would afford disappointed would-be candidates an enhanced level of protection.

Balabanoff is an important case on two levels; first, at the procedural level outlined above, where it demonstrates the availability of judicial review as a means to challenge the rejection of a nomination. Secondly, as we shall see below, *Balabanoff* demonstrates the vitality of the principles introduced by the RPPA 1998 and PPERA 2000 legislation and shows how even the humblest party candidate in a district council election is subject to the endorsement of the party hierarchy.

It is also beyond doubt, on the basis of the Margaret Thatcher case, *Sanders v Chichester* and *Balabanoff*, that a returning officer has the power and indeed the duty to reject a nomination paper that fails to be in good form. This matter will not be further examined. However the question remains as to the status of *Harford v Linskey* and that of Wright J's statement that there might be grounds for rejecting a nomination beyond the statutory grounds of informality in the form or presentation. It will be recalled that the matter was left open in *R v Returning Officer for the Parliamentary Constituency of Barnet and Finchley ex p Bennett v Thatcher*, and it was re-examined in *Sanders v Chichester*. It is necessary to provide a little of the background to *Sanders v Chichester* in order to point out the injustices which may arise in such cases. First, we need to note that the reason Richard Huggett stood as a Literal Democrat was in an attempt to wreck the chances of the Liberal Democrat candidate. The Liberal Democrat party came into being as a result of the merger between the Social Democrat Party (SDP), which was itself an offshoot of the Labour Party in its travails between 1979 and 1983, and the Liberal Party. Some members of the SDP and the Liberals were incensed by this merger because they saw themselves as separate parties with different programmes and resolved to stand against the new party; one such candidate, David John Morrish, stood in the interests of the Liberal Party in the 1994 Plymouth and East Devon European Parliamentary election and obtained over 14,000 votes.

Secondly, we need to note that the primary mischief caused or injustice done by Richard Huggett (Literal Democrat) was to Adrian Sanders (Liberal Democrat) and not to Giles Chichester, the winning Conservative candidate who obtained 74,953 votes, beating Adrian Sanders into second place with 74,253 votes. Given the closeness of the vote, Chichester was, perhaps, aided by Richard Huggett taking 10,203 of the votes arguably intended for Adrian Sanders. However, going down the route of a challenge by service of an Election Petition requires that the winning candidate be impugned. Chichester had done no wrong, but had innocently gained a margin over Sanders because, Sanders claimed, Huggett had tricked people into voting for Huggett instead of for himself. Whilst there can be no doubt that Chichester wished to hold onto his seat, it would have been politically inexpedient for him to refuse to join Sanders in a challenge to the election because he, Chichester, would then have faced an Election Petition. The case proceeded by means of 'case stated by consent' – which simply means that Sanders and Chichester joined forces to save expense and acrimony to bring the matter before the court. It will be argued in Chapter 6 below that the real harm to be addressed by the Election Petition is the harm which is done to society as a whole by the election offence. The candidate or candidates who are discomfited by, for example, cheating should not have any more say in the matter than the people as a whole.

In *Sanders v Chichester*, Dyson J considered the submission that the rule in *Harford v Linskey*, a case brought under the Municipal Corporations Act 1882, enabled a returning officer to reject a nomination paper not only on the statutory grounds concerning proper form, but also if it is 'on the face of it, a mere abuse of the right of nomination or an obvious unreality, as, for instance, if it purported to nominate a woman or a deceased sovereign' for in such a case 'there can be no doubt that it ought to be rejected, and no petition could be maintained in respect of its rejection'. Dyson J held that the rules for rejection of a nomination paper had *changed* since *Harford v Linskey* and the change limited the grounds upon which a nomination paper could be rejected. He observed that, for example, in the case he was considering Rule 12(2) of the 1983 Parliamentary Election Rules provided that 'The returning officer is entitled to hold a nomination paper invalid only on one of the (statutory) grounds' and that 'the rule in *Harford v Linskey* was *not* amongst those grounds'. (Emphasis added) It was argued before Dyson J that the case of *Harford v Linskey* had been followed in two cases, *Hobbs v Morey*[28] and *Evans v Thomas*,[29] and the rule was noted in *Watson v Ayton*.[30] However Dyson J observed that: 'In none of these cases did the Rules expressly limit the right of the returning officer to hold a nomination paper invalid to certain specified grounds.'[31]

Dyson J then proceeded to discuss the effect of the Margaret Thatcher case and took the correct view that the Court of Appeal had declined to express its opinion on the validity of the rule in *Harford v Linskey*. His operative conclusion on this point must be quoted in its entirety because, on the one hand, it seems to exclude the rule in *Harford v Linskey*, by providing that a returning officer may only reject a nomination paper for a statutory reason, whilst, on the other hand, he seems to allow that it may be rejected if it is 'manifestly a sham'. Dyson J said:

> We would hold that there is no power in the returning officer to reject a nomination paper on any ground other than those stated in Rule 12(2)(a)(b) or (c) [1983 Parliamentary Election Rules], unless the nomination paper is manifestly a sham. The words 'not as required by law' are sufficient to exclude descriptions which are illegal. The exclusion of sham nomination papers would deal with the example given by Wright J [in *Harford v Linskey*] of the deceased sovereign.

The words 'manifestly a sham' are capable of a sufficiently wide interpretation to allow the rule in *Harford v Linskey* back in, at least in respect to the Margaret Thatcher case (*R v Returning Officer for the Parliamentary Constituency of Barnet and Finchley ex p Bennett v Thatcher*). It is clear that a bearded man does not normally bear the name 'Margaret Thatcher', nor is a single flat in an ordinary municipal block normally called 'Downing St Mansions', nor is a political party normally called 'the Conservatory party'. Equally, it is hardly credible that a political party which chose to avail itself of the democratic process would freely

---

28 [1904] 1KB 74.

29 [1962] 2QB 250.

30 *In re Municipal Election for Berwick-on-Tweed Borough Council; Watson and Others v Ayton* (1946) 174 LT 216, (1946) 44 LGR 134.

31 All of the cases cited (*Hobbs v Morey*, *Evans v Thomas* and *Watson v Ayton*) were brought under the Municipal Corporations Act 1882 and the Municipal Corporation Election Petition Rules 1883.

admit that it wanted to make that process 'more of a farce'. This must be an abuse of process.

However that is not the end of the matter, because Dyson J went on to say:

> If we are wrong, and the *dictum* of Wright J is still good law, we are nonetheless of the view that the returning officer was not in breach of duty in not rejecting Mr Huggett's nomination paper. The description was not an 'obvious unreality'. There is obviously nothing unreal in the political description that he used. Nor in our judgment was it an 'abuse of the right to nomination'. The description may have been calculated to mislead some of the voters. On the face of it, however, for the reasons already given, it was no more, but probably rather less likely to mislead than would have been the description 'Liberal Democrat'. There was no exclusive right in Mr Sanders to the description 'Liberal Democrat'. The description 'Literal Democrat' was not an abuse of the right to nomination.[32]

Clearly this needs further interpretation. Dyson J says that 'the returning officer was not in breach of duty in not rejecting Mr Huggett's nomination paper'. This is a grammatically odd, although perfectly clear, construction; it deals precisely with the facts at issue and is, for that reason, admirable. The question of *Harford v Linskey* still remains open. This part of the judgment in *Sanders* could be interpreted to the effect that had the returning officer decided to reject Richard Huggett's nomination, she would not have been in breach of her duty either. By this reasoning, the question of what constitutes 'a sham' is shown to remain within the discretion of the returning officer. This is fully consistent with the later decision in *Balabanoff*. *Balabanoff*, it will be recalled, showed that questions of the validity of a nomination paper are to be determined by the returning officer. Where the returning officer rejects a nomination, that decision is subject to judicial review, but where it is accepted, no review lies. Dyson J goes on to say that in the judgment of the court, Huggett's nomination was not an 'abuse of the right to nomination'. However, this is not to the point because, if the question remains within the discretion of the returning officer it is not for the court to express any view as to whether they were right or wrong, but it should merely have asked whether the returning officer had exercised their discretion reasonably. At the time of the decision in *Sanders v Chichester*, the appropriate standard for the review was set out in *Wednesbury* – would a reasonable returning officer properly apprised of the facts take the decision to reject the nomination? It will be argued that this is no longer the appropriate standard of review – the test should now include questioning whether the rejection of the nomination is

---

32 This is most conveniently to be found on page E119 of *Schofield*.

acceptable in a democratic society. However the formulation of this test is a matter for Chapter 7 below.

Before proceeding further it seems useful to summarise the legal argument in a number of propositions.

1 A nomination paper which is good in form and does not constitute an abuse of nomination must be accepted by the returning officer.

2 A returning officer has the power to refuse a nomination paper which is bad in form or constitutes an abuse of the right of nomination. The phrase 'abuse of the right of nomination' is to be narrowly construed.

3 A returning officer's decision to accept a nomination paper is not susceptible to judicial review. Authority for this proposition is given by *Sanders v Chichester*.

4 A returning officer's decision to reject a nomination paper is susceptible to judicial review. Authority for this proposition is given by *ex p Bennett v Thatcher* (the 'Margaret Thatcher' case) and *Balabanoff*.

5 The test applied in *ex p Bennett v Thatcher* to exclude the nomination of Margaret Thatcher né Colin Hanoman –'what is in the best interests of the electors of Barnet and Finchley?' – is a particular application of the wider and correct test which should be applied in cases in which nominations are excluded. Where a nomination is excluded by a returning officer and the disadvantaged candidate challenges this exclusion by means of judicial review the test ought *not* to be 'Did the returning officer behave in a *Wednesbury* reasonable manner?', but *should be*, 'Are the interests of the electors in a democratic society best served by the exclusion of this purported candidate?'

6 It should be noted that the test is phrased in this way[33] so as to emphasise the fact that there should be a strong presumption in favour of the validity of a nomination.

7 Furthermore, and for the reasons explained by James Callaghan and in the argument set out above, the scheme of regulation first introduced by the RPPA 1998 and extended by the PPERA 2000 is both unnecessary and ineffectual. A determined spoiler candidate could still describe themselves as, for example, 'Tony B'liar, the Independent Labor Party Candidate and Prime Minister' on all

---

33 There is some discussion in Chapter 6 relating to *Morgan v Simpson* and concerning the way in which Lord Denning MR switches between the positive and negative phrasing of a question of statutory interpretation.

their election literature and, provided they confined themselves to 'Tony B'liar' and 'Independent' on the nomination paper, still stand properly nominated. Adopting the wider test canvassed in this chapter may allow the nomination to be struck out at least on the second or subsequent attempt at standing as a candidate.

Having considered the legal arguments and reached some tentative conclusions it is now time to return to the politics.

Discipline within political parties

Dyson J pointed out, in his concluding remarks in *Sanders v Chichester*, that in a number of jurisdictions, and he listed, amongst others, New Zealand, the Commonwealth of Australia, and the Republic of South Africa, there is a system of registration of political parties and a statutory provision limiting the ability of candidates to use the name of a political party. He concluded by saying that:

> It may be in the light of the present case that Parliament will wish to consider again whether a similar regime should be adopted for the conduct of elections in the United Kingdom.

Arguably these comments, together with the activities of Richard Huggett, 'Margaret Thatcher' and the others, led to the current unhappy state of the law.

We shall see in the next chapter what happened when a candidate, who was not wholly to the political taste of all the active members of a party, was imposed on them as their candidate by the central party machine. However, before the threads of the argument can be drawn together and a policy proposal submitted we need to examine the other root of the legislative framework originally introduced by the Registration of Political Parties Act 1998.

The focus must be upon the work of the Labour Party and Government because it was, after all the 1997–2001 government that designed and promoted the legislation. It may well be that the history of the other parties reveals a broadly similar story. It must be observed that the 1998 Act (numbered Chapter 48 of the Parliament) was an early piece of legislation introduced by the incoming Labour government; clearly the government thought that RPPA 1998 was a legislative priority even though the Labour Party had not been badly affected by spoiler candidates and the last major case had been *Sanders v Chichester* in 1994. Surely it could not rank with, for example, the National Minimum Wage Act 1998 (numbered Chapter 39 of the Parliament) and the Human Rights Act 1998 (numbered Chapter 42 of the Parliament) as a matter of social priority; however, it came into force before both of these Acts. It must also be remembered that the government had come to power in

May 1997, after 18 years in opposition, with a huge parliamentary majority of 179 and thus the ability to pass legislation freely. The Parliamentary Labour Party contained 183 newly elected MPs who lacked parliamentary experience. Given the opposition of an earlier Labour government to a similar measure, some other explanation must be sought for its passage.

The Labour Party had been characterised by divisions throughout its life.[34] Four examples from its hundred year history should serve to make the point. These stem, first, from the period 1900–05; secondly, 1929–31; thirdly, 1945–55; and, finally, in the run-up to the 1997 election.

From the beginning in February 1900 when the Labour Representation Committee (LRC) was formed, the party was split into more or less hostile groups.[35] Apart from the economic issues that divided many of the trade unionists, especially the Miners' Federation, from the rest of the party there was a major split upon the issue of the South African War. The Independent Labour Party and the communist Social Democratic Federation took the same position as many Liberals in opposing the war, whilst the Clarion group were strongly pro-war, the Fabians seemed to lack interest in it, and the trade unions were divided amongst themselves.[36] In the 1900 'Khaki election' 15 LRC candidates fought 16 seats;[37] its candidates were returned in two constituencies. Whilst Keir Hardy went on to become a 'One Man Party' and the 'Apostle of British socialism', the other elected MP, Richard Bell, the Secretary of the Amalgamated Society of Railway Servants,[38] was nominally a supporter of an independent Labour Party, but quickly left the party.[39]

The most obvious example of a fundamental split within the Labour party was evidenced by the 1931 general election where, following Ramsey McDonald's election in 1929 as the first Labour Prime Minister and the economic disaster of 1930, McDonald led a coalition of National Labour, National Liberal and National Conservative candidates into the

---

34 Put more pithily by Ben Pimlott, 1988, p 82:

> The history of this movement is littered with quarrels, splits and expulsions ... From the departure of the Marxist Social Democratic Federation in 1901 to the defection of the anti-Marxist S.D.P. eighty years later, there have been those who have dreamt of an alternative formation drawing away the labour movement's electoral base or building a movement of their own.

35 For a full account of the position in the early 1900s see Williams, F, 1950, Chapter 5.

36 In passing it may well be commented that in relation to the South African War, the Korean War and the Iraq conflict – *plus ça change*.

37 Keir Hardy fought both Merthyr and Preston, winning Merthyr and coming bottom of the poll in Preston.

38 He represented Derby, an early centre of railway development.

39 Quotations from Williams, 1950, p 137 and the caption to the frontispiece photograph of Keir Hardy.

1931 election against the Labour party. The Labour party lost most of its seats and spent the years until 1945 in the democratic wilderness.

The post-war Labour government led by Attlee is often seen in Labour party circles as the great reforming government of the century and has been the subject of apotheosis. Even Mandelson and Liddle draw attention to the fact that 'Labour governments have always coped with adversity, although none responded better than the 1945 administration which displayed extraordinary unity and coherence for most of its existence'.[40] In one sense it is difficult to categorise this statement as anything other than hyperbolic, for Clem Attlee, the 'modest little man with plenty to be modest about',[41] was beset by a plot to remove him from the leadership even before he was invited to form the government.[42] However, in another sense, Mandelson and Liddle are correct, for the real political difficulties for Labour did not arise until after the February 1950 election when, as a result of disagreements over the Korean War, rearmament, and Hugh Gaitskell's proposal to introduce some NHS charges, Nye Bevan, Harold Wilson and John Freeman resigned from the Cabinet.[43] Aneurin (Nye) Bevan was always a controversial figure within the party, having been expelled over the Popular Front to end appeasement in 1939, voting for the motion censuring the wartime coalition government after the fall of Tobruk in June 1942, attacking Attlee's record in the wartime coalition in September 1942, voting (together with an overwhelming majority of backbench Labour MPs) against the Labour frontbench's support for a delay in the implementation of the Beveridge Report in 1943, and subsequently resigning from the shadow cabinet and nearly being expelled from the party in 1955. Bevan was thus a thorn in the flesh of some elements of the leadership of the party. Beckett sums up the result of the 1955 election rather succinctly.

> Clem Attlee was popular and respected, but his party looked a mess. The result was: Conservatives 345, Labour 277, Liberals 6. For [Herbert] Morrison, [Hugh] Gaitskell and [Arthur] Deakin, this result could be explained in two words: Aneurin Bevan.[44]

---

40 See Mandelson and Liddle, 1996, p 236.

41 This dismissive comment about Clem Attlee is usually attributed to Winston Churchill, although there is good reason to attribute it to the *Daily Worker* journalist, Claud Cockburn. See Beckett, 2000, p 209.

42 See Beckett, 2000, pp 196–99.

43 For a full account, see Beckett, 2000, pp 285–88.

44 Beckett, 2000, p 303. For a fuller and more sympathetic account of the life and works of Aneurin Bevan, see Foot, 1975; Lee, 1980. Michael Foot was, of course, a political ally of Bevan, and Jennie Lee, apart from her own successful political career, was married to Bevan.

There are many further examples that could be given and these are admirably set out in Tudor Jones' *Remaking the Labour Party: from Gaitskell to Blair*,[45] but these will only add, admittedly valuable, detail to the short account given by Mandelson and Liddle.[46] Nicolas Jones alludes to the same point in his provocatively titled and polemical book, *The Control Freaks: How New Labour Gets its Own Way*.[47] Jones writes:

> Whenever Tony Blair has been accused at open meetings of becoming a control freak and of presiding over an autocratic party machine, his response has been brisk and to the point. He has asked the rank and file to remember the indiscipline of the 1980s when Labour was unelectable. In his judgement, the chaotic state of the party during those long years out of office provided every justification for a thorough overhaul; and in order to give the party the sharp professional edge, the leadership had to impose tight control over its structure and organisation. Indeed, so great had been the party's wish to escape from the horrors of the past that Blair had little difficulty in his early years as Prime Minister in silencing those voices at Labour gatherings who were starting to express criticism of his leadership.[48]

It is not surprising that the Labour party wished to renew itself and had to adopt defensive measures within the party to ensure that reforms which it considered necessary[49] were carried forward. Neither criticism nor endorsement is offered of these changes for the simple reason that they are matters which are rightfully the proper practical concern of members of the Labour party. It is for the Labour party itself to decide whether it wishes to endorse or reject any matter of policy from nuclear disarmament, to hunting with or without dogs, to nationalising the commanding heights of the economy. However, internal discipline has always seemed to be an issue for the party, most notably in the early 1980s when Mr Benn and Mr Healey fought for the deputy leadership. At the time of the 1983 general election the party was widely believed to have split irrevocably. No Labour leader could tolerate the schisms which had split the party and, as Tudor Jones, Mandelson and Liddle, and Nicholas Jones all clearly demonstrate, Mr Blair and his lieutenants moved swiftly to crush dissent when Mr Blair became party leader after the death of John Smith in 1994.

---

45 Jones, Tudor, 1996.
46 Mandelson and Liddle, 1996, pp 213–16.
47 Jones, Nicholas, 2001.
48 Jones, N, 2001, p 9.
49 The word order at this point is difficult. One alternative, 'necessary reforms', suggests that the reforms are endorsed. The phrase used, 'reforms which it considered necessary', is not to be taken as suggesting that the reforms were unwelcome.

Having demonstrated that it is quite understandable why the Labour party might wish to use the law to enforce party discipline there is only one more step necessary – to explain why they did it. In the next chapter we will see that in the Newark constituency there was friction between two groups both, no doubt, describing themselves as 'Labour party loyalists', and candidates stood as 'Old Labour' and 'Real Labour' in a number of seats. Furthermore, the story of Richard Huggett standing as a Literal Democrat is now brought into sharp relief. When the Liberal Democrat and Social Democratic parties merged, a number of members of both parties were bitter at losing the internal vote and saw themselves as the keepers of the true faith. Rather than going off and founding or refounding their own party or simply fighting the seat or seats, under the former name, the dissident group (which may just have amounted to Mr Huggett) resolved to act as spoiler candidates. Similarly the Labour Party was struck by 'the Blair revolution' and the party had every reason to fear that long-standing members of the party – probably on its political left – would do exactly the same thing. In these circumstances, since the candidate has every right to use their name and description on every piece of literature – leaving aside the ballot paper for the moment – it is a matter for the wronged party to deal with in their election literature. Clearly, the other competing parties will seek to exploit such divisions, but surely this is the stuff of politics.

It is asserted here that Labour was, in reality, using its parliamentary majority to push through legislation designed to protect its brand image. Its action is cognate with that which might be taken by the manufacturer of a 'fizzy drink' who wished to prevent others presenting themselves as, to use a helpful slogan 'the genuine article'. Only one brand of Labour was to be available in the electoral market.

Again it must be made clear that this is not an attack upon a particular political party. It is not denied, indeed it is positively asserted, that all political parties would behave in the same way in similar circumstances. The problem that is being addressed is not a question of which policies the Labour party (or, for that matter, any other party) ought to pursue, or which of its philosophical traditions it ought to follow,[50] but whether electoral law ought to be open to manipulation in this way.

The best evidence of the effect of the 1998–2000 changes in the law can be seen by reviewing the *Balabanoff* case. *Balabanoff*, it will be recalled, involved the rejection of the Liberal Democrat panel of candidates seeking election to Harrow Council, because of an apparent error by a local Liberal Democrat officer. He, apparently inadvertently, described

---

50 Mandelson and Liddle, 1996, pp 29–30.

the candidates in a way which did not accord with the certificate issued by the party's national nominating officer. This was an error for which the party paid dearly. However, the obvious danger is that parties will use the legislation to discipline dissidents within their own ranks rather than to protect themselves against outsiders. Suppose that a constituency party or district council group wished to take a radically different view from the national political party; the national party could override local wishes. An example will help to clarify the point. Suppose it is government policy to build, say, a wind farm within a certain district. There is vociferous local opposition and the ruling group on the district council, which is of the same party as the government, decides to oppose the development. At election time the nominating officer of the national party may decide to withhold the necessary[51] certificate from those candidates who backed the district party against the national party.

It appears plain that political parties are able to manipulate electoral law to their own advantage. This is not to discover, as did Winston Churchill, 'the sinister head of a future British Gestapo' sitting in the chair of the Labour party[52] – an assertion that might have been relevant and rhetorically powerful at the end of the Second World War, but seems melodramatic in modern Britain. The submission is, rather, that the political parties are able, in concert or by means of a large parliamentary majority with the authority that brings, to recast electoral law as a competition between branded political parties rather than as the means by which a free people govern themselves in their common and mutual interests. The Registration of Political Parties Act 1998 was the child of a political party and whilst it was revised, extended and incorporated into the Political Parties, Elections and Referendums Act 2000, this, too, was a wholly 'political act' in the sense that it was designed and built by members of parliament. True, this latter Act also brought about the birth of the Electoral Commission, but, as we shall see in Chapter 7, the Commission may easily be overridden by parliament.

This reveals that perhaps the most telling criticism that can be levelled against the electoral law of the United Kingdom is that it is the offspring of parliament. It has no special status as entrenched constitutional law and it may be changed, against the strong opposition of the House of Lords, by a simple majority in the House of Commons. This is wholly unsatisfactory. It was held, in *Ashby v White*,[53] that the law of elections precedes parliament. Parliament is, in a representative democracy, the organ of the people that governs on their behalf and it is

---

51 Under Rule 4A(1) of the Local Election (Principal Areas) Rules 1986.

52 Taylor, 1965, p 722.

53 (1703) 2 Ld Raym 938.

subject to their choice, which, as we have seen, ought to be exercised in the interests of the people as a whole. The problem with a market system is that, with very few brands on offer and the incumbents being able to control the content and identity of the brands, the democratic legitimacy of the parliament and the degree of interest in parliament falls.

Lees-Marshment has argued, as we saw in the first chapter, that the way out of this problem is for the political parties to engage in market-oriented strategies – 'find out what the people want and give it to them'. The main objection to her approach is that it leads to the dictatorship of the majority and not the governance of the country in the interests of all its members. Leaving electoral law in the hands of political parties who have subscribed to this theory could lead us into elections in which voting is quick and easy, requiring little physical or intellectual effort from the voters. Democratic governance is not so trivial a matter.

Chapter 5:
Election Expenses

Introduction

Has voting now become something of a commercial transaction? This question was raised in the first, introductory, chapter and has had a shadow presence throughout the following chapters. Do political parties compete in the same mode as purveyors of 'sofas and fizzy drinks'[1] for votes to bring them to power? This question is not the old sneering comment that 'British democracy is the best money can buy' – which implies that elections are simply a sham and that politicians are fundamentally corrupt – but, rather, whether the major actors – the political parties – have commercialised elections to the extent that they have become campaigns for marketing the political parties.

One would naturally expect the law that controls expenditure on elections to be at the forefront of the mechanisms designed to prevent electoral success from being bought. To state the obvious, advertising is big business simply because it works, and therefore political parties advertise to gain votes. However, the process of pouring money into political advertising and harvesting votes is viewed as akin to vote buying and therefore essentially corrupt. In the first part of this chapter the legal rules controlling election expenditure are surveyed.

The control of election expenditure

It is plain that bribery and corruption in elections were commonplace before the fundamental democratic reform of the 1832 Reform Bill and the legal prohibitions on vote buying;[2] Dickens' account of the Eatanswill election in *The Pickwick Papers* provides vivid illustrations of the routine corruption.[3] Gifts of various sorts – food and quantities of drink – seem to have been given to the townsmen and their families in attempts to secure the votes of the limited number of electors. Violence

---

1   See Chapter 1.
2   See, in particular, the 1854 Act, but it must be noted that this was not the earliest legislation prohibiting electoral corruption.
3   Dickens, 1992, Chapter 13.

and the use of drink and drugs to prevent electors' attendance at the poll were among the other techniques employed by the candidates. In fact, corruption was so widespread and so general that its differential effects were nearly nullified and it became almost an attractive feature of the election. Certainly the Pickwickians went to Eatanswill for the election entertainment.

Modern elections are, fortunately or not, much less entertaining and people do not welcome elections as an opportunity to receive the candidates' largesse. There is no bounty to be distributed and the doling out of even the most banal of 'goodies' – such as green parasols[4] – would, as we shall see, amount to at least one election offence.

The 19th century legal reforms directed against corruption were enacted in a period when political parties were relatively underdeveloped and there was a great deal less central control by each party over its own candidates. Whilst political control by central party machines was gradually established over the period of 150 years leading up to the end of the 20th century, it is quite clear that even in the late 20th century, there was no such legal entity as the Conservative Party, despite the fact that it had provided a number of governments. This, somewhat surprising, point was established in *Conservative Central Office v Burrell*,[5] in which the Conservative Party was found to be a loose amalgam of a number of separate bodies. The Party moved over the succeeding years to formalise its structure, but the underlying point is plain; in the past, political parties were much less monolithic. Parties have even found it difficult to protect their names against usurpers until the enactment of the Registration of Political Parties Act 1998 (see Chapter 4). Now consolidated into the Political Parties, Elections and Referendums Act 2000, this legislation has had the effect of centralising party governance. In earlier times, individuals, with or without the assistance of an election agent, were much more clearly responsible for running their own elections and so it was reasonable for them to be legally responsible for their own misdeeds. This was reflected by the imposition of criminal sanctions for corruption, such as the various forms of vote buying.

There are two levels of control imposed upon vote buying, the individual and the collective. These schemes interlock. First, at the individual level, the law provides a number of criminal offences with which those who seek unfairly and unlawfully to influence the voting decisions of others may be charged (and convicted). Persons convicted of these individual election offences are liable to ordinary criminal penalties

---

4   The example of a bribe given in the *Pickwick Papers*.

5   [1980] 3 All ER 42.

and the loss of their own vote for a considerable period. The most important of these offences are:

(1) bribery, the giving of money to corruptly influence a voter, as defined in s 113 of the Representation of the People Act 1983 (RPA 1983);

(2) treating, the provision of food and drink to corruptly influence a voter, as defined in s 114 of the RPA 1983; and

(3) undue influence, the threat or use of force or other menace to corruptly influence a voter, as defined in s 113 of the RPA 1983.

The punishment, as provided under s 168 of the RPA 1983, for these corrupt practices is imprisonment for a period of up to one year and/or an unlimited fine. Furthermore, according to s 173 of the RPA 1983 a candidate who is convicted of one of these offences is prohibited from holding elective office for a period of five years. Since such offenders are also likely to be political activists the latter penalty is highly significant. If they were, subsequently to the period of disqualification, to stand as an candidate in an election it must be beyond doubt that their wrongdoing would be revealed by their rivals and thus their chances of election severely curtailed.

Bribery in elections has been a criminal offence since early times[6] and seems to have been rife during the 19th century,[7] but it has not been possible to find any modern proven cases of such corruption so it must be judged that the law is effective. Furthermore the political space for such corruption has shrunk. Political parties are now in direct control of activity and it would seem unlikely that they would engage in such wrongdoing because of the serious consequences. Electoral politics has developed from being an individual concern into a corporate concern and it may be that the offences detailed above are of limited relevance, at least in so far as political parties are concerned. This is not, it must be strongly emphasised, be taken as an argument for the repeal of these provisions because, as has been argued elsewhere, including in this book,[8] the introduction of remote voting tends to lead, or may in fact have led, to the re-emergence of levels of individual corruption not seen since the 19th century.[9] It may well be that this sort of corruption would be best dealt with by the enactment of a short criminal statute with

---

6   See *R v Hollis* 20 St Tr 1225; *R v Vaughan* (1769) 4 Burr 2494.

7   See, eg, *Lichfield* (1895) 5 O'M & H 29; *Stroud (No 3)* (1874) 2 O'M & H 183; *Sligo* (1869) 1 O'M & H 302.

8   Birch and Watt, 2004, pp 60–72.

9   See *The Times* of 9, 10 and 11 June 2004 and Chapter 8 below.

clearly defined and modern[10] offences dealing with bribery and undue influence, rather than leaving the offences buried in a mainly administrative law statute.

The second level of legal control is imposed at the level of election funding or finance and applies not to individuals *qua* individuals, but to political parties and to their members standing as candidates. Clearly, an individual may stand as an independent candidate, but, it is argued, such a person should be viewed as a representative of a very small political party. The reason for this proposal is that the statutory mechanisms are designed around the model of competing political parties and the individual candidate is seen as out of the ordinary.

The law provides that only a certain amount of money may be spent upon an election campaign. This operates at two regulatory levels, first, the general election campaign in which the expenditure of political parties upon general campaigning is fixed by law. The scheme governing the general campaign expenditure of a political party upon a general election campaign was introduced by the Political Parties, Elections and Referendums Act 2000 (PPERA) and came into effect on 16 February 2001. The term 'general campaign expenditure' refers to the money spent by a political party upon the promotion of its own policies and programme, rather than upon the promotion of an individual candidate. Expenditure laid out on the promotion of an individual candidate is dealt with below, and an individual return of expenditure related to the promotion of that particular candidacy is required. It has been clear, since the leading case of *R v Tronoh Mines*[11] in 1952, that the expenditure of money on general election campaigning is not expenditure designed to secure the election of an identifiable single candidate or candidates and so is not chargeable to individual election expenses.

The statutory scheme imposes limits upon the relevant party's general campaign budget at election time. Prior to February 2001, there was no legal limit to the sum a registered political party could spend upon its election campaign; indeed, it needs to be recalled that prior to 1998 there was no scheme for the registration of political parties at all and parties could act at their free discretion. The registration scheme is discussed in Chapter 3. The scheme limiting expenditure extends to parliamentary general elections, European parliamentary elections, Scottish parliamentary elections, and elections to the Welsh National Assembly and to the Northern Irish Assembly, but not directly to expenditure on local government election campaigns. The financial

---

10 It is doubted whether issues of undue spiritual influence play much part in modern elections; see, eg, *Tipperary* (1874) 2 O'M & H 31; *Galway* (1869) 1 O'M & H 305; *Galway* (1874) 2 O'M & H 57.

11 *R v Tronoh Mines Ltd* [1952] 1 All ER 697.

limits are to be found in s 79 and Sched 9 of the PPERA 2000 and are subject to periodic increase.

The reason for the introduction of the scheme, and indeed the Act in general, relates to allegations that the Conservative party was receiving substantial contributions to its funds from overseas sources channelled through one of the party's vice-chairmen. These allegations were referred to the Committee on Standards in Public Life. The Government responded to the Fifth Report of the Committee with a set of far-reaching and wide-ranging proposals,[12] which resulted in the PPERA 2000. Details of the reporting requirements for these returns are contained in the 2000 Act between ss 80 and 84, depending upon the size of the expenditure, and the report, which must be made to the Electoral Commission, is available for public inspection.

The second and lower regulatory level governing election funding or finance serves to control the sum of money spent by individual candidates and their political parties on campaigns to return them to the relevant parliament, assembly or local authority. This regulatory scheme, which is contained in the RPA 1983, may be outlined as follows. There are two kinds of expenses, first, the personal expenses of a candidate, which are regulated by s 74 of the RPA 1983: they are not relevant to the present debate and will not be discussed. Secondly, there are the expenses in connection with the conduct or management of an election and these are regulated by s 76 of the RPA 1983. The expenses incurred in running an election must be claimed against the candidate or their agent and must, in accordance with s 78 of the RPA 1983, be claimed within 21 days of the declaration of the result and paid within 28 days after the declaration. Within 35 days of the declaration of the result a return of all the expenses incurred must be made to the returning office under s 81 of the 1983 Act. The 1983 Act provides for variation in these time limits in the case of, for example, an election for the Mayor of London.

Clearly, the rationale behind this legal control is that political parties and candidates should not be able to buy their way to political power. In the words of the Lord Chief Justice in *R v Jones; R v Whicher*:[13]

> The object, plainly, is to achieve a level playing field between competing candidates, so as to prevent perversion of the voters' democratic choice by significant disparities of local expenditure.

This can be seen as the intervention by the state in the vote 'market' in order to ensure a 'level playing field' or, perhaps more formally, the

---

12 *The funding of political parties in the United Kingdom: The Government's proposals for legislation in response to the Fifth Report of the Committee on Standards in Public Life*. Cm 4413, 1999.

13 *R v Jones; R v Whicher* [1999] EWCA 974. This is most readily found in *Schofield*.

conditions for free and fair competition. If that were the case it would seem that there is little to choose between the system of control of election finances adopted in the UK and that used in the USA. In the USA there is no limit upon the amount of money that may be spent by a candidate on their own election campaign, but there are very strict limits upon the size of donations which may be made to candidates – the rationale being that candidates should be free to use their own money to speak for them as loudly as they choose, but that the candidate or their election should not be bought by a third party who is not themselves standing for election. This was brought about by the decision in *Buckley v Valeo*,[14] in the US Supreme Court in an action brought under the free speech clause of the First Amendment. The US method of control seems to be much more like a market system than the British system. Clearly the sellers of 'sofas and fizzy drinks' ought to be free to spend as much as they like upon advertising in a market populated by rational consumers who can be trusted to see through the 'glitz' to the quality of the product beyond. The rationale behind the British regulatory scheme may be that it is simply inefficient to spend vast sums of money on a completely empty enterprise, such as losing an election, and candidates ought to be protected from their own folly. It should also be noted that, in the case of *Bowman v United Kingdom*,[15] an argument, similar to that run in *Buckley v Valeo*, succeeded before the European Court of Human Rights and led to an amendment of the 1983 Act.[16] In any event, the difference between the US and the British systems is of little consequence for the argument which follows.

The amount of money that may be spent upon an election campaign in Britain is tightly capped in two ways: first, and political parties will bear testament to this fact, by the funds available to the party. Parties are sometimes supported by individual donors, and this has been a matter of some controversy (although this is beyond the scope of the present work), but most election expenses have to be funded out of a parties' own income. Whilst there are proposals that political parties should be funded by the state, currently they are constrained by their own resources. This leads to difficulties which will be set out below. Secondly, as we have seen, there are tight legal limits. What happens when those legal limits are exceeded?

---

14 424 US 1 (1976). For analysis, see Barendt, 1985, pp 48–54.

15 *The Times*, 23 February 1998.

16 See s 75(1ZA) of the RPA 1983, introduced by s 131 of the PPERA 2000.

Breaking the legal limits on expenditure

The leading modern case in this matter is that of Fiona Jones, formerly Labour MP for Newark, and a discussion of her case forms the subject of this chapter. Fiona Jones, and her election agent Desmond Whicher, were prosecuted for offences that had at their base an allegation that the limits on election expenditure had been exceeded. Both Jones and Whicher were convicted at first instance, the convictions being overturned upon appeal. The question also arose as to whether Ms Jones should have automatically lost her seat in the House of Commons. This was resolved, in the negative, on the Crown side of the High Court. It will be argued here that *R v Jones; R v Whicher*[17] exposes the extent to which the British political system is dominated by the parties and demonstrates the extent to which its market nature is damaging to democracy. At the end of this chapter, a proposal to remedy the defect will be advanced. The facts surrounding the *Jones* case need some recitation and explanation because the case can really only be understood in its political context. The background to the case exposes the extent of collusion between the three main political parties that, it is argued, inhibits or prevents the law effectively controlling election expenditure.

The political background to *R v Jones; R v Whicher*

The following discussion of the political background of the *Jones* case is designed to add weight to the view that modern cases dealing with irregularities in election finance ought not to be dealt with as matters of criminal law, but ought instead to be addressed exclusively through the election courts using the election petition procedure. This is because, as will be seen, such irregularities are in fact matters of collective rather than individual responsibility and thus go to the organisation of the party's election campaign as a whole. It is the party, or the individual *qua* candidate, who should suffer the consequences of any wrongdoing rather than the individual themselves. As will be seen, however, recognising this would entail some far-reaching revisions to the law relating to election petitions.

Before entering the detailed discussion of the travails which beset the Labour Party in the period 1979–97 and which led to the Fiona Jones case, it is important to recall that all political parties pass through periods of eclipse. The Liberals were strongly in the ascendant during the first decade of the 20th century, whilst the Conservatives were in, apparently, terminal decline: however the Liberal Party almost disappeared as a

---

17 [1999] EWCA 974.

political force for a large part of the rest of the century. Furthermore, all parties have their dissidents – as was seen in the account of *Sanders v Chichester* (Chapter 4), where a member of the former Liberal Party, angered by the decision to merge the party with the Social Democratic Party, decided to stand against the Liberal Democrats as a 'Literal Democrat'. Just as the Liberal camp had its Richard Huggett, the Conservative party was faced with one Merrick who stood as 'the Official Byron Ward Conservative' against 'the Official Conservative party Candidate' in a Nottingham City Council by-election in late 1988.[18] It surely cannot be doubted that one may often find a 'local party riven by personal animosity'.[19] Personal animosity and political antagonism are sometimes indistinguishable. Lesley Mahmood (a member of the ultra-left 'Militant Tendency' of the Labour Party) stood in the interests of 'Walton Real Labour' in the Liverpool Walton constituency following the death of the leading left-wing Labour MP Eric Heffer and was insulted in the *Sunday Mirror* by Alastair Campbell, who wrote 'M stands for Mahmood, Militant and maggots ... Vote Kilfoyle (the Labour Party candidate) to kill off the maggots'.[20]

It is well known that Margaret Thatcher led the Conservative Party to victory in the 1979 general election and effectively ended the post-war social democratic consensus. Immediately after 1979, some sections of the Labour Party moved to the left, Michael Foot was elected leader and the party fought the 1983 general election on the basis of a manifesto sometimes termed 'the longest suicide note in history'.[21] The Labour Party was heavily defeated in the 1983 election and in the following two general elections, thus giving the Conservative party an uninterrupted run of 18 years of power. Whilst Michael Foot resigned after the 1983 defeat and was replaced as party leader by Neil Kinnock who, with the aid of other moderate socialists and social democrats, effectively defeated the Trotskyite left, resulting in their expulsion, it was left to Tony Blair and his colleagues to complete the transformation of the party from socialism to centre-left social democracy. The ideological centrepiece of this transformation, which for the socialist left amounted

---

18 See the unreported judgment of the Court of Appeal dated 2 November 1988 in *Patterson v Merrick and Hammond*.

19 See the penultimate paragraph in *Jones* [1999] EWCA 974 CA.

20 See Jones, N, 2001, p 165.

21 One Labour candidate, to the author's knowledge, adopted the manifesto with great enthusiasm. He published his personal statement developing these themes to such a degree that when it appeared under the title 'No Fudging' his election agent was heard to rename it 'No Fucking Votes'. The candidate in question, Julian Jacottet, who stood for election in the Oxford West and Abingdon constituency, did narrowly retain his deposit.

to iconoclasm, was the abandonment of Clause IV(4) of the party constitution.[22]

The other essential element of the political background to this case is the split that occurred within the Labour Party in the period leading up to the 1983 general election. Apart from the departure of three prominent members (David Owen, Shirley Williams, and Roy Jenkins) and one rather less prominent member (Bill Rodgers) of the core Labour party to form the Social Democratic Party (SDP), the rank and file of the party was divided. Some other members left to join the SDP, whilst those who remained expended a great deal of energy on ideological and doctrinal battles. These strenuous disagreements were rife during the early years of the Kinnock leadership, but, as year followed year of opposition, the battles diminished. The watershed was reached following the end of the Kinnock leadership, when after his resignation, brought about by the 1992 general election defeat, and the election of John Smith to a short leadership of the party, the Labour Party drew together, tired by years of political impotence. The party was now ready for its ultimate transformation into New Labour.[23]

This transformation – termed by its proponents 'modernisation' – of the Labour Party was greeted with a variety of responses. On the one hand, party membership blossomed with many new people joining the party and infusing it with fresh political enthusiasm, and on the other hand, many long-established members either left or adopted a 'bunker mentality' inimically hostile to the 'New Labour' project. Many constituency parties split on ideological lines, with the old left opposing newer members whom they saw as betraying the socialist traditions of the party. The newer members saw the old guard as being more interested in ideological purity than effective political power, and drew attention to the two most salient features of the preceding Thatcher/Major years, the splits in the party with constituency parties appearing to snipe at the parliamentary leadership and the public perception (real, imagined or in any event convenient) that 'Old Labour' socialism was old-fashioned, irrelevant and unelectable.

Such was the position in Newark in late 1996–early 1997. Many members of the constituency Labour party wished to select a prominent local trade union and Labour Party activist as their candidate in the forthcoming general election. They wished to emphasise their

---

22 Clause IV(4): 'To secure for the workers, by hand or by brain, the full fruits of their industry and the most equitable distribution thereof that may be possible upon the basis of the common ownership of the means of production, distribution and exchange, and best detainable system of popular administration and control of each industry or service.'

23 For a sympathetic account by some of the prime participants, see Mandelson and Liddle, 1996.

independence from Labour Party headquarters (derisorily known in these circles as 'Millbank' – the location of the party's London headquarters). Local Labour party activists commonly resisted the imposition of those whom they termed 'Millbank candidates'. On the other hand, some members of the constituency party, strongly supported by the national Labour Party, wanted to have a candidate more representative of the modern voter, more in tune with the concerns of the electorate and who was younger, more personally attractive, and who was, if possible, female. The party was conscious that female members of parliament were (and indeed remain to date) very much in the minority[24] and saw an opportunity to select a fresh female candidate.[25] Fiona Jones was selected as the parliamentary candidate. The Newark constituency Labour Party then split, with a number of party activists refusing to work for Ms Jones' election. Some members of the party remained loyal to her, seeing her as the properly selected candidate and the person most likely to be elected as Labour MP for Newark. Prominent amongst the Jones loyalists was Desmond Whicher, the former Labour Mayor of Newark, who had been a party activist for many years and who was, perhaps for that reason, detested by many on the left. Desmond Whicher agreed to serve as Fiona Jones' election agent after the resignation of her former agent. Desmond Whicher was a very experienced election agent and knew exactly how to husband the scarce resources available to the party. He was also well aware of 'the tricks of the trade' – as were indeed many of those who had deserted Ms Jones' camp.

The role of the election agent is pivotal to an election campaign. For most elections an agent must be appointed in accordance with ss 67 and 71 of the RPA 1983 although, by virtue of s 70, a candidate who fails to name an agent shall be deemed to act as their own agent. An early judicial view of the role of an election agent was that of Field J, in *Barrow in Furness*, in which he said:

> … a person shall be the election agent who shall be effectively responsible for all the acts done in procuring the election. The affairs of the election should be carried on in the light of day and a respectable and responsible man [*sic*], responsible to the candidate and to the public, should be there to do all that is necessary.[26]

---

24 See *Jephson and Dyas-Elliot v The Labour Party* [1996] IRLR 116; and the subsequent amendments to the law in the Sex Discrimination (Election Candidates) Act 2002. The House of Commons Research Paper 01/75 of 22 October 2001 contains much useful material.

25 Distastefully known to the boys of the tabloid press as a 'Blair Babe'.

26 (1886) 4 O'M & H 76.

The editors of *Schofield*,[27] reproduce the words of the Final Report of the Committee on Electoral Reform (Cmd 7286), which uses nearly the same words as Field J:

> The object of the requirement is that there shall be an experienced person responsible to the candidate and to the public for the proper management of the candidature and in particular for the control of expenditure. The employment of an agent is of great benefit to the candidate, and a competent agent can do much to promote due observance of electoral law. We see no reason for any distinction in this matter between parliamentary and local elections and every advantage in assimilation of the law.[28]

However, can this expectation be any more than a pious and wholly unrealistic hope? It is suggested that election agents are often chosen for their campaigning zeal, their ability to organise the candidate's diary and their capacity to motivate party workers, rather than their administrative or financial acumen. In one case, *McCrory v Hendron*,[29] the election agent was chosen simply because the agent who had supported the candidate (Dr Joe Hendron, the longstanding leader of the Social Democratic and Labour Party in Northern Ireland) in earlier elections had been so intimidated by threats of death and severe violence that he was not willing to assume the role again. Whilst it is highly unusual for election agents to be subjected to death threats and for them, in the light of those threats, to fail to perform their duties of financial administration adequately, it is rather more common for agents to be much more concerned with the political administration rather than the financial aspects of the campaign. Further, most agents in local government campaigns have little or no knowledge of electoral law and would be highly unlikely to be able to offer guidance to a candidate or otherwise 'do much to promote due observance of electoral law'. Agents are usually chosen for their political acumen and their willingness to work, rather than for their legal knowledge.

Finally, the editors of *Schofield* take the view that the relationship between a candidate and his or her agent is contractual and as such it ought to be reduced to writing. The authors of *Schofield* support this advice with good reason and authority,[30] but it is doubted whether it is often accepted. Furthermore, the editors of *Schofield* expose an interesting inconsistency in suggesting that the contract should be reduced to writing. If agents are supposed to be responsible to both their principal

---

27 At s 7.05.

28 Final report of the Committee on Electoral Law Reform. Cmd 7286 (London; HMSO, 1947), para 46.

29 [1993] NI 177.

30 *Parker v Robinson* (1835) 7 C & P 241.

and to the public, as in the *Barrow in Furness* case and the Electoral Reform Committee Report discussed above, it is difficult to understand why the relationship should be 'contractual' in the sense that it should be a wholly private relationship between the two parties (the candidate and the agent). It would seem to be like an employment contract on the one hand, whilst on the other hand, it would seem to be regulated by the law of elections. It may be that the reasons why such written contracts are rare are, first, that it would be expensive to have such contracts drawn up – such an expense being declarable as an expense of the election – and, secondly, there are few who would wish to be bound in this way.

The 'tricks of the trade'

It is difficult to run a modern highly competitive election within the tight financial cap imposed by the statutory expenditure limits. All forms of publicity are expensive and, whilst communication between party workers is now speedy and efficient due to the advent of the mobile telephone, its cost should be recorded as an election expense and telephone bills costs quickly escalate. Election agents, who are ultimately responsible both for the campaign and its financing,[31] employ a number of devices to subvert the effect of the expenditure cap. The most obvious of these, which was employed in the *Jones* case, is to design election expenditure so that it looks like expenditure for ordinary political campaigning. It is settled law that expenditure for 'ordinary political activity' is not chargeable to election expenses. The point was repeated in *Jones*:

> Election expenses are not incurred where a constituency party carries on its ordinary political activity otherwise than with reference to a specific election which is reasonably imminent, even though such activity has the ultimate aim of winning public support and gaining or retaining power in the constituency; nor are they incurred by a candidate who nurses a constituency.

In *Jones*, this sort of campaigning was said to have been through compiling a computerised database, whilst in many constituencies it is achieved by the setting up and distribution of a 'newsletter'. This is a more or less frequent publication containing pieces of political news and which is distributed to all or some of the households in the constituency, especially where there are votes to be garnered. A newsletter typically mentions the names of prospective candidates, at district, county or

---

31 See ss 67–71A of the RPA 1983; and the valuable discussion in *McCrory v Hendron* on the role of an election agent in administering the election on behalf of the candidate.

parliamentary level, and becomes more frequently published and distributed around election times.

The selective distribution of political materials, whether or not these amount to election materials, the arrangements for the funding thereof, and the distribution of the charges onto the various election expenses accounts, form an important part of the election agent's job. This particular 'trick of the trade' needs to be explained in detail.

Consider a district council election taking place in ten, more or less coterminous, wards with each of the wards containing 1,000 households, that is, 10,000 households in all. Say that a party election agent has sufficient funds to produce a total of 20,000 election leaflets. They know that three of the wards are 'safe' – they have well-established long-serving councillors representing their own party's interest; they also know that, barring a political miracle, three of the remaining seven wards are firmly in the hands of the opposition party. There are four highly contested wards. In an ideal world the election agent would like to produce one district-wide leaflet setting out the party's district-wide policy and two election leaflets for each of the party's ten candidates. This would amount to 30,000 leaflets, but the agent only has funds for two-thirds of that number. Furthermore, when the agent totals up the allowable election expenses, which are ward based and founded on the number of electors rather than the number of households, they find that the allowable expenses would only allow them to fund an average of just over two leaflets per household. How can the agent 'square the circle'?

It would be rational for the agent to arrange for the production of one district-wide leaflet (thus, 10,000 copies), one candidate-specific leaflet for each of the three 'safe' wards (thus, 3,000 copies), one candidate-specific leaflet for each of the three 'unwinnable' wards (thus, 3,000 copies) and two candidate-specific leaflets for each of the four 'winnable' wards (thus, 8,000 copies). Thus, the agent would need to produce 24,000 leaflets, which is both more than can be afforded and more than the allowable total election expenses will permit. So the agent would then go to the party's usual printer and negotiate a 'trade discount'. There is an excellent discussion of the legality or otherwise of 'trade discounts' in the leading case of *McCrory v Hendron*:[32] suffice it to say that ordinary discounts obtained in the course of trade are wholly lawful, whilst excessive discounts, which amount to a hidden subsidy for a political party, are unlawful. Our election agent negotiates with the printer that he will supply receipted invoices for 10,000 district leaflets, 3,000 'safe-seat' leaflets, 3,000 'unwinnable-seat' leaflets, and 8,000 'winnable-seat' leaflets and will adjust the price of the leaflets to bring

32 [1993] NI 177.

that order within the agent's budget. If the order was charged at the proper 'book price', it would exceed the allowable election expenses, but the 'ordinary commercial discount' brings it below the total sum that may lawfully be spent. The agent will then supply the printer with a proper written order for that number of leaflets and, on the back of an envelope, provide the 'real order' – 8,500 district-wide leaflets, that is, one for every household in the target seats and the 'safe' wards and some to be delivered in the 'unwinnable areas; 3,000 'safe-seat' leaflets ('we have to get our vote out'); as well as 8,000 'winnable-seat' leaflets, and 'as many unwinnable seat leaflets as you can produce for the money – we do not need to leaflet every house'. The rationale behind this double ordering is to spread the cost of the district-wide leaflet, which will be used most heavily in the target seats, across all the seats in the district and thus avoid exceeding the election expenses in the target seats. It may well be that the printer, apart from being a party supporter, also enjoys a 'wee dram' and he will receive a nice bottle of good single malt as a Christmas present – well away from election time. This should not be seen as reducing a serious problem of electoral law to a rather cosy anecdote – the matter of providing drinks after an election for activities performed during the election has been litigated on a number of occasions.[33]

Such deals and discussions take place every spring up and down the country and more or less all party agents are involved to a greater or lesser degree. More complex arrangements are undoubtedly made where districts span parliamentary constituency boundaries and one of the two constituencies in question is a winnable parliamentary seat. Ask a party activist of any political colour and they will admit that some activity of this nature goes on during most elections. It must be emphasised that no charge of generalised corruption or dishonesty is being made. National-level politicians sometimes put such occurrences down to the enthusiasm, or misplaced zeal, of individual party workers. There is no doubt that most business people or, indeed, most people in general look for the most economical way of conducting their affairs and if people who share a sympathy or interest come together over a business deal, it would be surprising if they did not co-operate in order to achieve mutually satisfactory results. No doubt the printers of, for example, programmes for football matches are often fans of the club in question. The reasoning that, as we shall see later in this chapter, was adopted by the Court of Appeal in *Jones*, is thus endorsed here to the extent that those engaged in the electoral process ought not to be convicted of

---

33 See, for example, *Brecon* (1871) 2 O'M & H 43; and *Cork (Eastern Division)* (1911) 6 O'M & H 31.

crimes of dishonesty unless they actually knew that their activity was dishonest in the light of the practices adopted by election agents in general and, nevertheless, deliberately continued with the dishonest conduct. It would be grossly unfair to criminalise those who had simply behaved in the way expected of their kind and whose behaviour had been endorsed by history. All the same, it will be argued below that the democratic process, properly regarded, should have no place for this sort of arrangement.

In 1987 Keith Ewing referred[34] to the 1960 study by Butler and Rose[35] and the 1965 study by Butler and King.[36] Commenting upon the latter study Ewing writes:

> Although these tactics were known to other candidates and their agents, those involved would not often apply for relief and in practice their opponents were not inclined to press an election petition to invalidate the result. The reason was given by Butler and King.[37]

> When Wedgwood Benn's agent had to go to the courts to seek relief for admitted overspending, a leading figure in another party commented, 'Many of our chaps overspend, but they're not such fools as to announce it in public'. In one or two cases the defeated side believed that it had clear evidence of overspending – but there were no petitions; fear of retaliation kept all parties from opening that Pandora's Box.[38]

Pinto-Duchinsky makes a similar point:

> An experienced election agent can normally find ways of stretching permitted expenditures. Printers are persuaded to give low quotations for election literature with the promise of further business after the campaign. Paper is purchased before the start of the campaign on behalf of the local party association and then sold to the candidate as second-hand stock. Election agents' fees are frequently artificially low. These devices can, where required, provide an extra 20% of expenditure.[39]

It will be seen that little has changed in respect of election spending and it is now time to see how the general law, the political background and the professional knowledge of an experienced election agent came together in the Jones case.

---

34 Ewing, 1987, pp 78–79.

35 Butler and Rose, *The British General Election of 1959* (1960).

36 Butler and King, *The British General Election of 1964* (1965).

37 Butler and King, 1965, p 224.

38 Quotation from Ewing, 1987, citing Butler and King (1965); see Ewing, 1987, p 78.

39 Pinto-Duchinsky, 1981, p 249.

The facts in question in *R v Jones; R v Whicher*

In *R v Jones; R v Whicher*, the central criminal charge – of which they were both convicted at first instance and subsequently acquitted on appeal – was that they had made a false declaration as to Ms Jones' election expenses contrary to s 82(6) of the RPA1983. It must be noted that the challenge itself appears, legally, rather odd. It appears, by virtue s 120 of the RPA 1983, that the sole means of challenge to the result of a parliamentary election is by means of an election petition. The Act says:

> 120 (1) No parliamentary election and no return to Parliament shall be questioned except by a petition complaining of an undue election or undue return ('a parliamentary election petition') presented in accordance with this Part of this Act.

However it is clear that the rules governing elections petitions are complex[40] and petitioners must strictly comply with the rules. The case of *Ullah v Pagel and Scallan, Ahmed v Kennedy*,[41] which involved petitions against the winners of some local government elections, makes this point very clear. Furthermore, whilst an electrical petition is heard in an election court,[42] which is an administrative court and therefore established to deal with matters of public law, the trial itself and the procedure for bringing an election petition appears similar to that of a trial in private law. Section 121 of the 1983 Act provides that the petitioner – a person who voted or had a right to vote in the election, or a disappointed candidate or a person who claimed to be a candidate at the election – shall mount a challenge to the successful candidate, who is referred to as the respondent. As we have seen in the preceding chapter, it may be that the successful candidate has been the innocent beneficiary of a dispute between two of the other candidates or, as we shall see in Chapter 6, it may be that all of the candidates have been the victim of mistakes by the electoral officials.[43] Quite apart from the complex rules for service, which tripped up the petitioners in the local government case of *Ullah*, there is the matter of security for costs. Under s 136 of the RPA 1983, a petitioner must put up security for the costs of witnesses or the respondent; these may amount to £5,000 in the case of a parliamentary petition. Furthermore, the petitioner may remain liable for the expenses of their own witnesses under s 143 of the RPA 1983 and for the conduct of their own case. It is therefore clear that it is unlikely that an ordinary

---

40 See, for the provisions governing petitions challenging parliamentary elections, the Election Petitions Rules 1960 SI 1960/543.

41 [2002] EWCA Civ 1793; [2003] 2 All ER 440

42 The provisions for the establishment of an election court to try a parliamentary election petition are to be found in s 123 of the RPA 1983.

43 See the discussion of *Morgan v Simpson*, in Chapter 6.

elector who has been disadvantaged by the conduct of an election would bring a petition.

It is quite understandable, therefore, that the dissident members of the Labour Party did not seek to challenge Ms Jones' election using an election petition. Instead they went to the police alleging that she and her election agent had deliberately submitted a false account of her election expenses. How were they able to make a plausible allegation that the account was false? Clearly the allegation must have been sufficiently well founded to convince the police to investigate and the Crown Prosecution Service to bring a prosecution. The dissident members of the Labour Party had been active in politics for many years and, it seems plain, they were well aware of the techniques used to disguise the true extent of election expenditure. They were also aware of two further facts: first, the likelihood that the election expenses will be checked by anyone is small and, secondly, the likelihood of challenge by election petition is even smaller.

The law, to be found in s 81 of the RPA 1983, requires that candidates and their agents make a return of election expenditure to the appropriate officer. This officer will be, in the case of parliamentary elections, the returning officer and, in the case of local government elections, the elections officer of the relevant district council. The appropriate officer has neither the power nor the duty to examine the returns of election expenditure and, given the reasoning to be found in *Sanders v Chichester*, where the court emphasised the undesirability of electoral officials becoming embroiled in matters of political controversy, it is highly unlikely that an officer would look at any return.

In the case of local government elections, until the beginning of this century it was likely that the returns would rest undisturbed in a file until they were thrown away. It remains unlikely that losing candidates will ever bother to check the election expenditure of a winning candidate unless the margin between the candidates is very small and some gross irregularity is suspected. It is doubted whether the returns of losing candidates are ever checked. The author is aware of one incident following the 1985 county council elections where, following the poll in early May, in which the candidate in question gained a derisory number of votes and was placed a poor third, no return was made until mid-August and that return was, to say the least, fanciful. The Electoral Commission has possessed a power since 2000 to call in returns of expenditure for inspection under s 87A of the RPA 1983, and so it may be that agents are now uniformly more scrupulous in submitting their returns.

The provisions for parliamentary elections are slightly more rigorous. The returning officer is obliged by s 88 of the RPA 1983 to write to the candidates' election agents informing them of the times at which the returns of expenditure are available for inspection and to place advertisements in the local newspapers advising the public of that fact. The returning officer is also obliged to alert the election agents and the public if no return of expenditure is made. If no return is made by the winning candidate they prevented from taking their seat in the House of Commons by virtue of s 85 of the RPA 1983. In the case of parliamentary elections, the returning officer has been obliged to forward all returns to the Electoral Commission under s 87A of the 1983 Act. This provision was introduced by the Political Parties, Elections and Referendums Act 2000 and so it was not in place in 1997. Accordingly, it is clear that Ms Jones' return of election expenditure was unlikely to be checked.

Secondly, it has been averred that it is likely that the election agents of all parties are engaged in practices that a zealot may find questionable. Since the primary legal provision is that the election is to be challenged by means of an election petition it is clear that, given the expense involved in bringing a petition, any wrongdoing would have to be egregious in order for it to be worth the petitioner's while. Funds are likely to be short and since litigation is always a risk, one would look for a pretty safe bet before proceeding. It is also the case that bringing a petition is likely to initiate tit-for-tat petitions in neighbouring constituencies or subsequent elections. It is submitted that it is unlikely that petitions are brought even in the case of serious wrongdoing. In support of this proposition it must be noted that the Liberal Democrat and Conservative parties did not bring a petition challenging Ms Jones' election, despite the fact that it was subsequently shown that the Crown Prosecution Service thought that there was sufficient chance of a conviction to allow the case against Jones and Whicher to proceed to trial.

The facts recorded by the Court of Appeal demonstrate how the defendants came to make out and file an allegedly false declaration. First, Whicher's legal duty as election agent for Jones was, under s 81(1) of the RPA 1983, to deliver to the returning officer a true account of the election expenses supported by receipted bills. Whicher duly made such a return, producing an account totalling £8,514.94, which was well within the cap upon election expenses provided by s 76 of the 1983 Act. Both Jones and Whicher provided a formal declaration, witnessed by a Justice of the Peace, under s 82 of the RPA 1983, that the return of expenses was, to the best of their knowledge and belief, a complete and correct return as required by law. The dissident members of the local party inspected that return and made a complaint to the local police that the return was incorrect and that both Jones and Whicher knew that it was incorrect. The relevant law is to be found in s 82 of the RPA 1983, where it is provided that the offence will be made out if the defendant(s) knowingly and deliberately make a false declaration. The dissident members of the party had directed the police towards evidence that the real figure for Ms Jones' election expenses was just under £22,000. Given that this figure is over two and a half times the declared figure, it is plain that it would be very difficult for the defendants to maintain that they had an honest belief in the veracity of the return. However, by the time the case came to trial, and during the trial itself, some of that excess expenditure had been explained or the allegations withdrawn by the prosecution.

The allegations pursued at the trial centred upon two items of expenditure; first, the rent of an office in Newark and, secondly, the use of a computerised database. The allegations will be examined in that order. The Labour party did not itself own premises in Newark; its facilities were owned by the Retford branch, and the candidate paid from her expenses a small sum of money for the use of those facilities. Additionally an office was rented in Newark and, it was said, the cost of the office was shared between the election expenses of Ms Jones and five county council candidates fighting an election on the same day. The period of office rental was quite long, stretching from February until just after the election on 1 May 1997. It would be of value to know whether the Newark constituency Labour party normally rented an office in Newark for the purpose of fighting the four-yearly county council elections and whether their campaign usually started in February. For the reasons set out in the introductory sections of this chapter, it would also be valuable to have the party's estimate of the likelihood of winning those county council seats.

In any event, it would seem to be settled upon the authorities that there is no clear date for the beginning of the election campaign and thus no clear date from which all the expenditure incurred in connection with the conduct or management of the election will count as election expenditure and thus will both be required to be returned and will be the subject of the statutory limit. The editors of *Schofield* take the view that:[44] 'No statutory time for the commencement of election expenses has been fixed. It is a question of fact in each case.' They support this view by a wealth of authorities spanning the years 1892 to 1965, in which a variety of courts have needed to determine the date of commencement of an election campaign. Clearly, this would make it very difficult to secure a conviction on an allegation that expenditure took place during an election campaign where the candidate was adamant that the expenditure preceded the campaign. Where the offence is only made out when the candidate had subjective knowledge of wrongful expenditure,

---

44 See s 7.08.

it is plain that a complete defence is afforded by the lack of such knowledge.

The Crown Court and the Court of Appeal

In the Crown Court at Nottingham, in front of Jowitt J and a jury, Jones and Whicher were tried for the submission of a false account. The prosecution's strategy was to bring up for examination each impugned item on the account and to seek to demonstrate that the amount entered was false and that Jones and Whicher knew that it was false. It would be unrealistic to expect that there would be evidence available to show that the defendants had deliberately lied, because the only paperwork which would be available would be that supporting their view of the events and the accounts. Many of the accounts were, indeed, internal to the Labour Party. Accordingly, the prosecution tried to show that the amounts charged were unrealistic or did not cover the entire period of Jones' candidacy.

In particular, the jury was asked to consider whether Jones was using one set of premises ('Paxton's Court') for the promotion of her candidacy for a longer period than she had claimed and disclosed upon her election expenses. The jury decided, on the basis of Jowitt J's direction,[45] that she had; presumably taking the view that once a general election was in the offing anything done by an identified candidate in public in connection with that candidacy was designed to secure their election. This would seem to be a common sense view. The jury was, in effect, asked to consider what Ms Jones was doing in the Paxton's Court office and came to the conclusion that she was acting as the Labour Party's candidate in the 1997 general election. They therefore concluded that the expenses of that office should, at least in part, be chargeable to her. Similarly with the question of the use of the database; the jury were invited to consider what use was to be made of the database. They concluded, on the basis of their common sense view of politics and elections, that such materials are used for the purpose of securing election. Whilst many, if not all, members of parliament hold regular surgeries and invite constituents to contact them by letter, the only time at which most members of the public come into contact with parliamentarians and their supporters is during the election period. It is therefore clear that if an ordinary member of the public was asked why the Newark constituency Labour Party maintained a computerised database of electors they would say – 'to get their candidate elected'.

---

45 Set out in the judgment in the Court of Appeal.

The Court of Appeal held that, since the beginning of the election period could not be determined with certainty, the decisions made by Jones and Whicher to include only those expenses incurred after a date ultimately of their own choosing, could not be classified as subjectively dishonest. In order to make out subjective dishonesty the prosecution would have needed to show that Jones and Whicher knew that they were wrongfully incurring expenditure during the election period. The Court of Appeal noted that evidence was given in the trial that the other candidates and election agents did behave or would have behaved in a like manner. Generally speaking, they all know that funds are short; they all know that they are required to do the best job that they can and, therefore, they do not think that they are behaving dishonestly when they operate the rules as an ordinary candidate or election agent does.

The legal test for dishonesty – which is the fundamental question at stake in *Jones* and *Whicher* – is best conceived in terms of the test formulated in the law of theft in the leading (though much criticised[46]) case of *Ghosh*.[47] Although the Court of Appeal did not frame the questions in this way it is clear that this reasoning underlies their judgment. The facts of *Ghosh* are irrelevant to the present discussion.

The *Ghosh* test requires the trier of fact (usually a jury) first to determine whether, in their own judgement, the accused acted honestly or dishonestly. Secondly,[48] if and only if they decide that the accused acted dishonestly, they must continue by asking whether the accused knew that ordinary people would view their (that is, the accused's) conduct as dishonest.

It would seem that the first question alone was asked in the Crown Court and the jury decided that the conduct was dishonest and therefore convicted Jones and Whicher. The Court of Appeal, in effect, asked the second question and decided that Jones and Whicher, both of whom were immersed in the electoral culture, believed that they were acting honestly. The Court of Appeal had no option but to overturn the convictions.

Analysis

It is agreed that the Court of Appeal's application of a purely subjective test to the question of the defendants' *mentes reae* is correct as a matter of criminal law. It would be monstrously unjust if defendants were convicted of crimes in circumstances where neither the courts nor the

---

46 See, eg, Griew, 1985; Williams, G, 1983, pp 726–30; Halpin, 1996.

47 [1982] QB 1053.

48 It being held in the later case of *Green* [1992] Criminal Law Review 292, that the two limbs of the test must be applied in this order.

expert practitioners could determine the boundaries of lawful behaviour. If a person would not have been convicted of theft (surely the paradigm example of dishonesty) if they had reasoned like Jones and Whicher, Jones and Whicher too must be acquitted.

The Electoral Commission has recommended[49] that election timetables – the periods between the calling of an election, the dates for nomination, the date of the poll, and so on – should be standardised between the various types of election and should be regularised in general. Clearly this is to be welcomed and the opportunity should be taken to insert into the legislation a clear date from which to compute the election expenses. However, it would be preferable if this date were sufficiently in advance of the date of the poll so as to prevent candidates incurring what are in effect election expenses just outside the election period. Alternatively, a list of costs, which should be recorded as election expenses, could be drawn up and included in legislation, such that a particular kind of expense is returnable as an election expense whenever it is incurred. The second of these alternatives is much to be preferred so as to avoid the problems of more richly endowed candidates and political parties distributing election materials immediately prior to the election period to the disadvantage of other parties.

More widely, it is submitted that the law in general takes the wrong approach to this question of election expenses in treating politicians as a class separate from ordinary citizens, having rules which differ from those applied to and by ordinary citizens. To apply this 'wrong approach' is, in the terms of this book, to apply the rules of the market or, in other words, to act neutrally between the political parties. This is market fairness, but it does not seem to be democratic fairness. The argument is set out in full below; suffice it to say at this stage that 'democratic fairness' is fairness in the sense that the political class (candidates, election agents etc) should be judged by the substantive standards set for all members of the community. Market fairness, on the other hand, allows political actors to be judged by the standards of fair conduct that they apply to themselves. An example might help to clarify the point. Say there are two racehorses in competition in a race. Both of the horses are obliged by the public rules to carry handicapping weights of 5kg. Their riders meet together before the race and agree that they will dispense with the weights. By so doing neither horse (nor rider) gains an advantage over the other. However the public is, in a sense, cheated, because they expected the horses to overcome the handicap. Whilst the degree of public interest in the probity of a horse race is limited, provided that the competition between the horses is fair; the public

---

49 See para 2.40 of *Voting for Change*.

interest in the probity of an election is, or should be, immense. This is because elections are the mechanism whereby the people choose the agents of their own self-governance; even if there is balanced or equal corruption, the mechanism of government is besmirched.

What is the problem?

The central charge then is that many sets of election expenses bear little resemblance to the sums of money which were, in fact, spent for the purpose of a candidate being elected. However, political parties keep, more or less, to the legal limits because they simply do not have the money to spend. Furthermore, most political parties are equally culpable. So, where is the harm? Ms Jones was acquitted of wrongdoing, Dr Hendron was granted relief. Why not simplify the law relating to election expenses, raise the limits on expenditure and thus remove the threat of criminality from a group of citizens who are, at the least, sufficiently public spirited to stand for election? Completing a return of election expenses is an onerous business and since there have been few real abuses since 1869, why not do away with the whole regulatory apparatus?

This sounds, at first hearing, suicidal for a democracy; surely it would lead to widespread corruption? It will be argued that it would be wrong to remove controls on election expenditure, but it is asserted the reasons for this go beyond the mere prevention of corruption, although this is itself a primary public good. It has been argued throughout this book that any corruption in elections is intolerable. However there may be an argument for removing controls on expenditure. First, it should be remembered that there are no limits on election expenditure in the USA, the control of corruption being imposed at the level of contributions to political campaigns under the doctrine set out in the *Buckley v Valeo* challenge to the Federal Election Campaign Act 1971. The Supreme Court took the view that the real danger to democracy was excessive contributions to political campaigns, rather than excessive expenditure. This point is already recognised in UK legislation.[50]

Secondly, it should be recalled that election expenditure is limited at least as much by the parties' lack of money as by the legislation. This fact has been averted to above and the point is well supported in the literature.[51] It may well be that the political parties' enthusiasm for remote electronic voting is, at least in part, driven by the fact that if one

---

50 See Pt IV of the PPERA 2000 – Control of donations to registered political parties and their members etc.

51 See Ewing, 1987, p 79. Ewing states the point baldly where he says: 'Finally, it seems clear that the spending limits are generally not now a serious constraint on the freedom of the candidates to reach the electorate.'

'votes by wire' it is highly likely that one will rely upon digital technology for a large proportion of one's political information, and the setting up of a party website is a relatively cheap way of disseminating political information.

However, it has been shown that, whilst the relationship between money spent and constituencies won is not simply positive, there is a high degree of correlation between expenditure and victory in a seat.[52] For that reason it is judged that there are good reasons for not abolishing the expenditure limits. Ewing writes,[53] following Rawls, that 'a just constitution sets up a form of fair rivalry for political office and authority' and argues that, whilst John Rawls did not develop this point, one of the ways this could be accomplished is by controlling 'expenditure from party funds'. It is clear from Ewing's work that he means money expended upon the financing of electoral campaigns. This sounds plausible, but it is, of course, the main point of attack of this book. It is submitted that a 'just constitution' does not 'set up a form of fair rivalry for political office and authority'; it provides a means whereby citizens can participate in their own governance. When we consider what these expenditure limits are, we can see the extent of the problem. Under the provisions of s 79 and Sched 9 of the PPERA 2000 the maximum permitted expenditure for general political campaigning by a political party contesting all of the constituencies in the Westminster parliament is some £20M. If we add to this the approximately £10,000 allotted under s 76 of the RPA 1983 for each individual candidate's election expenses we can see that the total sum available to be spent on elections by a single party contesting all the seats is of the order of £27M. As we have seen in the discussion of *R v Jones; R v Whicher*, this expenditure is supposed to be concentrated within the election period, but in fact it is supplemented by other expenditure, which may relate to the election, but which takes place outside the election period. If we take the guesstimate provided by Pinto-Duchinsky, which has not been controverted, and judge that this figure may be underestimated by, in the region of, 20% we are looking at an election expenditure of in the region of £32.5M per party.

This sum of money does not sound like a sum that might be spent persuading people of the validity of a set of political ideas that are in the best interests of the country as a whole; it sounds like a sum which might well be spent in advertising a brand. Indeed most election materials appear to be more like advertising materials rather than attempts at political argument or debate. When we recall that there is likely to be a

---

52 See the careful study by Johnston, 1987.
53 Ewing, 1987, p 182, citing Rawls, 1972, p 227.

cut in the duration of party political broadcasts,[54] which will reduce the scope for debate or explanation of party policy whilst leaving the ground clear for glossy advertising, there seems, from a democratic perspective, to be little to be said for allowing party campaign expenditure to continue at its present level. There would seem to be even less justification for implementing the reform advocated by the Houghton Committee,[55] Ewing[56] and Johnston,[57] which is to provide state funding for political parties, if all the parties will do with it is to advertise their supposed virtues rather than advancing political debate. This reform was rejected by the Neill Committee in its Fifth Report when it recommended that political parties should not receive public funding save for specific purposes. These recommendations were, in general, accepted by the government.[58] The two circumstances in which political parties should receive public money are in respect of their organisations in parliament[59] and for policy development grants for parties represented in parliament.[60] No doubt political parties would like public funding, but there would seem to be no reason to give it to them for it to be used as a form of subsidy to the advertising and publicity industry.

However, if political parties are to be obliged to use their own money to fund their publicity machines it is difficult, for the reasons set out above, to control their expenditure. How might this be done?

As to the level of general campaign expenditure, the statutory regime already exists within the provisions of the Political Parties, Elections and Referendums Act 2000, and the Electoral Commission has a well-developed reporting mechanism both for donations to political parties and campaign expenditure. At the level of individual constituencies and election campaigns, it is submitted that a more rigorous regime is needed.

---

54 See Chapter 1.

55 *Report of the Committee on financial aid to political parties* Cmnd 6601, 1976. The Houghton Committee recommended that (1) Annual grants be paid from government funds to the central organisations of political parties to support their work, and (2) some reimbursement of election expenses be made at local level.

56 See Ewing, 1987.

57 See Johnston, 1987.

58 See Chapter 6 of *The funding of political parties in the United Kingdom: The Government's proposals for legislation in response to the Fifth Report of the Committee on Standards in Public Life.* Cm 4413, 1999.

59 *Ibid*; see paras 6.6–6.10 for provisions relating to the Westminster parliament, para 6.9–6.11 for the Scottish parliament, paras 6.12–6.13 for the Welsh Assembly, and paras 6.14–6.15 for the Northern Ireland Assembly.

60 See paras 6.16–6.17; and s 12 of the PPERA 2000.

The role of the returning officer and the role of a citizens' jury

The importance of maintaining the neutrality of electoral officials between the parties fighting the election has been emphasised in a number of cases.[61] It should be beyond argument that electoral officials must not act or be seen to act in a partisan way. However, it is argued that within this concept of political neutrality, there are two conceptions which operate to different effects. It is submitted that one of these can, if it is to operate fairly, only be allowed to operate in the context of the other. These are, of course, the market and the democratic conceptions of fairness or political neutrality.

Where the returning officer or other electoral officials act to maintain fairness between the parties, they act like a referee in a boxing match. Low blows and other fouls must not be permitted, so as to ensure that one of the parties remains standing at the end of the bout having come through 'fair and square'. However, the point about elections is that they are not boxing matches; there is an overwhelming public interest in ensuring the best standards of public administration – the result has not only to be fair between the parties, it has to be fair to the world. It is submitted that where a returning officer detects some form of wrongdoing by one of the parties to the election, the returning officer ought to have a duty to bring this to the attention of the electorate. Clearly the mechanism exists – as we have seen in the case of Fiona Jones, where the allegations of corrupt practices were taken to the police.

It is accepted that the involvement of the police in those offences, which could be seen as 'political offences', is itself fraught with difficulties. If there are objections to electoral officials being seen to act in a way that could be viewed as politically partisan, these objections seem even more powerful when it comes to police action. It seems inherently undesirable for the police to be investigating the affairs of political parties although, where a criminal offence is involved, there seems to be little alternative. Where the party involved is in some way radical, for example, the Socialist Workers' Party or the British National Party, it would be easy for the party to claim that it was a martyr for its cause. Furthermore, one could well imagine some sections of the press objecting to police time being spent on looking at political parties when there are 'plenty of real crimes' for them to investigate. Where elections are seen as 'boxing matches' – competitions between parties rather than devices for selecting the best representatives of the public will – there may well be a tendency for electoral corruption to be seen as a

---

61 See, for example, the *Margaret Thatcher* case and *Sanders v Chichester*.

'victimless crime'. If a person stands for election, or enters a boxing ring, they must expect to be hit and, now and again, a blow might well be foul – *volenti non fit injuria*.[62]

It is therefore proposed that some alternative mechanism needs to be devised in order to provide for greater public scrutiny of election accounts. The first step to be taken is that ss 87A and 88 of the RPA 1983 ought to be extended to all elections. In the first place, it should be that the knowledge that returns of expenses will automatically be sent to the Electoral Commission will discipline election agents into producing election returns on time. In the second case, telling other agents and the public that the returns of expenses have been lodged and are available for inspection will increase scrutiny. These provisions would affect all candidates to an election.

The second step, which could be taken, and it is an obvious and simple step, is that a provision analogous to s 85 of the RPA 1983 could be introduced to prevent (any) successful candidates taking their seat on a council until the receipt of their election accounts has been confirmed. Clearly this provision would only affect winning candidates.

A more radical proposal, which might not be popular but which would have the effect of making all returns subject to public scrutiny, would be to hold a public scrutiny of all returns of expenses before a jury of electors selected at random from the electoral roll. All electors should be liable to sit on the jury whether or not they had voted in the election and the opportunities for recusal (that is, being excused from service) should be strictly limited. If election agents were obliged to justify their expenditure before a jury of citizens it would become obvious whether any malpractice had taken place because disparities of expenditure between candidates would become obvious and discounts on printing bills could be investigated. It is unlikely that printers would give special discounts to political parties if it became known that such cheap rates were available. The effect of political bias amongst the jurors could be minimised by submitting the election accounts of all the parties to the same panel of jurors, who could be obliged to reach their verdict on the acceptability of the accounts by a simple majority.

This could be combined with a proposal, made in a preliminary fashion by John Stuart Mill, to radically restrict the expenditure upon elections and subject them to some form of public accountability. Whilst this proposal would require some considerable modification to make it appropriate for today's circumstances, his words serve as useful starting point. Mill wrote as follows:

---

62 A volunteer cannot claim for harm occasioned by the mere fact that they have put themselves in harm's way. It is a classical tenet of the law of civil wrongs or torts.

Not only the candidate should not be required, he should not be permitted to incur any but a limited and trifling expense for his election. Mr Hare thinks it desirable that the sum of £50 should be required from every one who places his name upon the list of candidates, to prevent persons who have no chance of success, and no real intention of attempting it, from becoming candidates in wantonness or from mere love of notoriety, and perhaps carrying off a few votes which are needed for the return of more serious candidates. There is one expense which a candidate can not help incurring, and which it can hardly be expected that the public should defray for everyone who may choose to demand it – that of making his claims known to the electors by advertisements, placards and circulars. For all necessary expenses of this kind the £50 proposed by Mr Hare, if allowed to be drawn upon for these purposes (it might be made £100 if requisite) ought to be sufficient. If the friends of the candidate choose to go to the expense of committees and canvassing, there are no means of preventing them; but such expenses out of the candidate's own pocket, or any expenses whatever beyond the deposit of £50 (or £100) should be illegal and punishable.[63]

Clearly Mill's proposal would need to be expressed in terms of the modern law if it were to be brought into effect. First, it should be remembered that s 73 of the RPA 1983 provides that the only the candidate's election agent may lawfully make payments of the candidate's election expenses; thus there is a ready means of controlling the activities of the 'friends of the candidate' or even the opponents of the candidate.[64] However Mill's central proposal seems to be that the election expenses be defrayed out of the deposit put up by the candidate.[65] In order to achieve a worthwhile deposit out of which the maximum lawful expenditure could be met, we would need to look for a deposit of at least £10,000 in most constituencies for this is the expenditure limit in a general election under s 76 of the RPA 1983. We also need to note that the maximum expenditure for a parliamentary by-election is £100,000 under s 76(2)(c) of the RPA 1983.[66] Should we then call for a deposit of £10,000 or even £100,000? So to do would clearly disadvantage small parties or individuals for, even if they were able to

---

63 Mill, 1991, p 221.

64 *East Dorset* (1910) 6 O'M & H 41; *R v Hailwood & Ackroyd Ltd* [1928] 2 KB 277; and *DPP v Luft; DPP v Duffield* [1976] 2 All ER 569.

65 See Rule 9 of the Parliamentary Election Rules, Sched 1 of the RPA 1983. Currently the sum demanded is £500, and clearly this will not cover much of the election expenses which, as we have seen may amount to £5,483, together with an additional 6.2p for every entry in the register of electors to be used at the election under s 76(2) of the RPA 1983. Given a typical electorate of 65,000 the sum available is £5,483 + £4,030 = £9,513.

66 These limits are varied from time to time and are currently set by the Representation of the People (Variation of Limits of Candidates' Election Expenses) Order 2001.

say that they did not intend to spend up to the legal limit on expenses and were therefore legally permitted to provide a lower level of deposit, it may well be that they intended to raise their funds during the campaign. It is clear that a genuinely popular single-issue campaigner might wish to do this – a 'no bypass', 'save our hospital'[67] or 'no Cruise missiles'[68] – candidate should not be prevented from standing because they were unable to raise the deposit. It is suggested that in such cases an interest-free loan repayable at the time of settlement of the election accounts could be provided from the funds to be administered by the Electoral Commission. Candidates could then be obliged to deposit a sum up to that set as the maximum level of election expenditure with the returning officer and disburse their election expenditure from that fund under the supervision of electoral administrators and the citizen panel.

The argument contained in this chapter may now be summarised. Political parties and their agents are well versed and practised in avoiding the restrictions on election expenditure. Since it would appear that all the parties do it, to more or less the same extent, there is an argument which says that this is fair and the law should not be too ready to intervene. It is analogous to the jockeys who privately agree that they should all reduce their handicaps by the same amount. It is argued that this view should be rejected because the democratic process is a matter of public concern rather than the private concern of the political parties who engage in it. In the words of this book, it is a *democratic* process rather than a *market* process. To this end proposals are made to make election financing more transparent and subject to public control.

No + apple pie

---

67 Dr Richard Taylor, the independent MP for Wyre Forest, successfully fought the seat in 2001 on the basis of the campaign to save emergency health care facilities at Kidderminster Hospital. He obtained a majority of 17,630. Dr Taylor was returned to Parliament in 2005 with a reduced majority.

68 For example, Margaret Thatcher né Colin Hanoman, if he were a serious candidate and could provide answers to the challenges set out in Chapter 4 above. Ms Hipperson would certainly fall within the category of serious candidates who ought to be given the opportunity to stand.

Chapter 6:
Challenging the Result
of an Election

In this chapter we will focus upon the core use of election petitions; the raising of a petition to challenge some aspect of the conduct of an election that arises from some fault in the operation of the ballot. This excludes those cases discussed in earlier chapters, which focus upon abuses at the nomination stage (such as *Sanders v Chichester*[1] or the *Margaret Thatcher* case[2]), and the cases such as might arise on the facts disclosed in the Fiona Jones[3] case, that is, irregularities in election expenses. The discussion is structured in this way to isolate the faults that may arise in the process of voting; it will be argued that the case law relating to election petitions reveals that the judiciary is too deferential to elected authority and electoral officials. This operates, at best, in favour of the electoral bureaucracy and, at worst, to protect incumbents even where the fairness of their election may be seriously doubted. The statutory provisions and the style of judicial deference that is associated with those statutory provisions is, it will be claimed, firmly rooted in the 19th century and is wholly unsuited to a modern democracy. However, some may question why there is a need to consider the matter of election petitions at all in a book on electoral law, for election petitions are relatively rare events; indeed the majority of the election petitions of recent years are discussed in this book. If one compares the number of reported parliamentary election petitions in the vintage year of 1869, when there were more than 25, with the years between 1918 and 1951, when there were three, one might be tempted to conclude that this material is of purely historical interest. As against this, it is argued here that the law is framed at both a procedural and substantive level precisely so as to discourage the bringing of election petitions and, in fact, that more petitions ought to be brought; the law ought to be changed to facilitate the bringing of petitions. It is worthy of note that the phrases 'election petition' (that is, the procedural issue), 'illegal practice'

---

1 Queen's Bench Division (Election Court), 11 November 1994; *The Times*, 2 December 1994; *The Independent*, 16 November 1994; transcript.
2 [1983] CA, bound transcript 237.
3 [1999] EWCA Crim 1094. See Chapter 5 above.

and 'corrupt practice' (the substantive issues) simply do not feature in the Election Commission's *Voting for Change*. It is submitted that this is a serious omission.

The election petition is the primary route[4] for questioning the fairness of an election. It is argued that, in order for the law of elections to be in accordance with the general principles of the European Convention of Human Rights (ECHR), it should be interpreted in order to maintain and promote the ideals and values of a democratic society.[5] Further, the protection of rights guaranteed under the Convention, such as the right to a free and fair election of the legislature under Art 3 of the 1st Protocol to the Convention, must be 'practical and effective'.[6] Thus, as a matter of principle, the fairness of an election can only be tested where there is a procedure for testing its fairness before a court. This principle is supported by the case law of the European Court of Human Rights, but there is no direct authority in the decided case law for this principle. However, it will be argued here that the cases of *Matthews v UK*, *Golder v UK*,[7] and the points made concerning the availability of an effective remedy in *Chahal v UK*[8] and in *Conka v Belgium*,[9] support this proposition. These cases support the view that it is incumbent upon a state, where it provides a remedy for a wrongdoing, to afford applicants a realistic possibility of using the remedy.[10]

UK law has tended to develop in very much the opposite direction. It is sometimes said that judges should always hesitate to use their power to upset the result of an election. Authority for this proposition is to be found in cases spanning more than one and a quarter centuries. The classical statement of this doctrine is to be found in the *Warrington*[11] case, where Martin B said that the 'return of a member (of Parliament) is a serious matter and not lightly to be set aside'. Similar words are to be found in the judgment of Stephenson LJ in *Morgan v Simpson*.[12] This case is discussed at length below. Stephenson LJ said, in the context of a local government election petition, that 'an election is a serious – and expensive – matter and is not lightly to be set aside'. Furthermore,

---

4 See s 120 of the RPA 1983.
5 See *Kjeldson, Busk, Madsen and Pedersen v Denmark* (1976) Eur Ct HR series A vol 23 para 53; and the Preamble to the Convention.
6 See *Matthews v UK* application 24833/94 para 34; and *Conka v Belgium* case 51564/99.
7 Eur Ct HR Series A Volume 18 at para 28.
8 Case 70/1995/576/662.
9 Case 51564/99.
10 See, in particular, para 46 of *Conka*.
11 (1869) 1 O'M & H 42, p 44.
12 [1974] 3 All ER 722.

Lawton LJ, in the same case, referred to the 'unattractive possibility' of there being more election petitions.[13] Clearly it is right that the result of an election should not be challenged on the flimsiest of pretexts, for in a representative democracy some deference must be shown to the elected legislature or other authority that exercises power in the name of the people. If an elected person governs in the name of a sovereign people, that elected person dons, as it were, the mantle of their authority, or, alternatively, if the people have chosen, their will ought to be respected. That presupposes, however, that their choice has been exercised in way that is both fair and free. The problem addressed in this chapter is the question as to what amounts to a free and fair choice. A free and fair choice must be respected; a constrained and/or biased choice, which is no choice at all, must be overturned.

The legislative basis for an election petition is to be found in Pt III of the Representation of the People Act (RPA) 1983. The rules are complex and would certainly benefit from a thorough examination and redrafting in order both to modernise the rules and to clarify some issues. The law dates from 1868, for its wording is almost an exact copy of the relevant provisions of the Parliamentary Elections Act 1868.[14] This Act replaced the 1848 Act,[15] which was passed to amend the law for the trial of election petitions in the House of Commons in which forum, following the profound disagreement between the Lords and the Commons in *Ashby v White*,[16] parliamentary election petitions had been heard since 1704.

It is clear, from the local government election petitions case of *Ullah and Others v Pagel and Others; Ahmed v Kennedy*,[17] that the procedural requirements relating to the service of election petitions have to be strictly observed. The plain words of Art 3 of the 1st Protocol ECHR

---

13 This is Lawton LJ's final substantive comment in *Morgan v Simpson*, but it seems to have coloured his entire judgment. See [1974] 3 All ER 722 at 734g–h.

14 31&32 Vict. ch 125.

15 11&12 Vict. ch 98, *An act to amend the law for the trial of election petitions*.

16 See the comments of Josiah Brown, the reporter of the case in the House of Lords, which begin:

Scarce any judicial determination ever occasioned such a disturbance in both Houses of Parliament as the present. For, on the 25th of January 1704, the House of Commons resolved itself into a committee upon this business; and, after a very long and animated debate, the committee came to the five following resolutions, which were the next day reported, and agreed to by the House: …

(1703) 1 Brown 62 at 64, referring to Chandler's Debates vol 3, p 385. These resolutions made it plain that the House of Commons reserved the hearing of all parliamentary election petitions to itself and that for a court to hear them was a breach of parliamentary privilege. It is plain that such a procedure is open to grave abuse at the hand of parliamentary majorities.

17 [2002] EWCA Civ 1793; [2003] 2 All ER 440.

provide that the requirements for a free and fair election only extend to elections to a legislature, and thus local government election petitions fall outside the ambit of the Article; however it is surely beyond doubt that *Ullah* makes it certain that all election petitions will be subjected to the full range of stringent procedural safeguards. Do these procedural requirements amount to an effective barrier to those who wish to challenge the results of elections? This is a matter which may be tested before the domestic courts or, since Art 13 of the ECHR, which ensures the availability of an effective remedy, is not incorporated into English law by the Human Rights Act 1998, before the European Court of Human Rights. In any event, since the procedure for election petitions seems to be firmly rooted in the 19th century it is surely time for its examination and possible reform.

There are, furthermore, a number of wider points of policy, which will form the basis of the discussion in this chapter. There are two fundamentally separate types of fault that may give rise to a challenge. These may be simply labelled as, first, faults relating to the alleged wrongdoing of a candidate or candidates and, secondly, faults relating to the alleged wrongdoing of an election official. That is not to say that cases in which the two separate kinds of fault are inextricably mixed do not exist; indeed it will be seen almost from the outset that they are often inextricably mixed. First, when we consider faults relating to the wrongdoing of a candidate, we should note that it is sometimes more convenient for petitioners or other litigants to frame these in terms of an allegation of fault on the part of the election officials. Some challenges of this sort were considered in detail in Chapter 4 above. Richard Huggett, in one case, and Margaret Thatcher (né Colin Hanoman), in another, sought to spoil the electoral chances of other candidates. The problem with these cases for our present consideration is that, for a variety of reasons, they were not brought by means of ordinary election petition. *Sanders v Chichester* was brought by means of special case stated under s 146 of the RPA 1983, and *Thatcher* by means of judicial review, whereas here we need to consider a few mainstream election petitions in order to tease out some of the salient features.

The fault of the candidate

The first case for examination is that of *R v Rowe, ex p Mainwaring and others*.[18] Again, it must be noted that this election petition is slightly unusual in form. *Rowe* is a local government election case arising out of election petitions alleging that the respondents used undue means to

---

18 [1992] 4 All ER 821.

influence voters in an election in Tower Hamlets in May 1990. The petitioner alleged that the respondents had committed an election offence under s 115 of the RPA 1983.

Whilst such a petition is presented to the High Court under s 128 of the Act, it is tried by a Commissioner sitting under the provisions of s 130 of the RPA 1983. A parliamentary election petition is heard by two High Court judges on the rota for hearing such petitions, under s 123 of the RPA 1983. An appeal from the High Court may go to the Court of Appeal for final determination under s 157 of the RPA 1983, but the route of an appeal from a Commissioner is not at all clear from the Act. Clearly, a Commissioner is a creature of statute and their determination is not explicitly labelled as that of a superior court; in the absence, therefore, of some other means of review it would seem that, in principle, judicial review ought to be available.

In *R v Rowe, ex p Mainwaring and others*, Mr Commissioner Rowe QC heard the original petitions and dismissed them; his decision was then brought, on judicial review, before the Divisional Court where his decision was quashed. The matter then went on appeal to the Court of Appeal. This tortuous path in itself surely provides an example of the reason for enacting some procedural reforms for the hearing of election petitions. However, since the substantive matter did arrive in the proper court (the Court of Appeal) for final determination, it is clear that the case can properly be viewed as an ordinary election petition.

The facts are simple. The Liberal Democrat party produced leaflets in good form according to s 110 of the RPA 1983, in that they bore the name and address of the party agent publishing the leaflet. However, the leaflets were published under the title 'Labour News' and presented a collation of Labour party statements and policies collected by the Liberal Democrats over a period of time as if they constituted the Labour party election manifesto. The question was whether the publication of the leaflets amounted to the exertion of undue influence upon the minds of the electorate by means of the publication of a fraudulent device or contrivance. This is a particularly important case for it appears that there are no other reported cases on the substance as to what in law would constitute 'a fraudulent device or contrivance'.

The law provides, in the form of s 115 of the RPA 1983, that a person is guilty of the corrupt practice of undue influence if:

> 115 (2)(b) ... by abduction, duress or any fraudulent device or contrivance, he impedes or prevents the free exercise of the franchise of an elector or proxy for an elector, or so compels, induces or prevails upon an elector or proxy for an elector either to vote or to refrain from voting.

The Court of Appeal held that for the offence to have been made out the Commissioner would need to have held, as a matter of fact, that a voter was (or voters were) actually impeded in the free exercise of their vote. In other words, the attempted deception practised by the Liberal Democrats would have had to succeed in order for the respondents to be guilty. This decision was in line with the criminal law of the time; in particular it was said by Lord Morris, in *DPP v Ray*, that: 'For a deception to take place there must be some person or persons who will have been deceived.'[19] Since the Commissioner held otherwise, the Court of Appeal had no option but to decide that no undue influence had taken place. Farquharson LJ observed that if the sub-section (quoted above) had read 'any fraudulent device calculated to impede or prevent', the situation would have been different.[20]

It is submitted that the final observation of Nolan LJ (as he then was) is correct and that some attention to the substance of the statute, as well as the procedure, is overdue, and this is supported by the statements made by two of the judges in the case. Nolan LJ said:

> In conclusion, I would express the hope that in due course the legislature will reconsider the language of s 115. Some such provision is an essential part of the law's armoury in a democratic society, but the present terms of the section were framed in the last century, and may be thought to require revision by reference to the less blatant and less easily detected but no less effective methods of exerting influence which are available nowadays. I have it in mind in particular that the fraudulent pamphlet in the present case was plainly designed to mislead electors into voting against, or withdrawing their support from, the opposing party's candidates, and no one can exclude the possibility that it achieved some success, though this cannot be proved. It may be thought that the conduct of those responsible for the distribution of the pamphlet should in itself be sufficient to attract a penalty.[21]

Parker LJ's comments were, if anything, even more pointed. He said:

> Finally I should make it clear that in reaching this conclusion I give no sort of indication that I regard what was done by those who planned and took part in the scheme as other than reprehensible. It was, entirely correctly, thoroughly disapproved of by senior and more responsible members of the party but to no avail. Fortunately for its perpetrators the scheme has not been shown to have achieved its objective. But this does not change the fact that those responsible intended and attempted by a fraudulent device to impede or even prevent the free exercise of the franchise by a number of electors.[22]

---

19 [1973] 3 All ER 131, p 137.

20 See [1992] 4 All ER 821, p 827e–f.

21 At 830j to 831b.

22 At p 832 g.

These points are important because, contrary to one of the theses of this book, and this chapter in particular, they demonstrate that the judges do sometimes show a robust attitude in cases of electoral malpractice. It seems that in this case they were held back by the statute law. Since the judges were so critical of the respondents, it seems advisable to consider whether there are any purely common law provisions that might have permitted the election to be overturned on the grounds that the Liberal Democrat candidates in question conspired together, or attempted, to exert undue influence. The editors of *Schofield* state that '(a)s in the case of other corrupt practices "undue influence" was always an offence at common law',[23] but they do not give authority for this proposition. If it were the case that there was some robust basis for liability at common law it may be that an action, akin to that in *DPP v Shaw*,[24] could be mounted. In *Shaw* it proved impossible to secure a conviction under the obscenity legislation when Shaw published a directory of prostitutes, because the material in question fell short of the statutory definition of obscenity, but to adopt the oft-quoted *dictum* of Byles J[25] the justice of the common law was employed to 'supply the omission of statute' and Shaw was convicted of a novel common law offence of corrupting public morals. The statement in Schofield quoted earlier in this paragraph appears to stem from the speech of Lord Haldane LC, in *Nocton v Lord Ashburton*, that the courts of equity and common law exercised concurrent jurisdiction over matters of wilful deception from the earliest times.[26] It must be observed that most of the cases cited by the editors of *Schofield* date from after the passage of the Corrupt and Illegal Practices Prevention Act 1854 and so are of limited utility in determining the extent of purely common law liability in election cases. However, standard works on contract and equity, for example, confirm that in cases of property transactions there is no difficulty in setting aside bargains made where there is an unconscientious use of the power arising out of the relative position of the parties.[27] It is furthermore clear, from *Pasley v Freeman*,[28] that there is no requirement for the subject matter over which undue influence was exerted to be real property or to be the subject of a contract between the parties in question. It may also be arguable, on the basis of Holt CJ's judgment in *Ashby v White* that a vote

---

23 See s 14.04.

24 [1962] AC 220.

25 *Cooper v Wandsworth Board of Works* (1863) 14 CB (NS) 180, p 194. A similar principle can be found in the judgment of Holt CJ in *Ashby v White* (1703) 2 Ld Raym 938; see Plucknett, 1956, pp 246 and 339.

26 [1914] AC 932; see pp 946–57.

27 See Trietel, 1987, p 319, quoting *Aylesford v Morris* (1873) LR 8 Ch App 484 at p 491.

28 (1789) 3 TR 51.

is in any event property, but this may well be doubted in the light of the discussion in Chapter 2 above. The equitable jurisdiction seems to focus upon two sorts of cases. First, there are those where the persons who have allegedly been unduly influenced show identifiable weaknesses for, as Trietel says, 'equity may give such relief when unfair advantage is taken of a person who is poor, ignorant or weak-minded or is for some other reason in need of special protection'.[29] He cites, *inter alia*, *Evans v Llewellin*[30] in support of this proposition. However, this line of reasoning does not appear very helpful, for many would find it politically unacceptable to label a registered voter as being a member of one of these categories. Secondly, there are those cases in which there is a special relationship between the person who is allegedly influenced and the influencer.[31] Where there is a special relationship between the parties – such as that of spiritual adviser and disciple – the bargain may be set aside. The doctrines set out in the contract cases may be applied to those election cases in which undue religious or spiritual influence is brought to bear. In the 19th century there were cases, such as *Sligo Borough*,[32] where priests were heard to threaten to deny the sacraments to those who voted in a manner unacceptable to the Church. Yet, whilst there may have been some occurrence of this during the June 2004 European and local government elections, in that it was alleged that: 'Sajawal Hussein, a Labour councillor, claimed a voter was deceived into handing over her blank ballots: "One lady told me that somebody came saying that they were from the mosque nearby and people had sent them to collect those letters for the mosque. So she gave them the three envelopes which were not even opened."'[33] However, it is unlikely that there are many special relationships between voters and political parties. Accordingly it is thought unlikely that any action would lie at common law.

It is, furthermore, highly undesirable that a matter of election law should be left completely to the judges to decide. Therefore it is submitted that it is imperative that the statutory provision be changed so as to oblige the courts to overturn an election where there is clear evidence that the winning party has attempted unduly to influence voters. It is clear that a successful action against a losing party should not disturb the result of an election, because that would allow parties who were sure that they would lose the election to hold up the seating of the

---

29 Treitel, 1987, p 319.

30 (1787) 1 Cox CC 333.

31 See, eg, *Allcard v Skinner* (1887) 36 ChD 145.

32 See, eg, *Sligo Borough* (1853) 2 Pow R&D 256.

33 See *The Times*, 9 June 2004, p 6.

winning candidate. The imposition of some other penalty upon the losing party would be appropriate.

The substitution of words, such as those suggested by Farquharson, Nolan or Parker LLJ, into the statute would be appropriate, it is suggested, for three reasons. Their Lordships suggested that the offence would have been made out had the statute read:

> 115 (2)(b) ... by abduction, duress or any fraudulent device or contrivance, he impedes or prevents, *or by means of any fraudulent device attempts to impede or prevent* the free exercise of the franchise of an elector or proxy for an elector, or so compels, induces or prevails upon an elector or proxy for an elector either to vote or to refrain from voting. (emphasis added)

First, the present legal test is itself unduly sensitive and susceptible to fraud in the following way and for the following reasons. On the facts of *ex p Mainwaring*, there would have been nothing to prevent a fervent supporter of the Labour Party voting Liberal Democrat and then simply claiming that they had done so on the basis of the Liberal Democrat leaflet. Provided that they could maintain a consistent story in the witness box, the petition could have succeeded because then it would have been possible to give evidence that a vote had been unduly influenced. Cynics may think it surprising that the Labour Party did not ensure that some of its members behaved in that way. Whilst they are to be applauded for refraining from such behaviour, there would have been nothing for the party to lose and everything for it to gain: if Labour won the election despite being short of the sacrificial votes, it would gain the seat and, if Labour lost, it would succeed in the petition, a clear win/win situation. Thus the statute, as it is currently drafted, would seem to encourage, rather than discourage, dishonest behaviour and risks turning elections into a tactical race to the bottom. Elections ought not to turn simply upon the honesty and integrity of the contestant parties for, sooner or later, as the Liberal Democrat candidates themselves demonstrated, a less virtuous candidate will appear.

Secondly, there is a public interest in the fair conduct of elections. It is submitted that this means that the conduct of the parties to an election should itself be capable of withstanding the direct scrutiny of a court. By looking at the conduct, which may or may not be induced, amongst voters the courts are looking at an indirect measure of the problem. Why should those who use all their best efforts to wrongfully affect the result of an election fare better – by inadvertently choosing strong-minded victims – than those who choose weaker victims? Rather, it is the conduct that should be judged, not the result of the conduct.

Finally the provisions relating to undue influence stem directly from s V of the Corrupt and Illegal Practices Prevention Act 1854. This provides (and the 1983 Act continues to provide) that whilst force and the like or the threat of force etc shall of themselves constitute undue influence, it is only where the use of a fraudulent device or contrivance succeeds in its effect that it shall constitute undue influence. This undoubtedly reflects the concerns of the time. For example, in 1869 there were a large number of allegations of undue influence brought up in election petitions; amongst the most worrying cases being the *Blackburn* case[34] and the *Stafford* case.[35] Clearly the use of force or the threat of force, or the imposition or threat of imposition of a substantial penalty, in elections remains a most serious matter, but it is believed that such activity is now rare. However, in the June 2004 local and European elections there was a press report that '(i)n one case an employer allegedly told his staff that he would sack them all if they refused to support Labour',[36] so the law remains relevant today. It is suggested, however, that as campaigning for elections moves off the streets into a digital environment, the opportunities for the issue of fraudulent instruments that may deceive electors have increased enormously. For example, the practice of 'phishing'[37] – attempting to obtain customers' bank details and online passwords by means of false websites purporting to be operated by banks' security departments – has increased at an almost exponential rate during the period January 2000 to June 2004. It is submitted that the law ought to be developed in accordance with the times, and so it ought to include an attempt to interfere with the free exercise of the franchise within the definition of undue influence.

Undue influence has been presented here as a recent example of the way in which candidates can misbehave so as to bring the result of the election into doubt. It is clear that there is a wider range of corrupt and illegal practices in which candidates and their agents could indulge. It is clear, however, that these practices do not now occur with the same frequency as in, for example, 1869. Volume 21 of the *Law Times* records the following substantive election petitions in which various allegations of bribery,[38] treating[39] or undue influence were made: a group of

34 (1869) 20 LT 823.

35 (1869) 21 LT 210.

36 See *The Times*, 9 June 2004, p 1.

37 See www.webopedia.com/TERM/p/phishing.html.

 Pronounced 'fishing – the act of sending an email to a user, falsely claiming to be an established legitimate enterprise, in an attempt to scam the user into surrendering private information that will be used for identity theft. The email directs the user to visit a website where they are asked to update personal information, such as passwords and credit card, social security, and bank account numbers that the legitimate organisation already has. The website, however, is bogus and set up only to steal the user's information.

38 Now s 113 of the RPA 1983.

39 Now s 114 of the RPA 1983.

petitions centred on the *Northallerton* petition,[40] *Hereford*,[41] *Wigan*,[42] *Stafford*,[43] *Hastings*,[44] *Norfolk (Northern)*,[45] *Youghal*,[46] *Carrickfergus*,[47] *Drogheda*,[48] *Belfast*,[49] *Limerick*,[50] *Londonderry*.[51] There were also a number of other petitions. It is again suggested that the particular form of the election offences reflects the culture of the times and the precise form of the offence may well have changed over the ensuing 130–150 years. The facts of *ex p Mainwaring* do not appear to have occurred to the drafters of the 1854 Act any more than it is likely that the 1854 legislature considered that parents in 2004 might be 'voting for their daughters who are away at university'.[52] It is argued therefore that, despite the best efforts of the judiciary to enforce the spirit of the law, substantive amendment of the statute is necessary. This matter is discussed further in Chapter 8 in the light of the Electoral Commission's paper *Securing the Vote*[53] and the forthcoming Electoral Administration Bill.

The fault of the electoral officials

In turning to consider cases where candidates seek to overturn an election because of some mistake on the part of the electoral officials, it will be argued here that the courts are too ready to uphold the election result. The leading modern case is *Morgan and Others v Simpson and Others*,[54] and it arose from a local government election petition resulting from an election for a member of the Greater London Council held in Croydon North East in April 1973. There were three candidates and the result of the election, at least between the two leading candidates, was so close that there were several recounts. Out of the 23,691 ballot papers counted, the winning candidate, one Simpson, received 10,340 whilst the runner-up (Morgan) received 10,329, giving Simpson a majority of 11 votes. However, the returning officer had rejected 82 ballot papers; 38 because of some fault of the elector and 44 because the ballot paper was

---

40 (1869) 21 LT 113.
41 At p 117.
42 At p 122.
43 At p 210.
44 At p 234.
45 At p 264.
46 At pp 306 and 316.
47 At p 352.
48 At p 402.
49 At p 475.
50 At p 567.
51 At p 709.
52 *The Times*, 9 June 2004, p 1, quoting the words of Lord Greaves.
53 London, Electoral Commission, 2005.
54 Reports of the case are available at [1975] QB 151 [1974] 3 All ER 722.

not stamped with the official validating mark. At each of 18 of the polling stations operating in the election, a small number of ballot papers were not stamped, three of the polling stations accounting for 15 of the invalid papers. If the 44 void ballot papers had been counted, the result of the election would have been reversed. Miss Morgan would have received 10,360 votes and Mr Simpson 10,353, giving her a majority of seven. The matter was brought to the Divisional Court by way of agreed case stated, under the provisions of the Representation of the People Act 1949 now contained in s 146 of the RPA 1983.[55] The petitioners claimed that the election should be declared void because it had not been conducted substantially in accordance with the law. The decision of the Divisional Court to reject the petition[56] was then considered on appeal by the Court of Appeal which, it will be recalled, is the final court of appeal for election cases.

Whilst the provisions in question in *Morgan v Simpson* date back to s 13 of the Ballot Act 1872, the relevant law is now to be found in s 48 of the RPA 1983:

48 (1) No local government election shall be declared invalid by reason of any act or omission of the returning officer or any other person in breach of his official duty in connection with the election or otherwise of rules under section 36 or section 42 above if it appears to the tribunal having cognisance of the question that –

(a) the election was so conducted as to be substantially in accordance with the law as to elections; and

(b) the act or omission did not affect its result.[57]

Section 37 of the RPA 1949 used identical words, so there is no doubt that if *Morgan v Simpson* is correct it remains good law. However it will be argued that *Morgan v Simpson* is fundamentally flawed and should be overruled. At present, courts below the Court of Appeal are obliged to follow it.

It is argued that the proper reading of the section should be as follows:

If an election is not conducted in accordance with the law it is to be voided unless the error was so small as to mean that the election was conducted substantially in accordance with the law and the error committed did not affect the result.

The leading judgment of Lord Denning MR in *Morgan v Simpson* will be examined in detail; it will be argued that it sets in place, or buttresses, a

---

55 Then, s 126 of the RPA 1949.

56 [1974] 1 All ER 241.

57 See s 23 of the RPA 1983 for the analogous provisions for parliamentary elections.

legal regime that does not aid the control of abuse. In his recitation of the facts giving rise to the case, Lord Denning MR said that, in the polling station:

> There were directions for voters. They were exhibited on a printed notice at each of the polling stations. But rarely does anyone read them. I do not suppose that any of these 44 voters read them. These are three of the directions:
>
> '1   The voter should see that the ballot paper, before it is handed to him, *is stamped with the official mark.*
>
> 2   The voter will go into one of the compartments and, with the pencil provided in the compartment, place a cross on the right-hand side of the ballot paper, opposite the name of the candidate for whom he votes, thus X.
>
> 3   The voter will then *fold up the ballot paper* so as to show the official mark on the back, and leaving the compartment will, without showing the front of the paper to any person, *show the official mark on the back to the presiding officer,* and then, in the presence of the presiding officer, put the paper into the ballot box, and forthwith leave the polling station.'[58]

(Note that the directions to the voter are now to be found in almost identical terms in Rule 31(2) and Rule 31(3) of the Local Elections (Principal Areas) Rules 1986.)[59] This point is of the utmost importance, because, as can be seen by their plain words, these Rules apply to the actions of the voter. The presiding officer has, according to these parts of the Rule, almost a passive role. To return to the judgment:

> Now those directions are more observed in the breach than in the letter. Rarely does a voter look to see that the ballot paper is stamped with the official mark. At least I never do. Rarely does a voter go back to the presiding officer and show him the official mark on the back. At least I never do. Often enough the polling station is not suited for it. It is so furnished that the natural thing is for the voter to go straight from the compartment to the ballot box and put his paper in it – without showing it to the presiding officer. So I should think that the 44 mistakes were due largely to the fault of the officers in the polling stations and very little to the fault of the voters. If their votes are not to count, they are disfranchised without any real blame attaching to them.[60]

This lengthy quotation is necessary because it must be analysed. Some may dismiss it as an unfortunate, but harmless, excursion into folksiness,[61] others may view it as a robust and healthy dislike of

---

58 *Ibid.* Italics added.

59 SI 1986/221.

60 See [1974] 3All ER 722 at 724j–725d.

61 But, see Harvey, 1986, p 67, for an alternative view of Lord Denning's 'distinctive judicial writing style'.

overweening and unnecessary bureaucracy, whilst yet others may say that it demonstrates some contempt for the procedural safeguards deemed essential by parliament.[62] In any event, it is a judgment in the Court of Appeal, which is the court of final appeal in election cases; it lays down precedent.

First, to consider the principle that ballot papers must be validated before they are issued.[63] It may be thought that it is impossible to forge modern ballot papers or to steal them from the printers or electoral officials prior to the ballot,[64] and accordingly that the requirement for ballot papers to be validated before issue is unnecessary. However this remains an essential feature of election law and is to be found in Rule 31(1) of the Local Elections (Principal Areas) Rules 1986 and its predecessors back to the Ballot Act 1872. This Rule lays a clear duty upon the presiding officer. The Rule must be quoted in full:

31 (1) A ballot paper shall be delivered to a voter who applies for one, and immediately before delivery –

   (a) the ballot paper shall be stamped with the official mark;

   (b) the number and name of the elector as stated in the copy of the register of electors shall be called out;

   (c) the number of the elector shall be marked on the counterfoil;

   (d) a mark shall be placed in the register of electors against the number of the elector to denote that a ballot paper has been received but without showing the particular ballot paper which has been received; and

   (e) in the case of a person applying for a ballot paper as proxy, a mark shall be placed against his name in the list of proxies.

This Rule, or rather its predecessor, to be found in the 1st Schedule to the Ballot Act 1872, was considered in detail by the Court of Common Pleas in *Pickering v James*.[65] The brief note in *Schofield* section 9.16 says:

It is the clear duty of the presiding officer to see the official mark after the voter has marked the paper. It has been held that he should see the whole paper [giving *Pickering v James* as authority for this proposition].

Pickering v James is a most important case. It was cited to the Court of Appeal in *Morgan v Simpson*, but was not referred to in the judgments. It is argued that this was a critical error on the part of the judges because a

---

62 See Williams, DGT, 1986, especially at p 123.

63 See now, eg, Rule 20 of the Parliamentary Election Rules, Sched of the 1 RPA 1983.

64 However the same might well have been said regarding 'A' level examination papers; see http://news.bbc.co.uk/1/hi/education/3846711.stm.

65 (1872–73) LR 8 CP 489.

proper examination of *Pickering v James* would undoubtedly have had a major impact upon the decision in *Morgan v Simpson*.

Pickering v James stemmed from an election petition concerning a municipal election in Birmingham shortly after the passage of the Ballot Act 1872. It was alleged and proved in front of a Commissioner that the result of the election was affected by the inclusion of some ballot papers that had not been validated. This led the Commissioner to strike out some votes and make a declaration as to the law relating to the duties of the presiding officer in a polling station. The Commissioner's individual declarations were appealed to the Court of Common Pleas. Bovill CJ helpfully points out the three issues relating to the presiding officer's duty. Since this point is important and much depends upon it, his words are set out in full.

> In this case there are three allegations of duty upon which the plaintiff seeks to maintain this action. The first allegation is that it was the duty of the defendant, as presiding officer, to mark the ballot paper with the official mark, or rather, to deliver to the voter a ballot paper bearing such mark. The allegation which I will deal with secondly, though it does not come in that order in the counts, is that it was the duty of the defendant to be present at the polling station, so that each voter, before placing the ballot paper in the box, could shew [sic] to the presiding officer the official mark on the back of the ballot paper. Thirdly, it is alleged that it is the duty of the presiding officer to ascertain, before the voting paper is placed in the box, that it is properly marked with the official mark.[66]

Bovill CJ then goes on to say:

> There are no clauses in the Act, the rules, or the directions, that expressly impose any of these duties on the presiding officer. I am, however, of opinion, looking to the provisions of the Act, that there is clearly a duty cast on some person to deliver to the voters ballot papers with the official mark properly stamped upon them.[67]

This point is agreed by Keating J at p 505,[68] by Brett J at p 508,[69] and by Grove J at p 510 of the report.[70] Thus the four judges are unanimous that there is a legal duty cast upon the polling officials to ensure that there is compliance with the scheme set down in the 1872 Act. This duty, it is clear, continues into the schemes in the 1949 and the 1983 Act. The

---

66 At p 498.

67 At p 499.

68 Where he says, 'These duties, then, appear to me to be clearly imposed on some one, and in my opinion *prima facie* they are imposed on the presiding officer'.

69 Where he says, 'It seems to me, that *prima facie*, it is cast on the presiding officer; and that *prima facie* he undertakes it, when he accepts the office, by such acceptance'.

70 Where he says, 'The Act appears to me to cast these duties on the presiding officer for the time being.'

judges, in *Pickering v James*, do, however, differ on one point. Bovill CJ and Grove J think that the presiding officer may delegate some of their duties to one or more of the clerks who assist them at the polling station, whilst Keating and Brett JJ are of the opinion that the duties are cast upon the presiding officer in person. This difference between the judges appears to be of little importance for it is beyond doubt that the duty must be properly undertaken. It is submitted that the words of Bovill CJ accurately define the law when he says:

> The conclusion at which I have arrived, after the able argument on the subject, is, that the duty of delivering the paper with the official mark on it must rest with the person who undertakes that part of the duties connected with the election at the polling station; and I mean by that, not the person who generally undertakes that duty, but the person who in each particular case undertakes it, and consequently that the responsibility would rest on the presiding officer or the clerk, according as the one or the other did in point of fact deliver out the paper. [71]

It is therefore argued that the focus of Lord Denning MR, and indeed the entire Court of Appeal, in *Morgan v Simpson*, is upon quite the wrong point. Lord Denning MR characterises the failure to stamp the ballot papers as, in itself, a trivial point. He is quite clear that, were it not for the fact that the 44 unvalidated ballot papers affected the result of the election, he would have allowed the result to stand. He summarised the law in the following way:

> I suggest that the law can be stated in these propositions: (1) If the election was conducted so badly that it was not substantially in accordance with the law as to elections, the election is vitiated, irrespective of whether the result was affected, or not. That is shown by the *Hackney* case,[72] where two out of 19 polling stations were closed all day, and 5,000 voters were unable to vote. (2) If the election was so conducted that it was substantially in accordance with the law as to elections, it is not vitiated by a breach of the rules or a mistake at the polls – provided that it did not affect the result of the election. That is shown by the *Islington* case[73] where 14 ballot papers were issued after 8 pm. (3) But, even though the election was conducted substantially in accordance with the law as to elections, nevertheless if there was a breach of the rules or a mistake at the polls – and it *did affect* the result – then the election is vitiated. That is shown by *Gunn v Sharpe*,[74] here the mistake in not stamping 102 ballot papers *did affect* the result.[75]

---

71 At p 499.
72 (1874) O'M & H 77.
73 (1901) 5 O'M & H 120; (1901) 17 TLR 210.
74 [1974] 2 All ER 1058; [1974] 3 WLR 7.
75 [1974] 3 All ER 722 at 728d–f.

However, on the facts of the case, there is a failure to acknowledge that the breaches of the voting rules by the polling station staff are, in fact, very serious and amount to substantial breaches of their official duty, whether or not this affected the outcome of the particular election. This is shown by *Pickering v James*, in which it was demonstrated that the failure to provide the elector with a properly validated ballot paper amounts to more than one breach of the rules. It seems, from *Pickering v James*, that the duty upon the polling station staff is to provide the elector with a valid ballot paper, not an invalid ballot paper, the latter not being a ballot paper at all.

Lord Denning was able, by his typically folksy introduction to the facts, to categorise the matter as a simple slip. If he had said words to the effect that presiding officers have the clear legal duty to issue voters with valid or stamped ballot papers and, furthermore, have a duty to check that the papers are stamped before voters are permitted to place them in the ballot box and cited *Pickering v James* in support of those principles, he could then have gone on to consider more carefully whether 'the election was so conducted as to be substantially in accordance with the law as to elections'.

It is submitted that by structuring the judgment in this way the analysis would run: (a) the electoral officials have a duty to administer the election in accordance with the law, this includes a duty to ensure that the procedures in, and the arrangement of, the polling station facilitate legal compliance; (b) where the electoral officials are in breach of their legal duty, the court has a duty to consider whether the election can nevertheless stand. This is a reversal of the test applied by Lord Denning MR. How did he come to his test? Another lengthy quotation is required. Immediately after the quotation set out above he said:

> Such being the facts, I turn to the law. It depends on s 37 (1) of the Representation of the People Act 1949, which says:
>
> 'No local government election shall be declared invalid by reason of any act or omission of the returning officer or any other person in breach of his official duty in connection with the election or otherwise of the local elections rules if it appears to the tribunal having cognizance of the question that the election was so conducted as to be substantially in accordance with the law as to elections and that the act or omission did not affect its result.'
>
> That section is expressed in the *negative*. It says when an election is *not* to be declared invalid. The question of law in this case is whether it should be transformed into the *positive* so as to show when an election is to be declared invalid. So that it would run:
>
> 'A local government election *shall* be declared invalid (by reason of any act or omission of the returning officer or any other person in breach of his

official duty in connection with the election or otherwise of the local elections rules) if it appears to the tribunal having cognisance of the question that the election was *not* so conducted as to be substantially in accordance with the law as to elections *or* that the act or omission *did* affect the result.'

I think that the section should be transformed so as to read positively in the way I have stated.[76]

It is now clear what has happened. Lord Denning MR has actually *reversed* the statutory test, which dates back to s 13 Ballot Act 1872, and he does this on the basis of the gloss[77] provided by Leigh and Le Marchant.[78] Lord Denning MR plainly approves of the commentary offered by Leigh and Le Marchant for he calls it 'a valuable commentary'. He goes on to explain precisely why he thinks it is valuable, and the weight of this point cannot be overemphasised.

They transformed the negative into the positive in the way I have suggested.

'A non-compliance with the provisions of the Ballot Act, 1872, and schedules 1 and 2, or a mistake at the poll, will vitiate the election, *if it should appear that the result of the election was affected thereby*, but not otherwise, provided the election was conducted in accordance with the principles laid down in the body of the Act.' [79]

It is submitted therefore, that, even at this stage in the argument of this chapter, *Morgan v Simpson* should be read with very considerable caution for it affords too much deference to electoral officials. It is accepted that the case is correct in the result, but it provides the wrong balance in the law. Lord Denning MR placed great reliance upon the distinction to be drawn between the *Hackney*[80] and the *Islington*[81] cases. He argued that the failure to open two polling stations in *Hackney* led inevitably and correctly to the poll being voided, whilst in *Islington* a small mistake was condoned by the court and the poll stood. It is therefore important to look at the *Islington* case in more detail, for it seems that the case does not assist the Master of the Rolls' argument; indeed it goes in precisely the opposite direction.

---

76 [1974] 3 All ER 722 at 725d–g.

77 In the sense of 'to read a different sense into', *Oxford English Dictionary* (2nd edn 1936).

78 Lord Denning MR cites '*The Law of Elections and Election Petitions*, 2nd edn, 1874, p 97'. The author has been unable to check this authority.

79 [1974] 3 All ER 722 at 726h–727a.

80 (1874) 2 O'M & H 77.

81 (1901) 5 O'M & H 120.

The main point at issue in *Islington* concerned a polling station at which the doors were shut promptly at the close of poll at 8 pm to prevent further entry. There was a small queue of people inside the polling station, who had already applied for their ballots. These people were allowed to vote, although it would seem that meticulous records were kept of their time of voting and hence indicated that the presiding officer was genuinely unsure as to the law regarding such people. It is uncertain from the report whether 12 or 14 people were allowed to cast their ballots after 8 pm. In any event the winning candidate had a majority of 19 votes.

In the law report it says that:

> An election ought not to be held void by reason of transgressions of the law by a returning officer or his subordinates where the election was, in substance, conducted in accordance with existing election law, *and* the result, as regards the return of one candidate over the other, was *not shown* to have been affected by such transgressions; but, if the transgressions were such that the election was not fairly conducted, or if it were open to doubt whether it was so conducted and whether the return of a candidate was affected by them, then the election ought to be held void.[82] (emphases added)

It is submitted that in this case Kennedy and Darling JJ stated the law correctly in accordance with the statute. The law says that, if it is shown that the polling officials misconducted an election, the election ought to be voided unless it can be shown that their mistakes did not affect the result.

The *Islington* case gives the result which, it has to be said, it appears that Lord Denning MR desired, although the reasoning points in the direction of the result being an exception to the ordinary rule. However, there is at least one other case[83] that serves as authority for the proposition that an election should be voided where votes are received after the close of poll and, since the poll was conducted by secret ballot, there was no means of determining for whom the invalid votes were cast. This is the Irish case of *Gribben v Kirker*,[84] heard before Lawson J and Monahan CJ in the Court of Common Pleas in 1873. There were two matters for decision, the relevant one being founded upon the prayer

---

82 (1901) 17 TLR 210 at 210 col 2.

83 *Schofield* lists (at s 18.27 fn 19) another three combined cases, *Ipswich, Bantoft's* and *Beckham's* (1835) K & O 332, 380, 382, which have proved impossible to trace and which give authority to the proposition that: 'Votes received after the close of poll. Election held void.' However it is argued that pre-1872 cases are of little utility in furthering this discussion, which is founded upon the provisions of the 1872 Act.

84 It is set down in *Schofield* as *Cribben* [sic] *v Kirker*. It is, in fact, *In the matter of the Belfast (Cromac Ward) municipal election petition. Gribben & Others v Kirker* (1873) IR 7 Com Law 30.

that the election should be voided because '... a number of votes were recorded after 4 pm by voters who were within the polling booth before 4 pm, but did not vote until after that hour, ...' [85]

There is a single judgment in the case, which is so short that it may be quoted almost in its entirety, omitting the authorities. Monahan CJ said:

> The provisions of the statute requiring the poll to be closed at 4 o'clock, P.M. [sic] have not been complied with. The cases quoted are not applicable, and do not go the lengths of deciding that the result of the poll must be shown to have been affected by keeping the poll open after 4 o'clock , P.M. Mr Kirker was the senior Alderman. The election must be set aside. Each party to pay his own costs.[86]

This result would appear to be consistent with *Islington* because, contrary to the facts in *Islington* where a number of votes smaller than the margin between the candidates were cast out of time, here there were an unknown number of votes cast. This means that it could not be shown that the irregularity was of no effect. The irregularity was presumed in *Gribben* to have voided the ballot and, there being no evidence to the contrary, the petition had to succeed.

Gribben in turn confirms the analysis set out above and hence the larger argument offered here that *Morgan v Simpson* was wrongly decided not in its outcome, but in its reasoning. Put simply, Lord Denning MR may have been right, but for quite the wrong legal reason.

The view taken here is supported by the decision in one of the most recent election petitions to be heard in the courts. In *Considine v Didrichsen and another, In the matter of the Representation of the People Act 1983*,[87] Lord Denning MR's reversal of the words of the statute came in for considerable criticism in the Court. Since the matter was heard in the High Court, and not by the Court of Appeal, the Court lacked the authority to reverse *Morgan v Simpson*; instead it simply distinguished, which is to say declined to follow, *Morgan v Simpson* on the facts. The court held, in *Considine v Didrichson*, that because there was a small margin between the two candidates, the election should be voided.

The final case for analysis in this chapter is a modern election petition that stems from the 2001 general election. It would appear that there was wrongdoing on the part of the electoral officials and some of the party workers. The analysis of this case, which draws upon the analysis of *Morgan v Simpson*, will lead directly into the conclusions of this chapter.

---

85 *Ibid.*
86 At pp 30–31.
87 [2004] EWHC 2711 (QB); [2004] All ER (D) 365.

Joint fault

The issues that arise where there is alleged or proven wrongdoing on the part of both the electoral officials and party workers is demonstrated in *In the Matter of the Representation of the People Act 1983* and *In the Matter of the Parliamentary Election for Fermanagh and South Tyrone Held On 7 June 2001*,[88] which can most conveniently be referred to as *Cooper v Gildernew*. Michelle Gildernew, standing as the Sinn Fein candidate, was elected to represent the constituency by a majority of 53 votes out of some 51,974 votes cast, beating the Ulster Unionist Party candidate, James Cooper, into second place. James Cooper brought an election petition.

The relevant law governing the conduct of the election remains, in substance, that which has been under scrutiny so far in this chapter. Carswell LCJ, sitting in the Northern Irish High Court as an Election Court, set out the law as being contained in the RPA 1983, and the substance of the complaint as being that at St Martin's Primary School, Garrison, Co Fermanagh, where a total of 974 votes were cast, the presiding officer, under threats from supporters of Sinn Fein, issued ballot papers and permitted votes to be cast after 10 pm. The polls had been prescribed to be open from 7 am until 10 pm.

On the facts of the case Carswell LCJ held that there was fairly steady voting throughout the day, with a slacker period around noon. In the evening from about 7 pm, voting became more brisk and a queue of voters formed, which stretched along the corridor leading to the polling place[89] and out of the building into the school playground. It is to be presumed, given the layout of most primary schools pressed into use as polling places, that there was at least one set of doors capable of closure so that on any interpretation of the cases the poll could be said to be closable. Carswell LCJ held that, as a matter of fact, shortly before 10 pm the queue consisted of some 40 or 50 people. He observed that the presiding officer's duty was to close the poll at 10 pm by ceasing to issue any more voting papers. Carswell LCJ interpreted the *Islington* case to provide that valid ballot papers could be issued up to 10 pm, and provided that the voters marked them and deposited them promptly, the votes would be counted.[90]

---

88 Neutral Citation [2001] NIQB 36 (19 October 2001). Unusually for a case reported in transcript the paragraphs are not numbered. Ms Gildernew was re-elected in 2005 with an increased and clear majority.

89 The usual terminology holds that a polling place is the room in which a polling station, or polling stations, are situated. A polling station is the place where a presiding officer, assisted as may be by one or more clerks, checks the identity of voters and issues the paper; then there are booths for voting before the voter deposits the paper in the box in front of the presiding officer or clerk.

90 The authority being cited as *Islington* (1901) 5 O'M & H 120 at 129, per Kennedy J.

It is plain that Mr McGovern, the presiding officer, left his seat and announced that he would stop issuing ballot papers at 10 pm. There was some dispute about the time at which he made this announcement, but it seems to have been at some point between 9.55 and 10 pm. The police on duty at the polling place had become concerned by this time and had alerted the local police station at Enniskillen. The duty police officers told the senior officer at Enniskillen that they feared that they would not be able to keep order.

The police officers in the polling station gave evidence that ballot papers were being issued until 10.05 pm. Whilst there was again some dispute about the precise timing, their evidence was preferred to that of the presiding officer and the polling clerks who stated that the poll was closed promptly at 10 pm. Assuming that the correct time was 10.05 pm, the presiding officer then announced that the poll was closed and instructed the police to close the door. This closure of the poll was either strictly in accordance with the law – in which case there would have been no dispute – or it was a breach. It is submitted that, had the poll been closed at 10.05 pm and no further ballot papers issued, an election court could lawfully have found that the election had been held substantially in accordance with the law since there was some genuine confusion over the time and the result, whatever it would have been, would not have been affected by the failure to observe the law.

This closure of the door seems to have been done in accordance with the presiding officer's duty to keep order in the polling place as set out in Rule 33 of the Parliamentary Election Rules. The senior police officer on duty, one Sergeant Nixon, attempted to close the sliding door of the room; however it was blocked by some person and a number of people pushed their way into the polling place. Sergeant Nixon stated that he saw two people in particular orchestrating this push: Martin McGovern, a Sinn Fein polling agent, and Stephen Huggett, a Sinn Fein candidate in the local council election being held on the same day. He gave evidence that he heard Martin McGovern shouting that everyone must get in and exercise their right to vote.

There was clear evidence given in the trial that both the polling clerks believed that there was going to be trouble and Sergeant Nixon said in evidence that he believed that he could not control the situation and, rather than allowing that to happen, he allowed people into the room. In consequence of this the presiding officer reopened the poll at sometime between 10.12 and 10.15 pm. He continued to issue ballot papers until, it would seem, 10.23 pm when he was called away to the telephone and told firmly to close the poll. It is quite clear that he had no lawful authority to reopen the poll.

It is submitted that this serious breach of election law is sufficient, on the basis of *Islington* and *Gribben*, to void the election. However, Carswell LCJ used the law as set out in *Morgan v Simpson* to create the intellectual space to estimate the number of votes unlawfully cast. He did this on the basis of estimates from the polling clerks as to the time needed to issue a ballot paper and the average voting time during the day. Thus, he estimated, that about one paper could be issued each minute. If, first of all, we take his estimate that no more than 30 papers were issued outside the proper voting hours, we can see that 30 falls short of Ms Gildernew's winning margin of 53. However, it can be argued that, whilst making an estimate at all or making the estimate in this way in particular is a possible expansion of the doctrine set out in *Morgan*, there is no authority for such a procedure; indeed authority, in the form of *Gribben*, goes the other way and precludes the courts from making any such estimate.

Even if the analysis set out above – that the election should have been voided on the authority of *Islington* and *Gribben* – is incorrect, there are good grounds for voiding the election on the basis of the conduct of the Sinn Fein polling agent McGovern, the candidate Huggett, and the agent Timoney.

How can this analysis proceed? First, we should consider the conduct of the electors wrongfully admitted to the polling station. If their conduct had amounted to a riot, the only option open to the presiding officer would have been to adjourn the poll under Rule 42 of the Parliamentary Election Rules. This Rule would normally require the presiding officer to reopen the polling station on the following day, but, of course, there would have been no need and no authority to reopen the poll because it should have been closed before the (hypothetical) riot had taken place. However, the conduct seemingly fell far short of riot either at common law or in the meaning given to the word by the Public Order Act 1986.[91]

The editors of *Schofield*[92] take the view, on the basis of the *Nottingham Town* case, that a general riot, as opposed to a localised riot, would be required to void the result of an election.[93] A general riot seems to be a riot which affects all, or a majority of, the polling stations in an entire constituency. This seems to be the decision as reported in the case, but the *Law Times* report (as is usual with such reports) lacks precision and

---

91 It being acknowledged, of course, that the 1986 Act does not generally extend to Northern Ireland.

92 At s 18.27.08.

93 (1866) 15 LT 57.

detail. It may be that a localised riot would, if the result of the election were sufficiently close, be sufficient to upset the result of an election. However, the question of riot to one side, it is certainly the case that localised intimidation of 20 voters would be sufficient to upset the result of an election if it could be shown that the intimidation was operative at the time of the election.[94] Intimidation of a voter, presumably because it is much more personal than a riot – a general mêlée – seems to be regarded much more seriously by the courts and is the special subject of s 115(2)(a) of the RPA 1983. This states that a person will be guilty of exercising an undue influence over another:

> [i]f he, directly or indirectly, by himself or by any other person on his behalf, makes use of or threatens to make use of any force, violence or restraint, or inflicts or threatens to inflict, by himself or by any other person, any temporal or spiritual injury, damage, harm or loss up on or against any person in order to induce or compel that person to vote or refrain from voting, or on account of that person having voted or refrained from voting.

Section 115(2)(a) of the RPA 1983 may be sufficient to void an election if the general intimidation can be made out, if taken together with s 164 of the RPA 1983:

> (1) Where on an election petition it is shown that corrupt or illegal practices or illegal payments, employments or hirings committed in reference to the election for the purpose of promoting or procuring the election of any person at that election have so extensively prevailed that they may be reasonably supposed to have affected the result –
>
>   (a) his election, if he has been elected, shall be void, and
>
>   (b) he shall be incapable of being elected to fill the vacancy or any of the vacancies for which the election was held.
>
> (2) An election shall not be liable to be voided otherwise than under this section by reason of general corruption, bribery, treating or intimidation.

As we have seen, Bramwell B would have been prepared to void an election where 20 voters were intimidated and Willes J said that he would have been prepared so to do in the *Blackburn*[95] case, were a single voter intimidated.

---

94 Bramwell B, in the *North Durham* case (1874) 2 O'M & H 152, gives an example of a case in Windsor in 1874 in which he sat and in which he would have unseated a successful candidate who dispossessed 20 of his tenants who did not support him in an election, but for the fact that it was not proven that the threat of being turned out was operating at the time of the election.

95 *Blackburn* (1869) O'M & H 198.

The difficulty with applying these (rather weak) rules to the facts of *Cooper v Gildernew* are, first, it is not at all obvious that any actual voter (as opposed to an election official or a police officer) was intimidated so as to vote or refrain from voting; secondly, the modern statute seems focused on general corruption under sub-s (2) as a vitiating factor, although there are no modern examples of such corruption.

In answer to the first point, there are a number of observations to be made. It is plain that any Unionist present would have felt (at the least) rather uncomfortable and one wonders how many of the voters present were there because of vigorous and enthusiastic 'knocking up' by Sinn Fein. They had not troubled to vote earlier and it does seem unusual that they should wish to vote right at the close of poll given that the poll did not close until 10 pm. Furthermore, no evidence was given on the point of whether the police officers or the electoral officials themselves intended to vote shortly before the close of poll. If this was the case it may be that these officers were intimidated in their status of voters rather than in their official positions. This would void the ballot for the reasons set out above.

Most importantly, it seems odd that a polling official, who has a measure of control over the casting of a large number of votes in addition to their own vote, should receive less protection against intimidation than a voter who has only their own vote. Whilst the statute is silent on this matter, it must be the case that where a polling official is subjected to so much intimidation that he reopens the poll, in direct contravention of his statutory duty, then the law ought to step in. Whilst this may be a case for the judiciary to repeat the comment made in *ex p Mainwaring* that the legislature should step in, it may be appropriate for the common law to supply the omission of the statute.

This final observation goes to the point of general corruption by means of intimidation. An election simply cannot be regarded as free and fair where polling officials and police officers charged with keeping order at a polling station are so intimidated that they fear that they will not be able to keep order and reopen the poll. The view that judges ought to be ready to void an election in cases where widespread intimidation has taken place away from the polling station was set out in *North Durham*[96] by Bramwell B, who voided the poll where a committee room was wrecked, a vicar's house attacked, the prisoners released from a police station and a carriage thrown over a cliff. A further consideration is that the nearer the intimidation is to a polling place, the more ready the judiciary should be to void the election. This is because the whole purpose of having a specific polling place is to preserve the secrecy of the

---

96 (1874) 2 O'M & H 152.

ballot. Secrecy and security of the ballot cannot be guaranteed where intimidation takes place within the polling place. It is of particular concern where a political party effectively takes over a polling station.

Bramwell B made the point at the end of his judgment, in *North Durham*, that it is hard on that part of the electorate that did not misconduct itself for the election to be voided. He said that his reason for voiding the election was to prevent similar corrupt practices arising in the future. This sounds like some sort of utilitarian reasoning, but it can easily be stated in language more consistent with both the central theme of this book and the terms of Art 3 of the 1st Protocol to the ECHR. However, before this is set out in the conclusion of this chapter it is useful to record that there were a number of violent disturbances at polling stations in Derry during the European Parliamentary elections in June 2004. It is unclear who was responsible for these disturbances, which were roundly condemned by both the Mayor of Derry, Councillor Gearóid Ó'Éara and Mark Durkan the leader of the Social Democratic and Labour Party. As we shall see, there are pragmatic reasons both for voiding and endorsing elections marred by violence at the polling station, but, it will be argued, there are special considerations to be taken into account where the result is very close and the disturbances are caused by agents of the candidates in real contention for the seat.

Conclusion

The central argument set out in this chapter may be summarised in the following propositions.

1   Citizens take part in government by means of elected representatives.

2   Representatives can only lawfully be chosen by means of a free and fair election. Authority for this proposition is to be found both in Art 3 of the 1st Protocol to the ECHR and in the English common law; see, for example, the *North Durham* case.

3   If an election is challenged, this must be done through the election petition procedure.

Some further argument is needed at this point. In *Cooper v Gildernew*, Carswell LCJ said that Kennedy J, in the *Islington* case,[97] stated that it was for the successful candidate in an election, challenged by means of petition, to show that the result was not affected – but that he doubted this view and he was supported in this by the doubt expressed by the editor of Parker's *Law and Conduct of Elections* at para 19.92.[98] It seems

---

97 (1901) 5 O'M & H 120, at p 130.

98 The matter does not appear to be directly addressed in *Schofield*.

that this matter was settled by Streatfield J, in the *Kensington North Parliamentary Election Petition*,[99] a case brought by Sir Oswald Mosley in 1960. Streatfield J said:

> The question of the burden of proof does not, on the strict wording of s 16, really arise. If it did arise, it seems that, under the wording of the corresponding section of the Ballot Act, 1872, (Section 13 of the Ballot Act, 1872. The Act was repealed by the Representation of the People Act, 1949, s 175 and Sch 9.) the burden rested on the respondent: see *Islington, West Division, Case, Medhurst v. Lough & Gasquet* ((1901), 5 O'M & H at p 130, per Kennedy, J, delivering the judgment of the election court.) I think that with the changed wording under s 16 (3) of the Act of 1949 it is for the court to make up its mind on the evidence as a whole whether there was a substantial compliance with the law as to elections or whether the act or omission affected the result.

This point is important because, although we saw in Chapters 4 and 5 that there are shortcomings in the election petition procedure because it seems to share some of the characteristics of a private law procedure, this decision by Streatfield J emphasises the public law nature of an election petition. Streatfield J makes it explicitly clear that the court must decide the matter for itself, rather than one or other of the parties having to prove their case.

To continue with the key points:

4   There are faults in the statute law exemplified by *Mainwaring*, where we saw that in order to succeed in an action to annul an election for fraud it would be necessary to show that a person was, in fact, defrauded. The statute law is deferential to the interests of successful candidates.

5   It is submitted that *Morgan v Simpson* is wrong both as a matter of law and as a matter of policy. The judges are deferential to the interests of the elected candidate and too forgiving of the serious errors of the presiding officer. Lord Denning MR seems to take the view that the provisions of electoral law made by parliament are optional rather than mandatory. These lapses lead straight into the decision in the decision in *Cooper v Gildernew*.

6   It is submitted that the decision in *Cooper v Gildernew* is unsupportable. Here the presiding officer broke the law in the face of intimidation by agents of the candidate. It is submitted that the petitioner Cooper should have succeeded.

Some further explanation of this point is necessary. Quite apart from the fault of the polling officials who should, no doubt, have been better

---

99 [1960] 2 All ER 150; [1960] 1 WLR 762. Quotation from the All ER at p 153.

supported by the police, there was serious intimidation by the representatives of the winning party. Carswell LCJ said in the penultimate paragraph of his judgment:

> The incidents which took place at this polling station at the time when the poll should have closed were extremely reprehensible. It is understandable that electors who had waited for some time to cast their votes should feel angry at finding themselves deprived of the opportunity through no fault of their own. It may be that the holding of both elections on the same day threw a strain on the process which the resources of the polling staff could not bear, and we express the hope that the insufficiency will be addressed. No doubt there was a strong feeling of frustration among those who found themselves unable to vote. But nothing can excuse the scenes of threatening intimidation which took place, brought into being by supporters of the candidate who was eventually successful. Such behaviour is the negation of a parliamentary democracy.

Carswell LCJ's comments are entirely endorsed here – yet this makes it very difficult to understand why he decided the case in the way that he did. Surely, where the winning or the second placed candidates or their agents are engaged in wrongdoing that could be seen as 'the negation of a parliamentary democracy', judges should apply the highest levels of scrutiny to the election, especially where the margin between the candidates is within, say, 1% of the total number of votes cast. Clearly, such strict scrutiny must be used with discretion for fear that it might, where the result of the election is a foregone conclusion, tempt people into violent misbehaviour merely to upset the result.

Strong support for the view that the English courts are now ready and able to intervene can be found in the recent case of *Ghaidan v Mendoza*.[100] *Ghaidan* is a case relating to the Rent Act 1977 and concerns the issue of whether a gay man is able to take over the lease of a flat after the death of his partner in whose name the flat was rented. It is clear from the Act that a spouse would be able to take over the flat, but the law was much less clear about, or even hostile to, the position of a same-sex partner. However the case law of the European Court of Human Rights (ECHR) provides that gay partners should be afforded the rights given to opposite-sex partners. The House of Lords took the view that the Rent Act 1977 must be read in such a way as to reflect the jurisprudence of the ECtHR even though the Act under consideration was passed before the Human Rights Act 1998. It is therefore clear that any court seised of a matter brought under the RPA 1983 must consider the principles enshrined in Art 3 of the 1st Protocol. Surely it cannot be that an election as tainted as *Cooper v Gildernew* should be allowed to stand.

---

100 [2004] UKHL 30; [1984] 3 All ER 411.

Finally, the central argument of this chapter builds to some extent upon the argument advanced by Brigid Hadfield in her essay *'Does the devolved Northern Ireland need an independent judicial arbiter?'*[101]Hadfield argues cogently, but in the avowedly limited context of politically sensitive cases in Northern Ireland (such as the devolution case *Robinson v Secretary of State for Northern Ireland*[102]), that the judges should undertake hard-edged judicial review in 'litigation in which all of the parties have clearly different political perspectives'.[103] Hadfield, it is submitted correctly, dissents from the position taken by Kerr J in *In Re Michelle Williamson*;[104] Kerr J claimed that courts should not intervene in cases where decisions are taken in a political context informed by political considerations; Hadfield argues that it is the business of judges to intervene in these matters.[105] Election cases are paradigmatically ones in which the parties have different political perspectives and, following Hadfield, courts are bound to intervene. There is the one outstanding and overriding political perspective that the judiciary is bound to uphold under the terms of the ECHR, in general, and Art 3 of the 1st Protocol, in particular. There is an overriding public interest in ensuring that the people have their legislature chosen in a way that is clearly untainted by anti-democratic behaviour because, in the words of the *Greek* case,[106] 'in a democracy the majority has regard to the interests of all groups and people in the state'. It is argued that these interests can only be respected by ensuring that all elections are free and fair.

---

101 In Bamforth and Leyland, 2003, pp 133–56.

102 [2002] UKHL 32.

103 Hadfield, 2003, p 155.

104 NIHC 19 November 1999; Kerr J referred to this in *Robinson* NIHC 21 December 2001 reported at p 17 of the transcript; quoted by Hadfield, 2003, p 153.

105 Her argument is supported by the words of Carswell LCJ, dissenting in *Robinson* in the NI Court of Appeal. Transcript of 21 March 2002 at p 23 and quoted in her essay, Hadfield 2003, p 154.

106 12 YB 1 (1969) at 179.

Chapter 7:
The Problem and a
Possible Solution

Let us first recapitulate the argument so far. In Chapter 1 we saw how electoral law is always used for political ends. It is not neutral. We then looked briefly at the development of electoral law and focused in particular upon the developments during the 19th century and at the end of the 20th century. It was suggested that electoral law aspired to encompass a democratic model of a polity, and we looked at a formal model of democracy, which was found wanting. It was then suggested that there are two models of citizenship available to us – democratic citizenship and market citizenship. Evidence was presented in support of the view that political parties prefer to be treated as if they were market goods. Whilst some writers accept and promote this view, criticisms of the market approach were advanced on both the procedural and substantive levels. Finally, a model of the courts' approach to matters of electoral law was proposed and it was explained that this model would be further articulated and criticised in the following chapters.

In Chapter 2 we saw that, whilst people now possess a legal right to vote that is free from any requirement to own property, the work of John Stuart Mill contains a powerful objection to the notion of a right to vote. Saying that a citizen has the *right* to vote suggests that they may exercise that vote (or not exercise that vote) in accordance with their own desires. This implies that voting is a matter of market choice; the citizen buying one of the products on offer and then retiring from the democratic arena for the duration of the parliament. It is suggested that the 'right to vote' is better understood as the exercise of a power under a trust: the citizen should vote in accordance with their best view as to how the country ought to be governed in the interests of all of its citizens. This suggests that voting should be seen as an obligation to vote, rather than as a right. The argument in favour of the 'vote as obligation' also provides that the citizen should not be given any encouragement to vote for 'none of the above' by, for example, being given a 'none of the above' box on the ballot paper. Clearly, this means that the voter themselves ought not to act to achieve the same end by, for example, delivering a blank or spoiled ballot. This is because, to adapt the words of the cynical old saw, politicians will always win the election, and leaving the governance of the country solely in the hands of politicians is to substitute oligarchy for democracy. A refusal to vote is, far from being a quixotic gesture against the political status quo, merely a failure to behave in accordance with one's civic obligation.

In the third chapter we saw how the method of voting promotes a market notion of governance, as opposed to a democratic one. Whilst the secret ballot, mandated by the main international human rights instruments, has many virtues it re-emphasises the model of voting as being a matter of individual choice rather than a matter of civic duty. However, it is the best that can be achieved especially where it is exercised in a publicly supervised arena. The atomisation of the vote – where it is taken away from the public, impartially supervised arena, into the private family or social group – serves to strengthen the market model. This semi-secret vote is the least preferred option. The phenomenon of vote bartering, which is facilitated by, in particular, remote electronic voting, is shown to be a perversion of democratic choice.

It was argued that the state ought to work towards developing a voting model that obliges people to vote as citizens participating in a democracy. Whilst this will require an ideological shift on the part of the political parties who evidently perceive themselves to be beneficiaries of the market system (although further argument will be offered on this point), the mechanism of voting ought to be designed so as to promote democracy. In this seventh chapter the implications for the 'foundation model' proposed by the Electoral Commission[1] will be considered in detail.

In Chapter 4 we examined the legal process of the nomination of a candidate and saw that the common law might, and ought to, allow spoiler candidates to be denied access to the ballot paper. It was emphasised that this technique cannot and should not be used to exclude *bona fide* fringe candidates. The current techniques of legal control based upon the Registration of Political Parties Act 1998, as incorporated into the Political Parties, Elections and Referendums Act 2000, were shown to be designed to reinforce party discipline and thus to be a market-regulation measure, rather than a democratic-regulation measure. Parties can and do use the provisions to protect their own brand image.

It was argued in Chapter 5 that the control of election expenditure under the Representation of the People Act 1983 (RPA 1983) and the Political Parties, Elections and Referendums Act 2000 (PPERA 2000) models is nothing more than a hollow shell. Political parties are able to

---

1 See *Delivering democracy? The future of postal voting: the road ahead*, 2004, para 6.17 ff. The Electoral Commission's concrete proposals will be set out and discussed in Chapter 8.

avoid regulation and have been doing so for a number of years. It was argued that the involvement of the state, both bureaucratically in the person of the returning officer, and through the active involvement of the citizenry in a citizens' jury or board of scrutiny, in the supervision of election expenses will serve to control the market in political parties. If parties are prevented from spending huge sums on advertising, it may oblige them to expend greater efforts on policy explanation and the promotion of genuine political debate.

In Chapter 6 some further matters of substantive electoral law were considered. What principles should govern the disposition of an election petition occasioned by the fault of the electoral officials, the candidate(s), or the parties? It was argued that the courts should be more willing to overturn a defective election than seems to be the case at present. This is because a defective election is not a true election. The reason why the courts may be reluctant to void elections is because the annulment of an election may lead to a different result than the original result. In a market system this would not be fair because a market theory of elections supposes that the parties are in competition with one another and one party wins, whilst the others lose, an election. In this conception the election is thus, more or less, the outcome of the political process. The role of electoral law is, thus, like the Queensbury Rules or the Laws of Cricket, to ensure a fair bout or match. It was argued that this is an incorrect analysis of elections and election law. Democratic elections are the first stage in the process of governance. Election law is that body of law which provides citizens with their voice in governance.

How are these ideas to be drawn together? Let us consider 'Achilles' again. This character was introduced in Chapter 2 as a cipher for John Stuart Mill's straw man – 'the benevolent dictator'. Mill points out that our Achilles would not only have to be supremely intelligent, informed correctly at all times in the exact detail of the running of the state in all its branches and capable of choosing his lieutenants with perfect skill;[2] he would also need to be devoid of passion. Clearly no such person can exist. Is he just a figment of our imagination and a pointless exercise?

Achilles and the 'elective dictatorship'

So, John Stuart Mill drew attention to what can be called the recurrent 'democratic death wish'[3] to which citizens of a democracy appear to be prone, where they say, 'please can we have a benevolent dictator?' Mill's objection has been upheld amongst other objections. However, despite

---

2   See Mill, 1991, pp 55–56.
3   See above Chapter 2; and Mill, 1991, p 55.

the objections, the idea remains and holds some attractions. What are the attractions?

First, it is clear that being ruled by a benevolent dictator relieves the citizens of the responsibility of ruling themselves. Even where there is a representative democracy and most people do not have to carry any actual burden of administration themselves, it relieves them of the minor inconvenience of voting and, more importantly, the psychological burden of responsibility. If the dictator makes an unpopular, uncomfortable or downright unpleasant, though necessary, decision, the subjects (for they are not, in reality, citizens) can say that it was not their fault. It is clear that allowing someone else to rule is much easier than taking responsibility for ruling oneself. One might well rationally yield to authority because one is busy, concerned about making a mess of the enterprise, or simply lazy. It is also the case that, where one yields political (and other kinds of) authority to someone else, one has a ready scapegoat if and when things go awry.[4] It seems that the more power and authority we grant to Achilles and the less we reserve to ourselves, the more opportunity there is for things to go wrong because, as Mill pointed out, our Achilles can have neither sufficient information nor sufficient power to rule effectively. The more mistakes Achilles makes, the less faith we are likely to put in him. It may be that all parties are willing to assume their respective positions, but Achilles would be well advised to design an escape route. A suitable escape route for an Achilles faced with the practical limitations of government, such as the control of the uncontrollable,[5] would be to extol the virtues of limited government and then to lessen the responsibilities of government. This, perhaps rather cynical manoeuvre, may lessen citizens' expectations of government, but it seems likely that it would also reduce their willingness to vote for government. Governments may well say that they regret the fact that people do not vote, but they can find some comfort in a low turnout. As we saw in the first chapter, most of the defeats of sitting governments since the 1939–45 war may be ascribed to the failure of the outgoing government rather than the popularity of the alternative party.[6] A government returned to power in an election in which relatively few people bothered to vote might well conclude that at least the electorate thought that it was doing little about which to complain. Is it pushing this line of speculation too far to suggest that this may lead to an arrogance of power in the sense that governments may do much as

---

4   For example, see Raz, 1986, p 64, in which he considers the status of 'John is an authority on Chinese cooking'. Clearly, it is easier to follow John's recipe for, eg, crispy Sichuan duck than to have to work it out for oneself.

5   Such as the Minister for Drought appointed by the Labour government in 1976.

6   Crewe, 1988.

they wish provided that they do not overstep some line set by the electorate? Some examples of 'the line' being crossed would be, for example, the introduction of the community charge (or poll tax) in the late 1980s or the invasion of Iraq in 2003. Certainly a government with a secure parliamentary majority can do as it wishes and need not worry about the consequences until the next general election, by which time it may have been saved by fresh events.[7] However, this sort of 'elective dictatorship'[8] may well be doomed in the sense that it can be removed from office by the electorate and its policies reversed by an incoming government.[9]

The more interesting question, at least for the purposes of this book, is whether Achilles could, by manipulating election law, ensure the succession. As Sarah Birch and I noted in *Remote electronic voting: free, fair and secret?*,[10] 'the law governing elections has a profound effect upon the composition of the legislature'. A 'first-past-the-post' electoral system tends to produce a system in which there are relatively few political parties, and leads to single party governments. A system of proportional representation tends to lead to the fragmentation of political parties and towards coalition governments. The same point was made by Lord Hailsham, when he was considering the effect of methods of voting in defining the very nature of the political parties we have today.[11] He suggested that:

> ... parties, as they exist today, ... , are themselves, to a large extent, the product of the voting system, and not static groupings with an inherent right to separate representation whenever there is a general election. There are approximately 13 or 14 different systems of voting current throughout the world. Each one of these, if applied in Britain over a period of years, would produce party groups different from the present. There is no *a priori* reason to suppose that, after 10 years of a different system, any of the existing parties would exist at all in their present form. They are all groupings designed to produce results under the present system.

There seem to be three possible routes by which an Achilles could accomplish a reform of the electoral system so as to secure the succession.

---

7 For example, the 1979–83 government led by Mrs Thatcher was trailing in the opinion polls by a large margin until the war with Argentina precipitated by the Argentinian invasion of the Falkland Islands.

8 The phrase was coined by Lord Hailsham and explained in Hailsham (Lord), 1978.

9 The most obvious example being the repeal of the Industrial Relations Act 1971 by the incoming Labour government in 1974.

10 (2004) 75 *Political Quarterly* 60–72 at p 60.

11 Hailsham (Lord), 1978, pp 183–84.

The abolition of elections

The first of these routes is, it is hoped, highly unlikely in the modern British state and is, perhaps, best confined to the realms of fiction.[12] It is included for the sake of completeness and to demonstrate the full effect of Art 3 of the 1st Protocol ECHR.[13] This route would be nothing less than the complete abolition of elections.

Section 2 of the Meeting of Parliament Act 1694 provided that parliament should be prorogued and summoned afresh every three years; this period was extended to seven years by the Septennial Act of 1715 and shortened again to five years by s 7 of the Parliament Act 1911. The 1911 Act contained a restriction on its own use such that it could not be used to prolong the life of a parliament. In theory a sovereign parliament could prolong its life by means of a measure such as the Prolongation of Parliament Act 1940,[14] backed up by an Emergency Powers Act and a compliant House of Commons;[15] however, given any set of conditions short of a full-blown national emergency and a proximate threat to national integrity, it is unthinkable that this could ever happen again. Section 2(1) of the Parliament Act 1911 prevents such a measure being forced through the upper house by the use of the Act; although, as we shall see below, the Parliament Act has been used (or its use threatened) in electoral law matters on at least two occasions. It is also worthy of note that the amendments to the Parliament Act 1911 contained in the Parliament Act 1949, which reduced the delaying power of the House of Lords, were themselves forced into law by the use of the 1911 Act.[16]

It must be said that the postponement of an election to any tier of government would appear to be an extremely rare event; the most recent general postponement being that accomplished by the Election Act 2001. The local government elections due in May 2001 were postponed until 7 June (the date, as it transpired, of the general election) in order to avoid and minimise traffic across land affected by the outbreak of foot and

---

12 See Forsyth, 1984, p 89. Forsyth's reference to the Parliament Act 1911 is, of course, to s 2(1), which prevents the Act being used in relation to a Bill prolonging the life of parliament beyond five years. The point must be made that the relevant phrase in the 1911 Act as amended or (following the cogent argument of Samuels, 2003, pp 237–42) *purportedly* amended is original to the 1911 Act and is therefore beyond legal challenge.

13 The High Contracting Parties undertake to hold free elections at reasonable intervals by secret ballot, under conditions that will ensure the free expression of the opinion of the people in the choice of the legislature.

14 The last general election having taken place in 1935.

15 See, for a general description of the wartime arrangements, Calder, 1969, Chapters 2–5; and Taylor, 1965, Chapters XIII–XIV.

16 See, Samuels, 2003, p 238.

mouth disease.[17] It is at the very least arguable that the provisions of Art 3 of the 1st ECHR do not apply to local government elections because they do not appear to be part of the 'legislature' (as noted in Chapter 6); in any event, a delay of one month in a four year cycle of elections would appear to fall within the margin of appreciation[18] of a state's discretion as to a 'reasonable interval'[19] because it was for a short and definite period and due to a genuine and short-lived national emergency. It must be beyond doubt that a complete abolition of elections would be both politically unacceptable and legally unacceptable, however Samuels,[20] in summarising the arguments, writes that:

> ... , if the 1949 Act could be used unicamerally by the House of Commons to alter the timetable, that is reduce the delay from two years to one year, by the same token the House of Commons could unicamerally alter the five year provision, for example by extending the life of Parliament from five to seven (or whatever) years.

More worryingly Samuels reminds us that:

> The judicial declaration of incompatibility[21] under the Human Rights Act 1998 raises a similar potential conflict, though it does not of itself affect the validity of an Act of Parliament.[22]

Thus, if parliament really wanted to extend its life by abolishing elections it could, but unless it succeeded in packing the House of Lords with peers ready to accede to such a manoeuvre, it would need to amend the Parliament Act 1911 to remove s 2(1), breach the provisions of Art 3 of the 1st Protocol ECHR and thus be faced with both a Declaration of incompatibility and an adverse judgment in the European Court of Human Rights. Would a government, with whatever majority, be willing to proceed in this way? Surely only Frederick Forsyth would think so.[23]

---

17 An important economic disease of farm livestock, caused by a virus. The obvious joke quickly became tedious.

18 This point was made in Chapter 1, above, and refers to the point made in *Mathieu-Mohn v Belgium* 10 EHRR 1 and *Knight v Nicholls* [2004] EWCA Civ 68, in which it was made clear that Art 3 of the 1st Protocol does not impose any one standard of democratic method upon signatories to the ECHR, but allows them a wide discretion in compliance.

19 Recall the words of Art 3 of the 1st Protocol where they refer to elections being held at 'reasonable intervals'.

20 Samuels, 2003, p 238.

21 Under s 3(2) of the Human Rights Act 1998. For a helpful discussion see Feldman, 2002, pp 85–93. See the discussion of *A(FC) and others (FC) v Secretary of State for the Home Department, X (FC) and another (FC) v Secretary of State for the Home Department* [2004] UKHL 56, in Chapter 1 above.

22 Samuels, 2003, p 238.

23 *Ibid*, fn 12.

Altering the basis of representation

The second method of ensuring some form of succession would be to alter the basis of representation. Here the discussion of any proposed alteration to the basis of representation, such as a move from 'first-past-the-post' to some form of proportional representation, is conducted on a procedural level. There are merits and drawbacks in any form of electoral system and the discussion of these would, without doubt, require a book in itself, but this is not the place for such a discussion. Here the question is whether and by what means parliament could alter the electoral system (which would in turn end up altering parliament, as suggested above). The Representation of the People Act 1918 made some moves towards this aim following the recommendations of the Speaker's Conference of 1917.[74] Amongst a series of provisions[25] the Act provided for a number of pilots for a scheme of proportional representation based upon an extra member to represent a group of constituencies. The trials were never conducted.

Whilst it is clear that a form of proportional representation[26] is in operation for the European parliamentary elections, the elections to the Welsh Assembly and the Scottish Parliament and to the Greater London Authority, in order to provide some additional representation to those parties that have failed to secure seats by the 'first-past-the-post' method, a system of 'top-up seats' has been established. Registered political parties,[27] but apparently not individuals or unregistered parties, are entitled to submit lists of candidates from which party representatives may be elected to fill the additional seats. The method used is mathematically complicated, but the intention is to favour those parties whose candidates have not gained a seat by the 'first-past-the-post' method.[28] The usual method of election to seats in the House of Commons, the other legislatures and assemblies and to local government is still by the 'first-past-the-post' system and will remain that way until parliament decides otherwise.

---

24 *Conference on electoral reform: letter from Mr Speaker to the Prime Minister*, Cmnd 8463, 1917.

25 Including one that deprived conscientious objectors of the vote until 1923; see Taylor, 1965, p 160.

26 Note that the description used is 'a form of proportional representation', it is not claimed that the system of voting is 'true' proportional representation, but simply that the list system used provides minority parties (or, more importantly, minority *voters*) with additional representatives. See, too, s 4(5) of the Government of Wales Act 1998. Note that, by virtue of s 3 of the European Parliamentary Elections Act 2002, the method of election for Northern Irish MEPs is by single transferable vote.

27 Note that there is no provision for groups of individuals or unregistered political parties to contest the additional seats.

28 The complex rules for deciding on the allocation of votes may be seen at, eg, paras 6, 7 & 8 of Sched 2 of Pt II of the Greater London Authority Act 1999.

It is clear that parliament could decide to implement such a general scheme of proportional representation if it so chose. The 1917 Speaker's Conference and the Jenkins Commission[29] – which was set up following the Labour victory in 1997 – both recommended some form of proportional representation. There were other attempts at achieving reform in the intervening years. However the 1917–18 Speaker's Conference sets the scene. When the report was set before parliament the following happened:

> The House of Commons, favouring single-member constituencies, wanted the alternative vote. The House of Lords wanted proportional representation, which involved the grouping of constituencies. In the end, the university constituencies got a form of alternative vote which changed the result on nine occasions (depriving the House of Commons of JB Priestley in 1945).[30] Provision was also made for an experimental run of proportional representation in 100 constituencies of large towns which returned three or more members. This experiment was never tried.[31]

It is clear that during this period the attempt to introduce some form of proportional representation was blocked by the executive under Lloyd George against a majority of Liberal members of parliament; however the politics of the time make detailed analysis impossible.[32]

The other parliamentary and extra-parliamentary attempts to introduce some form of proportional representation may be mentioned briefly. Let us look first at the parliamentary position. The Speaker's Conference that reported in 1930 recommended the introduction of an alternative vote system.[33] A Bill was introduced by the Labour Government under Ramsay MacDonald, but this fell, together with the government, in 1931. Towards the end of the Second World War another Speaker's Conference on Electoral Reform[34] was convened, but again its recommendations were rejected. Finally, in 1967, the recommendations of the 1966–67 Speaker's Conference[35] were again rejected.

---

29 For details see its Report: *The Report of the Independent Commission on the Voting System* Cm 4090-I &II, 1998.

30 For a brief and somewhat wistful account of JB Priestley's political ideas and the fortunes of Common Wealth, see Calder, 1969, pp 631 onwards.

31 Taylor, 1965, p 159.

32 See, for an account, Taylor, 1965, pp 171–75.

33 Cmd 3636 (1930) *Conference on electoral reform: letter from Viscount Ullswater to the Prime Minister.*

34 Cmd 6534 (1944) *Conference on electoral reform and redistribution of seats: letter from Mr Speaker to the Prime Minister.*

35 Cmnd 3202 (1967) *Conference on electoral law: letter dated thirty-first January, 1967 from Mr Speaker to the Prime Minister.*

Secondly, there were at least four extra-parliamentary moves to secure reform. In 1976 the Hansard Society appointed a commission under the chairmanship of Lord Blake, which recommended a hybrid 'first-past-the-post' and 'party list' system.[36] In 1982, in the run-up to the 1983 election at which the Liberal–Social Democratic Alliance hoped to eclipse the Labour Party, a commission set up by the two parties produced a report calling for a complex system of 'community proportional representation'.[37] This simply disappeared from political sight.

Much the same fate met the Report of the Jenkins Commission. On 29 October 1998 the *Report of the Independent Commission on the Voting System*, produced by the Commission chaired by Lord (Roy) Jenkins of Hillhead, the former Labour cabinet minister and founder member of the SDP, was published. Its main recommendations were the use of 'preference voting' in electing constituency MPs, allowing voters to rank candidates in their own order of preference. In addition, county and city lists for additional MPs would be introduced, along with the use of 'open' rather than 'closed' or 'party' lists. An 'open' list allows the electors to chose which of each party's candidates they would like to see elected to the legislature, whilst a 'closed' or 'party' list allows the political party that nominated the list to determine the order in which the candidates stand and thus which are most likely to be elected. Although it was Mr Blair himself, on becoming Prime Minister, and in collaboration with Paddy Ashdown, the Liberal Democrat leader, who had set up the Jenkins Commission to look at alternatives to the 'first-past-the-post' electoral system, the Labour leader decided to abandon the proposals almost before the ink was dry.

Following the 2005 general election, the *Independent* newspaper has initiated a 'Campaign for Democracy' calling for electoral reform but, at the time of writing, it does not seem to be moving forward with any discernible velocity.

In all these periods of attempted reform, it is quite clear that the levers for changing the electoral system at the level of the basis of representation are quite firmly in the hands of the House of Commons and thus in the grasp of the government of the day or a parliamentary majority.

Amending electoral law

The third method for ensuring the succession is at the micro-level of electoral law. The problem with asserting that whenever a legislature

---

36 See *Report of the Hansard Society Commission on Electoral Reform*, 1976.

37 *Electoral reform: fairer voting in natural communities: first report of the Joint Liberal/SDP Commission on Constitutional Reform*, 1982.

enacts a provision of electoral law it is providing for its own succession, is that it sounds simply axiomatic. What else would a legislature be doing in enacting electoral law? Accepting, of course, that it might be legislating for elections to some other legislative or administrative body, it is otherwise inevitable that it will be legislating for its own successor. This point is not simply axiomatic because the party that was instrumental in passing the legislation will itself be one of the contestants in the following election. Some evidence is needed to show that there might be something sinister in attempts to change electoral law. This need not amount to an actual wrongdoing. Suspicion is all that is required to damage confidence in the electoral system.

In the past there have been allegations that the party in power at the time has tried to manipulate constituency boundaries to their own advantage. In *R v Boundary Commission for England ex p Foot and Others*,[38] the (then) leader of the Labour Party alleged that the Boundary Commission proposed to recommend constituency boundary changes that would unfairly deprive the Labour opposition of seats that it would otherwise expect to win in the (then) forthcoming general election. Whilst the application was dismissed as without foundation, it demonstrates that electoral law is a sensitive subject. This would suggest that there is a special burden upon a legislative body enacting electoral law, especially where the legislature is dominated by a party with a large majority and *especially* where that majority is dependent upon the executive. Recall the observation of Nicholas Jones set out, in part, above:

> The roll-call of constituencies [won] by Labour on election night included numerous seats where the winning candidates were the first to admit that they found it almost impossible to comprehend their success and could not believe that they really were on their way to the House of Commons. In their first few bewildering months at Westminster, the one bond that united all of the newcomers was a sense of discipline. ... The sheer enormity [sic] of Labour's overall majority of 179 seats gave the parliamentary party an air of invincibility. Rarely had there been such a large contingent of new MPs who were so anxious to demonstrate loyalty and so keen to allow their responses to be influenced if not controlled by the party machine.[39]

Recall, too, that the last *major* piece of election legislation before the election of the Labour government was the RPA 1983, which was broadly a measure reconsolidating the RPA 1949. The Labour Government has, with the aid of its large majority, brought forward a number of major amendments to election law, notably the Representation of the People Act 2000 and the Political Parties, Elections and Referendums Act 2000. These do not complete the list, but they are major components of the

---

38 [1983] 1 All ER 1099.
39 Jones, N, 2001, p 39.

reform of electoral law. The fact that the Labour Governments since 1997 have engaged in substantial electoral reform is itself worthy of note. It seems that more electoral reform has been performed in the last seven years than in the preceding 70. It is also noteworthy that this contrasts with major electoral reforms of the past, which were instigated by substantial public pressure rather than being initiated by parliament. As we have seen in Chapters 2 and 3, above, the Reform Act 1832 was brought about, in large part, by popular pressure instigated by the London Radical Reform Society and the Birmingham Political Union. The Chartist movement provided the impetus for the Ballot Act 1872 and the other reforming legislation of the time. The movement for women's suffrage was also a popular movement. The recent electoral reforms are unusual in so far as they are accompanied by popular political apathy rather than by agitation, as well as being party led.

It does not seem too outrageous to suggest that the elected members of political parties are likely to be more committed to the party line over matters of electoral law than perhaps any other kind of legislation. All of them owe their seat, at least in part, to the party machine that is staffed by those experienced in the running of elections. All of these MPs are going to get strong guidance from the party. Most importantly, there is going to be considerable pressure to repeat electoral success. Presumably the incumbent will wish to be returned to the seat; their party workers and activists will be looking for continued success. If the newly elected MP has remained on the back benches throughout their brief parliamentary career and then loses the seat in a general election, it is likely that they will find it difficult to get another seat in parliament unless there is a by-election in the seat that has recently been lost. Even if the seat is safe, there will be considerable pressure from other members of the parliamentary group (especially those with smaller majorities), the party itself , and its supporters (both individual and institutional) in the country. The temptations to tinker with the electoral system to produce some sort of advantage must be very considerable.

For all these reasons there is, in principle, a strong case to make electoral law into a special category of legislation that cannot be made, amended or otherwise controlled by parliament. Notice that this is wider than 'cannot be governed by the majority party'; for, where the parties are able to collude in electoral matters and where they act as a number of competing brands rather than as mechanisms for allowing the people to govern themselves, control of the basic mechanisms for legislating electoral law should actually be taken away altogether from parliament.

Since taking away the making of electoral law from parliament appears to be an attack upon the fundamental law-making power of the sovereign parliament, some strong justifications are needed for the proposal. First, we need to recall that the courts in *Ashby v White*[40] held that an election is 'precedaneous' to parliament and is the foundation upon which the authority of parliament rests. If, as has been argued throughout this book, there is some doubt about an election, it ought to be overturned – and this principle ought to apply *a fortiori* to election law itself. If there is any doubt about the fairness of election law it ought to be subject to the strongest scrutiny. The argument here is not that the law fails to be fair between the parties, but that it fails to be fair to the people.

Who should make electoral law?

An inter-party consensus?

In 1948, Winston Churchill observed that changes in electoral law should not be imposed by one political party upon another, but should be settled 'by an agreement reached either between the leaders of the main parties or by Conferences under the impartial guidance of Mr Speaker'.[41] However, we have seen above that the Speaker's Conferences have been particularly ineffectual in securing changes to electoral law because the parties have voted down their recommendations. The idea of some sort of deal between party leaders (*a fortiori* 'between leaders of the main parties') is inimical to the notions of democracy set out in this book. This would sustain the market nature of our current political system and ensure that politicians and parties remained remote from the people

The House of Lords?

Perhaps the power to make electoral law should be given to an unelected second chamber – the House of Lords. It is somewhat surprising to note that the unelected House of Lords has arguably, and at least patchily, demonstrated over the course of 300 years a more rigorous approach to election law and the preservation or furtherance of democracy than the elected House of Commons. A limited argument of this sort has been advanced, at least in relation to the recent history of electoral law, by the editors of *Dod's Political Communications*.[42] This claim, or at least the strongest reading of this claim, will be doubted below, but it is worthy of exploration.

---

40 (1703) 2 Ld Raym 938.

41 HC Deb Col 859, 16 February 1948.

42 See *Dod's Political Communication online* at http://www.first-web2.co.uk/ engine.asp?lev1=0&lev2=383&menu=1&showPage=article&ID=1313 , heading 'House of Lords' in the 3rd para of the report.

As we have seen above, the first battle between the two Houses was over *Ashby v White* in 1704. The House of Commons claimed, under the Bill of Rights of 1689, a unique right to regulate membership of the House of Commons. It has to be said that it is difficult to find a legal foundation under the Bill of Rights 1689 upon which the House of Commons' Resolutions were based. The only two relevant provisions are:

That election of members of Parliament ought to be free;

That the freedom of speech and debates or proceedings in Parliament ought not to be impeached or questioned in any court or place out of Parliament.

It would seem that, in *Ashby v White*, Holt CJ's judgment gave effect to the first principle. Holt CJ's view was that the election of members of parliament ought not to be subject to parliamentary control. His judgment was that the law provided that the determination of whether an election was fair was one for the ordinary (that is, general) law, not for the law of parliament to decide. We can easily see that the objections of 1868[43] raised to the hearing of election petitions in parliament were just as telling in 1703–04. Clearly, the second principle of the Bill of Rights, as set out above, was not engaged by Holt CJ's judgment, because at the time of the judgment there was no 'speech, debate or proceeding' in parliament. The House of Lords, which then fulfilled its role as the Supreme Court by debate and voting on the floor of the House, held that electoral cases concerning the parliamentary franchise should be resolved in the ordinary common law courts. The Commons purported to reverse this by a Resolution. This was a bluff because a Resolution does not affect the law – it is not a law-making act. They did not attempt to do it by Act of Parliament, presumably because in the pre-1911 parliament the House of Lords would have declined to pass any such Bill and it would have been lost. This might well have led to the packing of the House with Lords more sympathetic to the Commons' position. Some examples of this practice are set out below.

The Lords' preference for proportional representation at the time of the 1918 Representation of the People Act has already been noted; this returned to the forefront during the consideration of that which became the European Parliamentary Elections Act 1999, which was eventually only passed by the application of the Parliament Acts 1911 and 1949. The passage of the Act was halted in the Lords because a sufficient number of peers voted against the government's preferred scheme for the distribution of seats in the upcoming European Parliamentary elections.

---

43 See Chapter 1.

It is unclear whether all of them voted against the government's scheme because they genuinely believed in the alternative system of proportional representation, or because they believed it to be inherently more democratic, or whether they supported it because they simply believed that it would deliver their own party more seats in the European Parliament, or simply because of their die-hard Euroscepticism and they saw the chance to vote for a wrecking amendment. In any event, the government was obliged to use the Parliament Acts in order to pass its legislation.[44]

This is not the end of the matter. The most recent blocking manoeuvre practised by the Lords upon the Commons was over the European Parliamentary and Local Elections (Pilots) Act 2004. The summary in *Dod's*[45] provides a useful starting point for the discussion.

> It is a curiosity that the unelected House's most stubborn resistance to the Commons is often displayed on electoral matters. They inflicted a defeat on the government on the conduct of the first GLA (Greater London Authority) elections in 2000. This year they took the government to the wire over the European (Parliamentary) and Local Elections (Pilots) Bill. This bill was designed to permit experimentation in the 10 June elections with different methods of voting to assess their impact on turnout.[46] The Electoral Commission had recommended that all postal voting should be trialled in only two English regions, whereas the government had proposed four. The Lords sent the bill back to the Commons five times in an attempt to insist on taking the Electoral Commission's advice. The government refused to give way – by the end of the exchanges perhaps more on grounds of the principle of resisting the Lords than on the substance of the disagreement. On the sixth refusal of the Commons the Lords backed away from a constitutional crisis, just in time to allow the pilots to go ahead for the 10 June elections. It would once have been held to be constitutionally impossible for the 'ping-pong' between the two Houses to have continued for so long.

It is a matter of speculation as to why the Lords allowed the measure to pass. It could be that they were threatened with the use of the Parliament

---

44 This was only the third time the amended Act had been used. It was used for the Parliament Act 1949 itself, the War Crimes Act 1991, the EPEA 1999 and subsequently in respect of the Sexual Offences (Amendment) Act 2000. It has now been used in respect of the Act to outlaw the hunting of wild mammals with dogs and this has precipitated the challenge, brought by hunt supporters, to the legality of the Parliament Act 1949. This matter has now been resolved by the House of Lords in *R (on the application of Jackson) v Attorney General* [2005] HL 56 in which nine Lords of Appeal held (on 13 October 2005) that the Parliament Act 1949 was of full legal effect. This settles the argument set out above.

45 *Ibid*, fn 35.

46 This needed primary legislation because the trial was to be performed in the European Parliamentary election. Trials in local government elections have been conducted, under s 10 of the Representation of the People Act 2000, since May 2000.

Acts, although if the Parliament Acts had been used, the Lords would still have been able to delay the Bill for sufficiently long to prevent it being used in the June 2004 elections.[47] As we shall see below, the traditional threat used by governments denied their legislation by a stubborn House of Lords was to go to the monarch to have sufficient peers created to pack the House and thus get the legislation through. The use of this device was threatened in 1832 with the first Reform Act, and in 1910–11 with the 'People's Budget'. However, the old threat of packing the House of Lords by the creation of sufficient peers to pass the measure seems quite empty for two reasons. It could not have been accomplished in time for the Pilots Bill to pass and the House of Lords is currently under reconstruction in any event. If the Lords, most notably the Liberal Democrat peers, were sufficiently convinced of their own arguments, there is no obvious reason why they did not 'stick to their guns' and defeat the measure. However, it seems that the matter is not that simple.

The point is, of course, that the peers themselves are, and always have been, highly politicised. In the debates surrounding the passage of the English and Welsh Reform Bill in 1832,[48] the Lords made a number of amendments in favour of their own economic interests before rejecting the Bill entirely. Their acceptance of the Bill was only secured by pressure being applied, by the Commons, to William IV to threaten to create sufficient new peers to pass the measure.[49] It is notorious that the Lords' refusal to pass Lloyd George's great reforming 'People's Budget' of 1909 led directly to pressure being put on George V who agreed, if necessary, to create sufficient new peers to ensure the Budget's passage in the Lords.

The House of Lords has repeatedly demonstrated that it is every bit as 'political' as the House of Commons. The House of Lords is fettered by the Commons; it was defeated over the 1832 Reform Act, the People's Budget, the 20th century Acts pushed through using the Parliament Act and, one might add, effectively defeated in *Ashby v White*. We can also see the House of Lords has been extensively remodelled over the years since 1997 and it is by no means clear where the process is going to end; thus the House of Lords is subject to reconstruction at the will of the Commons and this makes it inherently unsuitable as the author or source of electoral law.

---

47 The Act only received Royal Assent on 1 April 2004, leaving returning officers with slightly more than two months to complete the arrangements. The necessary Order implementing the all-postal ballots was not made until 27 April 2004, and so many of the necessary arrangements could not be made until the beginning of May.

48 It must be remembered that there were separate Reform Acts for Scotland and for Ireland. For a useful summary of their provisions see Woodward, 1962, p 87.

49 For a full account, see Woodward, 1962, pp 76–87.

The Electoral Commission?

The Electoral Commission was established by Pt 1 of the PPERA 2000. It has a wide range of responsibilities in electoral matters. The responsibilities most relevant to the current discussion are set out in ss 6 and 7 of the Act. Section 6 of the PPERA 2000 requires the Commission to keep certain maters under review and to report upon them to the government. At its own instigation it may review and report upon:(a) matters (including the law) relating to elections and referendums; (b) the redistribution of seats at parliamentary elections; (c) the registration of political parties and the regulation of their income and expenditure; and (d) political advertising in the broadcast and other electronic media. The Secretary of State, charged with overseeing electoral matters, may ask the Commission to review and report upon a wider range of matters, provided that they are not matters devolved to the various regional assemblies.

The Commission has a wide range of responsibilities under s 7 of the Act. Section 7 requires the Secretary of State to consult the Electoral Commission before making delegated legislation with respect to a wide range of electoral matters, including regulations under the European Parliamentary Elections Act 2002 and the Representation of the People Act 1983.

It would be natural to think that such an expert body would be a prime candidate for making electoral law. However the discussions surrounding the European Parliamentary and Local Elections (Pilots) Act 2004 not only provide another reason for removing the government's power to rewrite election law; they clearly demonstrate the reasons why the Commission cannot at present be regarded as a serious candidate for authorship of electoral law.

The Electoral Commission advised that two regions be designated as 'all postal ballot regions'. The Electoral Commission's own account of the affair is helpful:

> 3.6 In September 2003 the Government introduced the European Parliamentary and Local Elections (Pilots) Bill to provide for the piloting of innovative voting methods at the June 2004 elections. Prior to this, there was no statutory basis for using non-traditional voting methods in relation to European Parliamentary Elections. It should also be noted that the legislation applied only to the 2004 elections, not to future European parliamentary elections.
>
> 3.7 Following the introduction of the Bill, the Commission was *directed by Government to recommend up to three European Parliamentary regions* [emphasis added] that would be suitable to run pilots in 2004 and to consider which one of these would be most suitable to incorporate an e-voting element. The commission launched a consultation exercise on

25 September 2003 and published its recommendations in *Electoral pilots at the June 2004 elections*[50] on 8 December 2003.

3.8 We recommended that the North East and East Midlands were, respectively, highly suitable to undertake an all-postal pilot scheme. Four other regions were named as potentially suitable for piloting, although we were not able to make a positive recommendation that the government proceed to designate them as pilot regions. These regions were, in order of suitability, Scotland, Yorkshire & the Humber, North West and West Midlands. The Commission recommended that no region was suitable to undertake an e-enabled pilot scheme.

3.9 Following the submission of these recommendations, the Government announced on 16 December 2003 that it would be taking forward the Commission's recommendations to hold all-postal pilots in the North East and East Midlands at the June 2004 elections. The Government also accepted the Commission's recommendation not to proceed with electronic voting pilots in the June 2004 elections. The Government announced, on 21 January 2004, that it intended that two more regions, Yorkshire & the Humber and the North West would also pilot all-postal voting at the June 2004 elections. Following extensive discussion in both Houses of Parliament, the European Parliamentary and Local Elections (Pilots) Act 2004 designating these four regions as all-postal pilot areas for June 2004, this received Royal Assent on 1 April 2004. The European Parliamentary and Local Elections (All-Postal) Pilots Order 2004 was made on 27 April 2004.[51]

The long quotation is useful because it demonstrates that the government was quite prepared to treat the professional opinions of the Electoral Commission, as well as the electoral officials surveyed, with little more than contempt (in the sense of considering something to be of little account or worthless, rather than vile). First, the words 'directed by Government to recommend up to three European Parliamentary regions' surely indicate the Commission's view of the relationship between the government and the Commission. It would seem that even the Commission views itself as an executive arm of government, rather than of parliament or of the people. Secondly, the Commission fulfilled its remit to 'recommend *up to three* European Parliamentary regions' – it recommended two. Thirdly, it provided a 'reserve list', going beyond its remit. Then the Government announced that it intended to add two more trial regions, thus extending the list to four, one greater than the Commission's remit. Fourthly, the Commission reported that the Government had also announced that 'Yorkshire & the Humber and the

---

50 Electoral Commission, 2003.

51 See *Delivering democracy? the future of postal voting*, 2004. The quotation is from page 18, paras 3.6–3.9.

North West would also pilot all-postal voting'. These two regions were second and third upon the Commission's reserve list: the proposal to include Scotland as 'first reserve' was abandoned.

There were a number of problems with the European parliamentary elections and the local government elections, which were held on the same day. There were a large number of reports of fraud, and reports that voting papers did not arrive on time. Many of these reports now appear to be unfounded, because there have been relatively few election petitions, but the perception at the time was very unfavourable. The Commission's analysis of the results of the all-postal voting pilots appears to indicate that they were correct in their assessment that only two regions should have been subjected to pilot schemes. Whilst some of the difficulties encountered in the pilots were undoubtedly due to the short period during which electoral officials, printing companies and the postal system had to prepare for the ballots,[52] the main difficulty seems to have been that the public lost confidence in all-postal ballots. The reasons for this seem to be centred upon the procedures for applying for postal votes, the handling of postal votes by the local authorities or by party workers,[53] and the integrity of the system.[54] In any event, the Electoral Commission's recommendation is unequivocal and damning:

> The Commission recommends that all-postal voting should not be pursued for use at UK statutory elections. We further recommend that there should not be any further piloting or rollout of a form of voting that relies overwhelmingly on the dispatch and return of ballot papers by post.[55]

This is a plain reversal of the Commission's recommendation published in 2003 in *The shape of elections to come: a strategic evaluation of the 2003 electoral pilot schemes*,[56] where the Commission proposed that the government make all-postal voting the norm for local government elections.

---

52 See para 4.32 of *Delivering democracy?*

> The form of the pilot was also finalised too late to allow for its effective implementation. Late decisions on the exact design of the voting process saw Returning Officers left with no time for adequate planning and procurement processes. The Commission itself was not able to finalise the training materials it was separately funded to produce, with the result that pilot regions received a lower level of service than non-pilot regions at a time when they could legitimately have expected more support. The time available for Royal Mail to plan and organise the logistics was reduced. Crucially, the time available to test improvements and modifications to IT and print systems was almost non-existent.

53 See *Delivering democracy?*, paras 4.75–4.82.
54 See *Delivering democracy?*, paras 4.83–4.104.
55 Highlighted insert to *Delivering democracy?*, para 6.15.
56 Electoral Commission, 2003.

Whilst it was made clear above that the Commission has a duty to submit reports to the government on matters under their purview,[57] that it must be consulted in other matters,[58] and that the government must take account of their views, the general position is that the government may, at least as a matter of law, ignore the Commission. This may be politically difficult, but in circumstances where the government has a large parliamentary majority, the government may simply ignore the opposition if it tried to insist upon following the Commission's advice where the government were minded to reject it.

This position might well be compared with that set down in Pt 12 of the Criminal Justice Act 2003, dealing with the government's relationship with the Sentencing Guidelines Council in relation to fixing the lengths of prison sentences, which gives the Council far more authority than the Electoral Commission. The intention in making the Sentencing Guidelines Council powerful and independent was to give people faith in the criminal justice procedures and to ensure that the rights guaranteed under Arts 5 and 6[59] of the ECHR were respected. It may be suggested that making the Electoral Commission powerful and independent would show an intention to respect Art 3 of the 1st Protocol. At present, the Commission seems to be little more than an executive and advisory agency of the government. This is the current fundamental weakness of the Electoral Commission.

The point is made even more clearly in the government's response to *Delivering Democracy?*, entitled *The Government's response to the Electoral Commission Report: Delivering Democracy? – the future of postal voting*.[60] The government, in the shape of the Office of the Deputy Prime Minister, completely rejects the Electoral Commissions view that all postal voting should be abandoned. They say that the reported problems were whipped up by aggressive reporting in the news media and seem (as noted above) to have resulted in very few substantiated complaints. Furthermore the government notes that people seem to like the opportunity to vote by post, as evidenced by the increase in electoral turnout. Whilst the government agrees that, at least for the present, general elections should not be conducted by means of an all-postal ballot, requires that there should be a continuation of postal voting in local government elections. The government has asked the Electoral Commission to return to the position advocated in *Voting for Change* and asked that provisions for all-postal voting be incorporated into the

---

57 See ss 5 & 6 of the Political Parties, Elections and Referendums Act 2000.
58 See s 7 Political Parties, Elections and Referendums Act 2000.
59 The right to liberty and the right to a fair trial respectively.
60 Cm 6436 of December 2004.

Electoral Commission's Foundation Model for voting which was due to be published at the end of March 2005. In the event, the paper, entitled *Securing the Vote*, was published in early June 2005.

In these circumstances it is difficult to discern the purpose of the Electoral Commission. It was asked, or rather *directed*, to produce a plan for a widespread trial of all-postal voting. The Commission was ignored. It was asked to evaluate the ballot, and again was ignored. The Office of the Deputy Prime Minister appears to have taken over its substantive functions, leaving the Commission as a mere talking shop. At present therefore, and despite its obvious expertise, there seems to be little practical possibility of the Commission becoming responsible for election law.

However, making the Electoral Commission into a truly independent body with the power to draft legislation and present it to parliament for endorsement or, alternatively, rejection by a super-majority, would be a welcome although radical change, perhaps on a par with the passage of the 1832 Reform Act.

The argument is not yet complete because the proposal will not be that parliament should have no say at all in the drafting or enactment of electoral law, but that a special procedure should be adopted when making electoral legislation. Before this argument can be made in full, it is necessary to return to a consideration of the perceived gap between parliament and the people. The discussion is speculative for this is not a work of empirical political science. It is an attempt to offer an explanation for the 'deep sense of disconnection with political process and disillusion with the political class'.[61] The discussion is designed to be a spur to further research rather than an answer.

The market model or who is Achilles?

The issue is neatly encapsulated in the very words 'political class', used by Rallings and Thrasher in the quotation immediately above. The suggestion is that there is now a political class in Britain that is separate from the mass of the population; it is self-contained and self-perpetuating. The market system of elections is designed to ensure that, so far as possible, people 'buy' with their votes one of the *prêt à penser*[62] packages on offer. For the majority of the citizenry, voting is not a matter of participating in the process of self-government; rather it is a matter of

---

61 Quotation from *Delivering democracy?*, para 3.11 The words are themselves a quotation from Rallings and Thrasher, 2003.

62 By analogy with *prêt à manger* food and *prêt à porter* clothes. I am grateful to Olivier Moreteau, Professor of Comparative Law, Director of the Edouard Lambert Institute of Comparative Law, Université Jean Moulin Lyon 3, for, in quite another context, giving me the idea for the phrase.

choosing a 'monarch' or, better, a ruling oligarchy. The name 'Achilles' could well be given to any of the heroes of the political class who are put up for sale, like so many 'cans of fizzy drink or sofas', and who are supported, not by those who wish to argue and challenge the ideas of government,[63] but by a group of myrmidons.[64]

The charge, then, is that Achilles (as a cipher) is simply a remote political class that has effectively usurped power from the people.

To suggest, or to confirm suggestions, that there is a remote political class may seem like a mouse of an idea. The novelty of the idea, as set out in this book, is that there is a strong link between electoral law and the promotion and maintenance of a political class. It is also a matter of political importance in two senses; the first sense is the purely political, and its explanation justifies a brief excursus into the realms of party politics. After a consideration of the political, we will return to a consideration of electoral law.

Alienation and politics

The sense of alienation that the populace feels from the political class produces some surprising political effects, in addition to the fall in electoral turnout. The rise of far-right political groups in some northern English cities is well known, but it would appear that the rise of the Independent Working Class Association (IWCA)[65] is a better model of the problem of alienation from the main political parties. This is not to claim that there are any similarities in political ideology between the IWCA and the far right.[66] However, whilst neither the far-right parties, such as the British National Party (BNP), nor the IWCA would thank the author for making the point, both groups focus upon crime affecting working class people and the lack of services provided for them. The BNP (and the other far-right groups) blames these problems upon allegedly unrestricted immigration and asylum seeking by 'bogus' refugees, whilst the IWCA blames the Labour government for being fixed upon 'middle-class concerns'. The far-right has an uninterrupted,

---

63 See, eg, Jones, N, 2001.

64 Little, Brown and Trumble, 2002, give the uses of the word: 1. (with capital M) one of a warlike race of men inhabiting Thessaly, who followed Achilles to the siege of Troy. Used of Achilles himself; 2. a faithful follower or servant. Now chiefly *joc(ular)*; 3. in a derogatory sense: an unscrupulously faithful attendant or hireling; a hired ruffian.

65 A political party registered under the terms of the Political Parties, Elections and Referendums Act 2000. See http://www.iwca.info/ for information on the party.

66 Stuart Craft, the IWCA's first councillor, is sometimes slurred by suggestions that he has links to the far right, a calumny he fiercely rebuts, drawing attention to his activism in anti-fascist organisations. See the *Oxford Times* 9 July 2004.

though schismatic, history going back to 1918[67] and a fixation with racist and anti-Semitic ideologies, whilst the IWCA describes its ideological roots as resting in 1970s trade union collectivism and dates its roots from 1995, which date it identifies as the Labour Party's abandonment of the working class.[68] However the political ideologies are not important for the following argument.

The IWCA caused astonishment in East Oxford in June 2004 when it increased its representation to three seats on Oxford City Council.[69] Oxford East is the parliamentary seat currently held by the former Secretary of State for Work and Pensions, Andrew Smith, and there is some speculation that his resignation from the cabinet was prompted by his desire to hold on to his seat in the face of a challenge from the IWCA.[70] Mr Smith lives in Blackbird Leys, Oxford, which is the centre of IWCA activity, and his wife is one of the councillors for the ward, which was always seen as one of the country's safest Labour council seats. One of the main speakers for the IWCA is Stuart Craft, the first IWCA candidate in Britain to win a council seat. The *Oxford Times* published an article which illuminates something of the IWCA's political position:

> … Mr Craft, an Oxford bus driver, sees little reason, however to concern himself with satisfying the curiosity of the mainstream political parties.
>
> Pursuing the interests of the working class is the mission, and the stated method is to pursue it 'with no consideration for, and regardless of, the consequences to the existing and political structures' [*sic*].
>
> The contempt he feels for the mainstream parties, he says, is now widespread on Blackbird Leys, the estate where he grew up and now lives with his wife and son.[71]

It could be argued, and here a challenge is offered to the political scientists, that the relative, but limited, success of the minor parties, such as the IWCA, is due to their willingness to engage with everyday issues of governance and their use of traditional methods of political campaigning 'on the doorstep'.[72] This point is brought into relief by the words of John Lister, a Trotskyism whose views correspond with the IWCA in some respects, where he says that:

---

67 Thurlow, 1987.

68 Much of this information is taken from '*A party that stands a class apart*', reproduced from the *Oxford Times* article of 9 July 2004 and reprinted on the IWCA website at http://www.bliwca.fsnet.co.uk/clssaprt.htm.

69 Holding its seat in the Northfield Brook ward and taking a seat from Labour in each of the Blackbird Leys and Churchill wards.

70 If Andrew Smith had secured all the votes cast in favour of the IWCA in May 2005 he would have increased his majority over the Liberal Democrats from 963 to 1855. His majority in 2001 was 10,344.

71 Quotation from '*A party that stands a class apart*', *Oxford Times*, 9 July 2004

72 See http://www.iwca.info/news/news0022.htm for a comment on the IWCA's campaign strategy.

It seems to me that the very factors that have formed the basis of the IWCA's success so far – their heavy focus on very local issues in parts of the Blackbird Leys and Wood Farm estates – would suggest that they would have little interest in contesting a parliamentary seat, ... it would, inevitably, involve them seeking votes from very large parts of the city which, by their measure, are 'middle class'. What we have is a popularist [sic] organisation that relates to people's day-to-day living pressures rather than offering a political programme. In fact it does not appear to have one. If you look at the newsletter, it is virtually all about drug dealers, drug users, difficulties with problem families and inadequacies in tackling street lighting and repairs. The IWCA's definition of politics appropriate to the 'working class' seems to leave no room for even relatively basic issues which interest and involve many working-class people, such as education and the improvement of the NHS.[73]

Lister seems to have missed the point, as apparently the Oxford Labour Party has, that the essence of politics is, in a democracy, dealing with the people's concerns. The members of the IWCA are elected to Oxford City Council, which has control of the housing stock and deals with repairs and housing issues; presumably they are communicating with their constituents about matters that they think will interest them. The point is, as Lees-Marchment has correctly observed,[74] it is for political parties to respond to the electors' agenda; the difficulty is when they respond to sectional demands from within that agenda. Mr Craft and his colleagues seem, in the views of the electors of Blackbird Leys and Wood Farm, to be addressing the real issues.[75]

The alienation from electoral law

This seems to have taken us some distance from the problems of electoral law: Mr Craft's sentiments do not suggest that the problem with political disengagement has anything directly to do with the structure and institutions of electoral law, but, on the contrary, has everything to do with politics. Nonetheless, the government and, so far as it has an independent existence, the Electoral Commission see their tasks as delivering electoral renewal and revival of political participation through revising the techniques of voting, in particular, as we shall see below, by the introduction of a 'foundation model' for future elections. The point is, it is argued, that the government's programme of electoral reform is having the opposite effect by actually adding to the degree of disillusionment and disengagement. Whilst there is some evidence that

---

73 Quotation from 'A party that stands a class apart', Oxford Times, 9 July 2004.

74 Above, Chapter 1.

75 See, further, the interview with Lorna Reid, the IWCA's candidate for the London mayoralty, at http://www.iwca.info/news/news0026.htm.

the government/Electoral Commission programme is raising turnout slightly, from 37.11% in the non-pilot regions in the European Parliamentary Elections to 42.42% in the all-postal pilot regions,[76] there seems to be little evidence that the alterations in voting methods are having any effect upon the hard core of non-voters. Indeed, although there is no empirical evidence on the point, the very form of (the appropriately named) *remote voting* itself articulates disengagement with the business of democracy by contrast to the traditional act of voting.

It is useful to recall, at this point, some of the material presented in the first three chapters. We saw that in 1430 the franchise was restricted because people showed too great a readiness to vote. Those (particularly the Levellers) who argued for a greater measure of democracy in the aftermath of the Civil War were put down, first, in debate by Henry Ireton and, later, more forcibly, by Oliver Cromwell and Thomas Fairfax.[77] The development of the modern, nearly universal, franchise was brought about by the popular democratic movements of the 19th and early 20th centuries – the Political Associations, the Chartists and the Women's Suffrage movement. All of these movements were popular causes, accompanied by demonstrations, civil disobedience and, in the last resort, civil or military conflict. These movements led to changes in, or substantive consolidations of, electoral law. The latest changes to electoral law have, as we have seen, been marked by a complete lack of public enthusiasm. The reform of electoral law is a government only, or at least a government sponsored, project. Electoral law ought to be a 'hot

---

76 These figures should be compared with the average turnout across the European Union of 46% in the European Parliamentary elections; itself a record low figure. Data from *Delivering democracy?* at paras 3.15–3.16. The comment relating to the London European Parliamentary and Mayoral/Assembly elections is somewhat chilling and supports the view expressed in this book.

In London where European Parliamentary elections were held alongside London Mayor and Assembly elections, the European Parliamentary turnout was 37.65%. Turnouts for the London Mayoral and Assembly elections were around one percentage point lower.

It might well be added that on the last occasion the author fought a District Council seat in Banbury Ruscote, the following result was achieved 'Labour councillor Mr Bob Watt retained his Ruscote seat with a much increased majority – the turnout in his ward was about 48 per cent', *Oxford Mail*, 4 May 1990.

77 The pithy summary from the Channel 4 history website needs little addition.

Three soldiers are executed at Burford, Oxfordshire, following mutinies by Leveller soldiers in Salisbury, Aylesbury and Banbury. Mutineers from Salisbury and Aylesbury join forces near Abingdon and head west, but are overtaken by Thomas Fairfax and Oliver Cromwell, who defeat the rebels at Burford. A much smaller group of mutineers from Banbury are defeated at Wellingborough. This marks the end of effective radical politics in the army.

See http://www.channel4.com/history/microsites/H/history/guide17/timeline28.html. For a full scholarly account, see Brailsford and Hill, 1961.

topic', but it is almost completely submerged, largely absent from law school curricula, and ignored by nearly everyone.[78] What can be done?

The Electoral Commission's 'foundation model'

Whilst the Electoral Commission has reversed its initial position and said that it cannot support the further piloting or rollout of specifically all-postal balloting in statutory elections,[79] it does wish to proceed with electoral modernisation.[80] It says that 'we support further pilots of genuinely multi-channel elections'[81] and recommends the development of a 'new foundation model of voting for statutory elections and referendums.'[82] The government has said that it does not support this abandonment of all-postal voting and it wishes the Commission to integrate all-postal ballots into its foundation model.[83] In any event there is a shift in thinking from all-postal or all remote voting to multi-channel voting. Multi-channel voting means that electors will be able to cast their ballots by a variety of means.

However, before we can consider the Electoral Commission's proposals some preliminary comments can be made. First, it has proved impossible to get the government to respond to questioning on the legality under Art 3 of the 1st Protocol ECHR of remote (electronic or all-postal) voting. It may be surmised that they have legal advice to the effect that multi-channel voting is compliant with Britain's obligations under that Convention. The question as to the legality has been set out above, in *Human Rights and Remote Voting by Electronic Means*,[84] *Remote electronic voting: free, fair and secret?*[85] and in *Legal issues concerning the implementation of electronic voting*.[86] The government does not seem inclined to answer these points. It would be useless to submit a request for information under the Freedom of Information Act 2000 because legal advice supplied to the Government for the formulation of policy is exempt from the disclosure provisions of the Act under s 37. However,

---

78 The Campaign for Democracy sponsored by the *Independent* has, at the time of writing, secured relatively few supporters.

79 *Delivering democracy?*, para 6.15.

80 *Delivering democracy?*, para 6.16.

81 *Delivering democracy?*, para 6.17.

82 *Delivering democracy?*, para 6.16.

83 *The Government's response to the Electoral Commission Report: Delivering Democracy? – the future of postal voting*, Cm 6436 of December 2004.

84 Watt, 2003, pp 197–208.

85 Birch and Watt, 2004, pp 60–72.

86 http://www.local.regions.odpm.gov.uk/egov/e-voting/01/index.htm.

the Joint Parliamentary Select Committee on Human Rights is aware of the arguments I have raised.[87]

No favours are being claimed here, in fact quite the opposite; the argument is that the government should publish its legal advice for all to see. It is acknowledged that the arguments presented in my earlier publications may be wrong. They are, however, arguments and no more. As Sedley LJ pointed out, in *Knight v Nicholls*,[88] the matter can only be resolved in full before the European Court of Human Rights. It is submitted that it is essential that the legal advice be published. Elections are a matter of public concern for all the reasons set out in this book and it cannot be acceptable that the legal foundation for any change in electoral law remains confidential. It is submitted that all arguments about electoral law should be made in a wholly public arena. These are not matters of state secret, indeed they are matters of absolute public concern.

Secondly, the intention is to have this model available for piloting from September 2005, or at the May 2006 English local government elections and again in May 2007, with a full scale test available in the May 2008 London Mayoral, Greater London assembly and English local government elections.[89] It is suggested that the timetable is alarmingly short for two reasons. The Commission's working party has until the end of March 2005 to report. A consultation paper was prepared around Christmas 2004. Simply asking the public for ideas about a new foundation model for elections, without any kind of guidance from the Electoral Commission, is pointless. It is submitted that the matter ought to be submitted to the public because the design of an electoral system is central to self-governance. It is, of course, conceded that many members of the public will lack the detailed technical knowledge of the designers of the system, but since, as the Commission point out throughout *Delivering democracy?*, any voting system has to be acceptable to the public, it is essential that there is plenty of time for public consultation. The second reason for the submission that the timetable is too short is that the Commission wishes the scheme to be ready for piloting in September 2005 at 'by-elections'. If by this the Commission means parliamentary by-elections, rather than at local council by-elections in single isolated wards – in which case the proposed pilot will be both extremely expensive and will, for the reasons set out in *Delivering*

---

87 See the Eighth Report of the 2003–04 Session of the Select Committee on Human Rights. http://www.publications.parliament.uk/pa/jt200304/jtselect/jtrights/49/4906.htm.

88 [2004] EWCA Civ 68; see, especially, paras 37–39.

89 *Delivering democracy?*, para 6.25. See, too, para 30 of the government's response. The government is uncertain whether this timetable will prove feasible.

democracy? as to scale, be of very limited value – it will need primary legislation because s 10 of the Representation of the People Act 2000 extends only to local government elections. Given the Government's difficulty in getting the European Parliamentary and Local Elections (Pilots) Act 2004 through Parliament, and given the difficulties with those elections and the adverse report in *Delivering democracy?*, the task will be more difficult next time; there will be no parliamentary time for the necessary legislation. However, a general election was announced in April 2005 and the reform procedure brought to a halt. The government has now laid an Electoral Administration Bill before parliament and it is expected that it will encounter considerable opposition. In any event the Department of Constitutional Affairs has said that the resulting Act will not be brought into force before June 2006.

Thirdly, as we saw in Chapter 3 above, the Joint Select Committee on Human Rights had some concerns about the European Parliamentary and Local Elections (Pilots) Bill (Now the 2004 Act). Presumably they will wish to scrutinise any elections legislation very carefully, especially where this contains provisions for multi-channel voting. It was observed above that the Government has, as is usual in these matters, not published their legal advice.

For all these reasons, the Electoral Commission and the Government should review its timetable for the production and testing of the foundational model. It is accepted that a foundational model of elections is needed and it is agreed that the Electoral Commission is the body best placed to produce it, subject to the caveats regarding public consultation set out above. It is submitted that the Commission ought to institute a longer term project for the rewriting of electoral law and it is suggested that a new method for adopting their proposals should be instituted.

A proposal for the reform of electoral law and its embedment in a constitutional settlement

In the past, reforms of electoral law have been forced on the government by popular pressure. Today it is the other way around, with the government now trying to interest people in voting and passing legislation to encourage them so to do. Yet, in order for people to be encouraged to vote they have to feel that their vote makes a difference and that they are engaged in the political process – which is ultimately the process of self-government. How can the process of electoral law making be brought closer to the people? Presenting politics and voting in terms of *prêt à penser* products for which voter-consumers can shop online is not the answer; indeed, it merely exacerbates the problem

The establishment of the Electoral Commission in 2000 was, at least potentially, a great step forward. However, as the forgoing discussion of the foundation model illustrates, the Commission is being pressed by the Government to do too much, too quickly and without involving the wider public in consultation. The Electoral Commission had some polling conducted that showed that people were happy with all-postal ballots.[90] However, it is suggested that this is not a true guide to public opinion because the whole picture has not been put before the public. If people are asked whether they prefer the convenience of postal voting to the inconvenience of a trip to the polling station it is hardly surprising which they will choose.

Electoral law does not need a quick fix. The preparation of a foundation model is important and the Commission should set a realistic timetable extending over at least two years. This will allow time for proper public consultation, which must extend well beyond the established political parties. However, it is also important that the Commission should obtain an authoritative legal view on the acceptability of alternative methods of voting. It was proposed in earlier work[91] that the Government should ask the Crown to refer the matter of alternative voting mechanisms to the Judicial Committee of the Privy Council under s 4 of the Judicial Committee Act 1833, which procedure was followed in *Re MacManaway*.[92] It is argued that the Electoral Commission should be asked to produce a comprehensive independent report on the modernisation of Britain's electoral laws and to propose legislation in the form of a draft Bill. This draft Bill should then be placed before the Queen with a request that it be referred to the full judicial committee under the s 4 of the Judicial Committee Act 1833 procedure.

It must be observed that the matter is one for the Queen, acting, it is to be presumed, upon the advice of her ministers, to refer to the Judicial Committee and not for the House of Commons itself to refer the matter to the Privy Council. The latter suggestion was made by Mr Anthony Wedgewood (Tony) Benn in *In re Parliamentary Election for Bristol South East*,[93] and is contrary to the plain words of the Act, although it accords with Tony Benn's views of political sovereignty. The important point about s 4 Judicial Committee Act 1833 procedure, apart from the authoritative nature of the judgment, is that (contrary to the *Bristol South East* petition case) the cost is borne by the public. It is submitted that all

---

90 See para 13 of *The Government's response to the Electoral Commission Report: Delivering Democracy? – the future of postal voting*, Cm 6436 of December 2004.

91 See Watt, B, http://www.local.regions.odpm.gov.uk/egov/e-voting/01/index.htm.

92 In *re MacManaway and In re The House of Commons (Clergy disqualification) Act 1801*, [1951] AC 161.

93 [1964] 2 QB 257.

costs in the matter of the determination of the legality of voting procedures should be borne by the public purse because it is a matter affecting all citizens equally. It has already been argued that the costs of election petitions ought similarly to be a public cost.

The Judicial Committee should subject the draft Bill to strict scrutiny in accordance with the approach set out by Lord Walker in *R (Pro-Life Alliance) v British Broadcasting Corporation*,[94] rather than the approach set out in *Associated Provincial Picture Houses Ltd v Wednesbury Corporation*.[95] Lord Walker took the following approach,

> I will highlight four principles which Laws LJ (in *International Transport Roth Gmbh v Secretary of State for the Home Department* [2003] QB 728, at 765–767) put forward (with the citation of appropriate authority) for the deference which the judicial arm of government should show to the other arms of government: (1) 'greater deference is to be paid to an Act of Parliament than to a decision of the executive or subordinate measure' (para 83); (2) 'there is more scope for deference "where the Convention itself requires a balance to be struck, much less so where the right is stated in terms which are unqualified" (per *Lord Hope in R v Secretary of State for the Home Department, Ex p Kebilene* [2000] 2 AC 326, 381)' (para 84); (3) 'greater deference will be due to the democratic powers where the subject matter in hand is peculiarly within their constitutional responsibility, and less when it lies more particularly within the constitutional responsibility of the courts' (para 85); (4) 'greater or less deference will be due according to whether the subject matter lies more readily within the actual or potential expertise of the democratic powers or the courts' (para 87).[96]

In relation to these four principles: (1) the Report of the Electoral Commission and its draft Bill would not be an Act of Parliament and therefore does not require deference to be paid to it; (2) the right in question, that contained in Art 3 of the 1st Protocol of the ECHR is, upon its face, an absolute right. Even before the entering into force of the Human Rights Act 1998, the right to vote was recognised as a fundamental right in English law. This point was made in *Ashby v White*, albeit in terms of an absolute right affixed to property and, more importantly and without qualification, by Lord Donaldson MR in *Hipperson*. Thus no deference need be paid to the Electoral Commission's interpretation of that right; (3) it is submitted that, despite the Resolutions of the House of Commons in 1704, the point remains that the determination of election law is within the proper constitutional responsibility of the courts; finally, (4) the determination of whether a

---

94 [2003] UKHL 23; [2004] 1 AC 185.

95 [1948] 1 KB 223.

96 [2003] UKHL 23; [2004] 1 AC 185, para 131.

scheme for accomplishing a lawful act (such as voting) is within or outside the law, as laid down in the Human Rights Act 1998 and the ECHR, must rest with the courts and, as we saw in *Knight v Nicholls*, ultimately with the European Court of Human Rights.

Clearly this is not to argue that the courts should go through the scheme provided by the Electoral Commission and undertake a review of its merits. All they are required to do is to examine whether the scheme measures up to the standard required to give full weight to the citizens' voice in a democratic society. This accords with the view taken by the House of Lords in *Ghaidan v Mendoza*, where they measured the Rent Act 1977 against the standards of the ECHR.

Neither is it to argue that parliament should be excluded from the process. It is desirable that the Judicial Committee should give a fully reasoned opinion, so as to alert parliament as to the principles to be observed in framing electoral legislation. Furthermore, there may well be options left open by the Electoral Commission – any or all of which may be acceptable to the courts – and it is quite right that parliament should have the opportunity to debate these options. Since, as we have noted above, governments with large majorities are able to push legislation through, some form of special majority or a measure of cross-party support ought to be required for the passage of the Bill.

It may be desirable for the resulting Act, following a full debate in parliament, to be approved by a special majority, but in any event it is argued that the final draft of the election law should be subject to approval in a referendum. It is submitted that such a referendum would have two important purposes. Clearly its formal purpose would be to secure the approval of the electorate for the electoral law. However, such a referendum would require a great deal of publicity, especially if the terms of the referendum were such that the electoral law required that it obtained the positive approval of more than half of the electorate. The engagement of the citizenry with electoral law may thus be secured.

A Burkean epilogue

This chapter effectively brings to an end the theoretical aspects of this book. In the final chapter we look at some practical matters, namely the judgment in the Birmingham City Council election petitions stemming from the two disputed wards fought in 2004 and the publication of the Electoral Commission's 'foundation model'. It seems appropriate to end the theoretical consideration with a brief discussion of the work of a writer who is usually seen as far removed from the liberal political tradition which has been advanced in this book. The purpose of this discussion of the work of Edmund Burke is to demonstrate that democratic renewal should not be seen as the concern of only one side of the political spectrum. The idea that democratic government is a matter of the engagement of all voters in the business of governance is of long standing. Burke shows how government is not to be regarded as the triumph of one set of political views over the alternatives, but is to be seen as the epitome of a deliberative process involving all citizens.

Generations of politics undergraduates have undoubtedly taken the view that Edmund Burke was a reactionary, patrician and undemocratic character.[97] However his *Speech to the Electors of Bristol of 3 November 1774* – too often paraphrased as a statement of the principle that members of parliament are not delegates, but representatives – is, in fact, both far more complex and far more enlightened. His position on the line between reaction and radicalism is, for the purposes of this argument, irrelevant, for here there is no endorsement of any political party.

We need to be clear about the distinction between delegates and representatives because it returns us to the heart of the debate between the market and democratic conceptions of citizenship. A delegate is, in the Burkean sense, a person who goes to parliament to argue for the views and interests of their constituents. This is, in fact, the conception of citizenship urged upon us by Lees-Marshment. In her view political parties should find out what the people want and then adjust their policies to suit them. The alternative conception is that of a Burkean representative – a member sent to parliament to consider the issues of governance – a representative person chosen by their peers to deliberate matters and act on their behalf.

It is suggested that just as electors ought to consider carefully who should govern on their behalf, members of the legislature ought to be in a position to carefully consider legislation. Thus the democratic model ought to run from the top to the bottom of a democratic polity.

What should such a representative 'look like'? Burke suggests that members should not be guided by personal friendships with members of the electorate. It ought to be recalled that Burke was one of the two Whig candidates returned to parliament by the electors of Bristol in 1774. His running mate, Henry Cruger, had thanked his friends for electing him to parliament and had said that he was 'the servant of my constituents, not their master, subservient to their will, not superior to it'.[98] Burke repudiated this view, saying that he was returned to parliament not to fulfil the mandates of his electorate, but to take part in parliament.

---

97 See Bromwich, 2000, p 10. Bromwich writes:

However embarrassing the admission would become on both sides, the truth is that Burke was a hero to radicals through most of his parliamentary career. Yet to call Burke a dissident suggests too narrow a reading of his politics. It is no better than the usual error of treating him as the father of modern conservatism.

98 Bromwich, 2000, p 48.

> Parliament is not a congress of ambassadors from different and hostile interests; which interests each must maintain, as an agent and advocate, against other agents and advocates; but parliament is a deliberative assembly of one nation, with one interest, that of the whole; where, not local purposes, not local prejudices ought to guide, but the general good, resulting from the general reason of the whole. You chuse [sic] a member indeed; but when you have chosen him, he is not member of Bristol, but he is a member of parliament. If the local constituent should have an interest, or should form a hasty opinion, evidently opposite to the real good of the rest of the community, the member for that place ought to be as far, as any other, from any endeavour to give it effect.[99]

Burke's view is, in effect, the position that has been stated a number of times in the present book. It is a key articulation; a proper expression of the principle of a representative democracy. Currently, electoral law fails to support this principle, delivering instead the choice between finished products, like 'cans of fizzy drink or sofas'. Lord Scott said, in *R (Pro-Life Alliance) v British Broadcasting Corporation*, as follows:

> One of the disturbing features of our present democracy is so-called voter-apathy. The percentage of registered voters who vote at general elections is regrettably low. A broadcasters' mind-set that rejects a party election television programme, dealing with an issue of undeniable public importance such as abortion, on the ground that large numbers of the voting public would find the programme 'offensive' denigrates the voting public, treats them like children who need to be protected from the unpleasant realities of life, seriously undervalues their political maturity and can only promote the voter-apathy to which I have referred.[100]

It is suggested that these words can be adapted to sum up the core argument presented in this book. Thus – it is clear that one of the disturbing features of our present democracy is so-called voter-apathy. The percentage of registered voters who vote at general elections is regrettably low. The problem is that political parties treat voters as consumers who must be consulted once every five years in the most convenient fashion, which is least likely to engage their critical faculties, and then exclude them from the political process. Those parties, who treat voters like children who need to be protected from the unpleasant realities of life, seriously undervalue their political maturity and thus promote the voter-apathy to which I have referred.

---

99   Bromwich, 2000, pp 55–56.
100   [2003] UKHL 23; [2004] 1 AC 185, at para 99.

Chapter 8:
The Immediate Future

The May 2005 general election provided us with some of the breathing space which was requested in the preceding chapter. The Electoral Commission published its proposals for a Foundation Model for elections at the end of May 2005 in its paper *Securing the Vote*[1] and the government announced its intention to bring forward an Electoral Administration Bill in the Queen's Speech.[2] The Department of Constitutional Affairs swiftly responded to *Securing the Vote* and the Electoral Commission published a summary of the 45 main proposals made in the paper together with the Department's responses. Thirty-two of the Electoral Commission's proposals have been accepted immediately by the Department, whilst 11 have been highlighted as rejected, although in the text the Commission notes that many of their proposals have not been squarely addressed. The remaining two proposals are, according to the Commission, still under consideration by the Department. On the face of it this looks like a victory for the Commission but, as is argued throughout this book, it can be seen as a coming together of elite groups without popular involvement. This is further indicated by the speed of the transaction between the Commission and the Department. Furthermore the government re-elected in May 2005 has, despite its reduced majority, sufficient support to push the measure into legislation in the next parliamentary session. It does not appear likely that there will be widespread public consultation. The main themes of the joint Electoral Commission–Department of Constitutional Affairs approach are set out below.

---

1   London; Electoral Commission, 2005.
2   Legislation will be brought forward to encourage greater voter participation in elections while introducing further measures to combat fraud and increase security.

However, before we proceed to examine the proposals in *Securing the Vote* we should examine in detail the decisions in the Birmingham Election Petitions[3] deriving from the June 2004 City Council Elections.

The Birmingham election petitions were brought to contest City Council elections held in the Bordesley Green and Aston wards in June 2004. It was alleged that the elections in these wards were tainted by serious irregularities in the handling and completion of postal voting papers by the some of the candidates and their agents. The election results were overturned by an Election Court presided over by Commissioner Mawrey QC on 4 April 2005 on the grounds that the winning (Labour) candidates had engaged in corrupt and illegal practices and, more tellingly that the elections should be avoided for general corruption under s 164 Representation of the People Act 1983 (RPA 1983). The voiding of an election for general corruption is a very rare event indeed. The only clear case of general corruption which has been reported is the *Borough of Bridgewater*[4] in 1869. It seems clear from Commissioner Mawrey's judgment that the whole issue of postal voting, and perhaps other forms of remote voting, must be closely scrutinised after the election before the Foundation Model can be finalised. This book will, it is hoped, serve as a contribution to the forthcoming debate surrounding the Foundation Model. Such a debate should not, for the reasons set out in this book, be restricted to parliament.

---

3 *In the matter of a Local Government Election for the Bordesley Green Ward of the Birmingham City Council held on 10th June 2004 and in the matter of a Local Government Election for the Aston Ward of the Birmingham City Council held on 10th June 2004*. Election Court Unreported. Uncorrected Judgment of 4th April 2005. I am extremely grateful to John Owen of the Elections Department of Birmingham City Council who supplied me with a copy of the uncorrected judgment. See too, *R (on the application of Afzal) v Election Court* [2005] EWCA Civ 647 in which the penalty imposed upon Mr Afzal was removed. However the final paragraph of the judgment of the Court of Appeal is telling:

>   46 The Commissioner was faced with a large volume of complex evidence. He was under time constraints having regard to the need to resolve an election Petition promptly and the fact that there is a one-year time limit for most electoral offences. His judgment, extending to 185 pages, is a model of clarity. His findings of general corruption and of personal corruption on the part of the three Bordesley Green Labour Party respondents and the other two Aston Labour Party respondents have not been challenged. The procedural shortcomings that we have identified in relation to the manner in which he dealt with the case made against Mr Azfal should not be permitted to distort the overall picture painted by the Commissioner's otherwise admirable judgment.

4 (1869) 1 O'M & H 112. However reference is also made to the matter in *Guildford* (1869) 1 O'M & H 15 and *Lichfield* (1869) 1 O'M & H 22 in which it was held not to have taken place and in *Borough of Worcester* (1906) 5 O'M & H 212 in which it would seem that the election was avoided for general corruption.

The Birmingham Election Petitions

Election petitions were lodged against the successful Labour candidates in the Bordesley Green and Aston wards of Birmingham City Council alleging that the councillors had only succeeded in the election by corrupt means. In particular the allegations promoted by the People's Justice Party and the Liberal Democrats said that the victorious candidates had fraudulently obtained a number of postal ballot papers, and completed and submitted them. This would amount to the election offence of personation under s 60 RPA 1983[5] and is a corrupt practice, ie, one of the most serious election offences.

The essence of the allegations was that some of the candidates and their helpers were involved in filling in postal votes for electors. For example, the impugned Labour candidates in the Aston election were caught in a warehouse with a number of voting papers in front of them. To use the words of Commissioner Mawrey QC who described what happened when the police raided a warehouse where, it was alleged ballot papers were being completed:[6]

> 501 Taking as my starting point that I am satisfied that there were open envelopes and yellow ballot papers visible on the table when the police arrived, it seems to me that there are only two real possibilities as to what the men present were doing:
>
> (a) they were filling out blank ballot papers; and/or
>
> (b) they were examining properly completed ballot papers with a view to altering or destroying those which did not vote Labour.
>
> 502 Both these activities constitute personation and consequently both constitute corrupt practices. I am quite satisfied that these men were not at the warehouse for any innocent purpose and that they were engaged in corrupt practices.
>
> 503 I am unable to make any finding as to how many ballot papers were involved. It is known that, at about 4.00 am on 9th June 2004, the police took possession of 275 B envelopes which were subsequently delivered to Mr Owen but whether they represented the totality of the documents present in the warehouse on the first occasion the police called, I have no idea. All I can say, therefore, is that *at least* 275 ballots were involved.

5   Section 60(1) A person shall be guilty of a corrupt practice if he commits, or aids, abets, counsels or procures the commission of, the offence of personation. (2) A person shall be deemed to be guilty of personation at a parliamentary or local government election if he – (a) votes in person or by post as some other person, whether as an elector or as proxy and whether that other person is living or dead or is a fictitious person.

6   The quotations are taken from the numbered paragraphs in Commissioner Mawrey's judgment.

504 From this it follows that I am satisfied that each of the three Labour Party Respondents, together with Mr Zulfiqar Khan and the Najibs, father and son, were engaged in corrupt practices on that night. That said, I see no purpose in naming either the two Najibs or Mr Tariq Hussain in my report. At worst, they were mere foot soldiers in this fraud: the generals were the candidates and their 'Ward organiser'.[7]

Whilst it is doubted whether the examination 'of properly completed ballot papers with a view to altering or destroying those which did not vote Labour' does in fact amount to the offence of personation as stated in paragraph 502. It appears to be an offence under s 65(1)(b) RPA 1983[8] which carries, on summary conviction a fine and/or a sentence of imprisonment. However, that having been said, the point of principle remains. It is quite clear from the facts held in the Birmingham case that the operation of remote voting systems is fraught with practical difficulties. Foremost amongst these is the point revealed in the Birmingham petitions that representatives of a political party, in this case the Labour Party, were involved in the collection of postal votes from electors prior to the votes being received and counted by the electoral officials. These practical difficulties, or opportunities for fraud, are in addition to the doctrinal difficulties set out in this book, in particular the averred incompatibility of a remote voting system with Art 3 of the 1st Protocol to the European Convention on Human Rights (ECHR). Whilst the Convention does not apply to local government elections because local government is not a legislature – which is the body mentioned in the Protocol – it is quite clear that Commissioner Mawrey's warning in par 703 of the judgment is highly apposite. If this level of electoral fraud had prevailed in the May 2005 general election it is beyond doubt that election petitions would have been brought and the courts obliged to consider the ECHR point. It will be seen in the Birmingham judgment, at par 717, that the Commissioner concluded that the mechanisms for realistically dealing with electoral fraud are simply non-existent. If the Commissioner is correct in this conclusion, and it is argued that he is,[9] it follows that the mechanisms for ensuring that the general election will be free and fair within the terms of Art 3 of the 1st Protocol ECHR are similarly lacking.

---

7   Quotation from the numbered paragraphs in the uncorrected judgment.

8   A person shall be guilty of an offence, if, at a parliamentary or local government election, he fraudulently defaces or fraudulently destroys any ballot paper, ...

9   See, too, the judgment in *R (on the application of Afzal) v Election Court* [2005] EWCA Civ 647 which supports the view that the irregularities in Birmingham went to the root of the electoral process despite the procedural fault which vitiated Afzal's penalty.

Commissioner Richard Mawrey QC's judgment is concluded by a summary of his opinion of the current state of UK remote voting law. It is hoped that this will convince the Electoral Commission to abandon attempts to introduce remote voting and prompt the courts to examine the ECHR point thoroughly in any forthcoming Parliamentary Election Petition. Given that Commissioner Mawrey heard all of the evidence in the Birmingham case he must be acknowledged as the leading expert on the ways in which the electoral system may be manipulated. For that reason it is useful to quote his concluding words in their entirety. No further endorsement is required. The concluding paragraphs read:[10]

> 703 It must be heartrending for Mr Owen (Birmingham City Council's Elections Officer – author's addition) to see massive electoral fraud committed, almost before his eyes, knowing that he was powerless to do anything about it. What is more he knows that, as no steps have been taken to improve the situation, he may face a re-run of the 2004 débâcle in the forthcoming General Election.

> 704–711 (omitted).

> 712 The conclusions of what I realise is a very long judgment are as follows:

> (a) The election for the Bordesley Green Ward on 10th June 2004 was avoided by corrupt and illegal practices on the part of the three Labour Party Respondents

>> (i) Mr Shah Jahan

>> (ii) Mr Shafaq Ahmed

>> (iii) Mr Ayaz Khan.

> (b) The election for the Bordesley Green Ward on 10th June 2004 was also avoided for general corruption within section 164 of the Representation of the People Act 1983 in that corrupt and illegal practices for the purpose of promoting or procuring the election of the three said Labour Party Respondents have so extensively prevailed that they may reasonably be supposed to have affected the result of such election.

> (c) The election of each of the three said Labour Party Respondents for the Ward of Bordesley Green shall be void under sections 159(1) and 164(1)(a) of the said Act.

> (d) Each of the three said Labour Party Respondents shall be incapable of being elected to fill any of the vacancies for the Ward of Bordesley Green under section 164(1)(b) of the said Act.

---

10   Quotation from the numbered paragraphs in the uncorrected judgment.

(e) The election for the Aston Ward on 10th June 2004 was avoided by corrupt and illegal practices on the part of the three Labour Party Respondents

(i) Mr Mohammed Nazrul Islam

(ii) Mr Muhammed Afzal[11]

(iii) Mr Mohammed Amin Kazi.

(f) The election for the Aston Ward on 10th June 2004 was also avoided for general corruption within section 164 of the Representation of the People Act 1983 in that corrupt and illegal practices for the purpose of promoting or procuring the election of the three said Labour Party Respondents have so extensively prevailed that they may reasonably be supposed to have affected the result of such election.

(g) The election of each of the three said Labour Party Respondents for the Ward of Aston shall be void under sections 159(1) and 164(1)(a) of the said Act.

(h) Each of the three said Labour Party Respondents shall be incapable of being elected to fill any of the vacancies for the Ward of Aston under section 164(1)(b) of the said Act.

(i) The claims of the Petitioners in the Bordesley Green Petition against the Returning Officer have not been made out to the standard required by section 48(1) of the said Act and are dismissed.

(j) The claims of the Petitioners in the Aston Petition against the Returning Officer have not been made out to the standard required by section 48(1) of the said Act and are dismissed.

(k) There is reason to believe that corrupt practices have extensively prevailed at the elections of 10th June 2004 throughout the area of Birmingham City Council.

713 …

Afterword

714 In this judgment I have set out at length what has clearly been shown to be the weakness of the current law relating to postal votes. As some parts of this judgment may be seen as critical of the Government, I wish to make it clear that the responsibility for the present unsatisfactory situation must be shared. All political parties welcomed and supported postal voting on demand. Until very recently, none has treated electoral fraud as representing a problem. Apart from the

---

11 Mr Afzal was successful in his appeal against the penalty imposed in *R (on the application of Afzal) v Election Court* [2005] EWCA Civ 647.

Electoral Commission, whose rôle I have described above, the only voices raised against the laxity of the system have been in the media, in particular *The Times* newspaper, and the tendency of politicians of all Parties has been to dismiss these warnings as scaremongering.

715 In the course of preparing my judgment, my attention was drawn to what I am told is an official Government statement about postal voting which I hope I quote correctly:

> *There are no proposals to change the rules governing election procedures for the next election, including those for postal voting. The systems already in place to deal with the allegations of electoral fraud are clearly working.*

716 Anybody who has sat through the case I have just tried and listened to evidence of electoral fraud that would disgrace a banana republic would find this statement surprising. To assert that "The systems already in place to deal with the allegations of electoral fraud are clearly working" indicates a state not simply of complacency but of denial.

717 The systems to deal with fraud are not working well. They are not working badly. The fact is that there are *no* systems to deal realistically with fraud and there never have been. Until there are, fraud will continue unabated.

It cannot be sufficiently emphasised that the main problem identified by Commissioner Mawrey is the opportunity for political parties, or unscrupulous candidates representing political parties, to commit electoral fraud. It is not claimed or even remotely suggested that the national Labour Party endorsed this, or any, level of electoral fraud, indeed the impugned candidates were expelled by the Party and their legal representation withdrawn at an early stage in the proceedings. It must also be mentioned at this stage, before we enter the detailed discussion of the 'agreed' proposals that there are two other problems which have been identified with remote voting – the susceptibility of the vote to peer pressure from family or friends – and, most importantly, the personalisation of the vote.

Securing the Vote: the Electoral Commission's proposals

It was noted earlier in this chapter that there is no apparent substantial difference in opinion or approach between the Electoral Commission and the Department of Constitutional Affairs regarding the next stage in reforming the UK's electoral laws. The principle of 'postal voting on demand' discussed in Chapter 7 has been conceded by the Electoral Commission and the main thrust of the paper – reflected in Recommendations 7–22 and 39–42 – is to attempt to control the abuses of the process. It is not intended that the discussion set out below contains a full account of the Electoral Commission's proposals. Some of the proposals deal with minor matters of electoral administration whilst others are broadly uncontroversial. The focus here is upon matters considered at length earlier in the book. The Commission's proposals – broadly accepted by the Department – fall into five main classes.[12]

(1) Electoral registration (Recommendations 1–5, 30)

(2) Voting procedures at the polling station (Recommendations 6, 31–38)

(3) Postal voting (Recommendations 7–22, 39–42)

(4) Proxy voting (Recommendations 23–24)

(5) Electoral administration and general anti corruption measures (Recommendations 25–29, 43–45).

Electoral registration

The proposals suggest that household registration should be replaced by individual registration and voters should be required to provide individual means of identification to the Electoral Registration Officer in addition to their name and qualifying address when registering to vote. It would become a criminal offence to fail to supply such information or to supply false information. The electoral registers would be constructed and maintained electronically; the submission of identification details would facilitate telephone or online amendment. Electoral Registration Officers should have new powers to investigate objections to registrations (including objections raised by themselves) at any time.

The deadline for registering to vote for a particular election should be moved so that it is the same date as the close of nominations. This would mean that voters would be able to join the appropriate Register up until 11 working days before polling day in parliamentary elections and up to 19 working days before the poll in other elections

Clearly individual registration is much to be preferred to household registration because that lessens the possibility that subordinate members of the household will be left off the register; however whilst it is currently a criminal offence not to register to vote actual prosecutions are few. It has been reported that in a sample of 500 students in 1997, only 75% were registered to vote.[13] Perhaps electoral registration could

---

12   In their paper they use seven headings but these lack logical clarity.

13   See Huggins, R 'The transformation of the political audience' in Axford B and Huggins R (eds) *New Media and Politics*, 2001, London: Sage at p 129. Huggins' chapter contains some useful comments on electoral registration by young people

be enforced by some form of fixed penalty system but the problem is that any form of electoral registration depends upon the person having a known contract address of some sort and this contact address has to be known by the electoral authorities prior to registration in order for the threat of sanction to be meaningful.

Despite the practical difficulties however the Electoral Commission's proposals are to be welcomed because they may succeed in facilitating a compulsory system of voting and in lessening the opportunities for domestic pressure.

Voting in the polling station

The Electoral Commission has proposed that the controls against personation should be strengthened with Presiding Officers being empowered to make more searching enquiries of those who wish to vote and to require evidence of identity. Clearly this must be welcomed. Furthermore, in Recommendation 26 (and apparently as a direct result of the Birmingham cases) the Commission has recommended that police officers should have the power to arrest persons whom they reasonably suspect of personation at whatever location they find them. This must be supported for the reason made plain throughout this book; corruption must not, in the interest of all citizens, be allowed to taint the electoral process.

The second proposal that is worthy of note is that provision should be made within the legislation to allow young people accompanying voters to be admitted to the polling station at the discretion of the presiding officer. This, too, must be welcomed although it must be recognised that many presiding officers already allow this to take place. Presiding officers also sometimes admit non-voters (such as foreign students of election law) to polling stations. Why it is thought necessary to restrict admission to young people accompanying voters is unclear; there seems to be no good reason why relays of schoolchildren undergoing citizenship education should not be admitted in order to familiarise them with the administration and conduct of elections provided that the presiding officer is confident that order can be kept in the polling station.

Some of the Commission's proposals are directed to the general supervision and oversight of the electoral process. There is, at present, no opportunity for international or national Election Observers to enter polling stations and the Commission itself is broadly excluded from practical oversight, although it has a statutory duty under the Political Parties Elections and Referendums Act 2000 (PPERA) to report on electoral administration. One of the main arguments in this book has been that elections must be closely supervised in the interest of the whole polity. These proposals seem to increase the levels of scrutiny.

Postal voting

Increasing the level of supervision of postal votes is one of the main themes of the Electoral Commission paper. The present Labour government and its predecessor have made their commitment to postal voting on demand absolutely clear.[14] Accordingly it is unsurprising that the Department of Constitutional Affairs has accepted most of the Commission's proposals. Those which have not been explicitly accepted seem not to have been directly discussed by the Department. The most important postal voting proposals are set out below in the Commission's own words:

7   All postal vote applications should include personal identification details collected at registration (we recommend date of birth), as well as the applicant's signature. Electoral Registration Officers in Great Britain should verify the personal identification details provided on all postal vote applications against those collected at registration. Electoral Registration Officers should also be able to refer to records of electors' signatures to verify any doubtful applications.

8   The deadline for electors to apply for a postal vote, or to change their existing postal vote delivery details, should be moved from six to 11 working days before polling day to allow more efficient and accurate production of postal ballot packs.

9   Once individuals are required to provide a signature and other identification details as part of the registration process, electors should be allowed to indicate an application for a postal vote or other remote voting method on the registration form.

10 The law should be revised to provide that postal vote applications must bear the return postal address of the Electoral Registration Officer at their normal place of business; or, if an alternative option is needed, the address of a central sorting house which is operated independently of political parties.

The latest in this list is one of the most important proposals to come from the Commission and seems to be a direct outcome of the Birmingham electoral petitions. However it is surprising that the proposal does not go much further. The problem in Aston and Bordesley Green was that the impugned candidates and their helpers were collecting marked and

---

14   See the discussion in Chapter 7.

unmarked postal ballot papers from electors. These were subjected to interference – by being filled in or by being destroyed. However it was quite clear that political parties throughout the country were engaged in the collection and handling of postal votes. One of the questionable practices used by the political parties in a number of elections was for party workers to canvass armed with applications for postal votes and invite their supporters to complete them. They would then submit the postal vote applications in bulk. This would facilitate a second stage in the process. After the postal votes had been issued by the electoral administrators to electors, party workers would then visit all those who had applied for postal votes and those who already had postal votes and urge their supporters to mark the voting papers and hand over the completed and sealed ballots. The reasoning was that if voters could be persuaded to complete the ballot by a party worker and then hand it over, the voter would not have the opportunity to forget to vote or to forget to post the ballot paper in time for it to be counted. Presently there is nothing illegal in this practice and it is beyond doubt that it will increase turnout because votes are collected from those who would not otherwise venture near a ballot paper. The Commission's proposal does not seem to render illegal the second step in the process and it would seem, from Commissioner Mawrey's findings in the Birmingham petitions that the second stage process gives just as much as an opportunity for abuse as the first stage. The other way in which the electoral process could be corrupted is by the political party making wholly fraudulent applications for postal votes by using non-existent electors or by making applications in respect of real electors but in respect of false addresses which would then act as collecting points for ballot papers to be completed by the electoral cheats. The problem with allowing political parties such access to ballot papers is that it can give rise to the appearance of unfairness and thus reduce trust in the election process. It is therefore quite clear that the only acceptable way for postal voting applications to be made and processed – if they are to be permitted at all – is for individual electors to make applications for postal votes individually and for political parties to be denied access to bulk supplies of postal voting application forms at any stage of the process. The forms should not be made available to political parties to distribute during the canvass. It is beyond doubt that the political parties will object to the proposal made here because they see themselves as the 'big players' in the political process – those with the responsibility to mobilise the vote. The argument in this book is, of course, against this view; political parties are part of the consequence of the political process rather than drivers of politics.

The Commission's proposal, which has been endorsed by the Department of Constitutional Affairs, that there should be a new electoral offence designed to prevent fraudulent applications for postal votes, with the maximum penalty being a custodial sentence in line with the penalties for personation, is to be welcomed insofar as it goes. The problem with the proposal is that it individualises the offence and places the culpability onto the individual perpetrators. It is suggested that where political parties are engaged in the offence – as would seem to be the case in the Birmingham case outlined above – that the party itself should bear the penalty. It is impractical to imprison all the members of a party and it would seem to be unjust to gaol, for example, the party's Nominating Officer, but it is quite possible to bar the party from contesting any election in the relevant electoral division for the period of five years prescribed as the period of disenfranchisement consequent upon conviction for a corrupt offence:

The Commission's Recommendations 14, 15 and 19 are of the first importance. The first suggests that plain English guides are sent out with postal voting packs. This can only be of assistance. Fifteen and 19 are reproduced in their entirety:

15 The current declaration of identity should be replaced with a new security statement to accompany postal ballots. This security statement should include a statement signed by the voter that they are the individual to whom the ballot paper was addressed, and the voter should also give their date of birth. The security statement should not require any form of witness signature. It should include a clear explanation of the role and use of the declaration, in particular the fact that failure to complete the statement will render a ballot paper invalid.

19 It should become a legal requirement that secrecy warnings are included on postal voting literature; these warnings should be specified in law.

These provisions go some way towards ensuring that remote voting is treated with the same level of secrecy as voting in the polling station The wording of the secrecy warning is important and should be the subject of wide political and, in accordance with the aim of this book, *public* debate. It is therefore firstly proposed that the statement starts by making it clear that:

The aim of securing secrecy of the ballot is to ensure that all citizens have a full opportunity to participate, through their freely chosen representatives, in the governance of the country.

This is, for the reasons set out in this book, to be preferred to, for example:

The aim of securing secrecy of the ballot is to ensure that all citizens have the opportunity freely to participate in choosing the government.

It is suggested that the preferred form of this statement contains a thinner ideological commitment than the second draft. It is more consistent with a state of free, self-governing, and rational individuals than the second form which posits a distance between the superior governing class and the inferior governed. However it does not (and should not) say anything about the scope of government or about its 'size'; these are more properly the subjects of political debate between the parties vying for government.

It is proposed that the statement should continue by pointing out that electors should fill in their own ballot papers in accordance with their own judgement and should not allow others to dictate how they should vote. Whilst other people may well have important and valuable things to say about politics and the way that the country should be governed, the voter's own judgment is that which should determine the way in which they vote. Voters should not allow someone to watch them whilst they vote nor should they allow them to inspect their completed ballot paper. In no circumstance should a voter give their blank or completed ballot paper to someone else but should return it to the Returning Officer by an approved means. For the avoidance of doubt it should be made plain that interfering with another person's vote is a serious criminal offence.

Recommendation 27, which has not been approved by the Department of Constitutional Affairs, is also of use here. It deals with the law of 'undue influence'.[15] The Electoral Commission has recommended that the law of undue influence which has been discussed throughout this book, should be amended to make the nature of the offence clear. The nature of influences upon a voter is, of course and at first sight, a matter of controversy[16] and it may be for this reason that the Department has not yet approved the recommendation made by the Commission. However it is argued that there is a simple explanation of the offence of undue influence which makes the reason for its criminalisation plain and suggests a way in which the law can be clarified. Herring writes, after giving an example, that the paradigm form of blackmail that it is 'a threat to do a completely lawful activity'. His example is 'A tells S that he will tell S's husband that she is adulterous, and invites her to give him some money to prevent him

---

15   See s 115 Representation of the People Act 1983.

16   For a survey of the justifications given for the crime of blackmail, which at first sight seems to be congruent with 'undue influence' see Herring, J, *Criminal Law: Text, cases and Materials*, 2004, Oxford: OUP at pp 584–588.

informing on her'. Both of A's actions are lawful when performed in isolation, but together they amount to blackmail. A person who unduly influences another voter says to them, 'Vote for x, rather than for your own choice y or I will impose an otherwise lawful sanction upon you.' This is, in effect, saying that unless you let me vote for you I will sanction you. Depriving another person of their vote and voting in their place is, as we have seen, personation which is in itself a criminal offence. A simple clarification of the law of undue influence could be undertaken and a statement added to the postal voting pack to say that: 'Telling someone how to vote and threatening them with an unpleasant consequence is equivalent to voting instead of them and is a serious criminal offence.'

There are other matters which are discussed in *Securing the Vote* and in the Commission's follow up paper, but the foregoing seem to be the most important.

At the end of this book it remains simply to say that the forthcoming Electoral Administration Bill offers a chance to encourage greater citizen participation in governance rather than simply 'greater voter participation in elections'[17] and it is hoped that the government will seize the opportunity.

---

17 See Chapter 8 n 2 above – the quotation is from the Queen's Speech.

Bibliography |

Government Publications

All published by the Stationery Office: London, in the year shown

Conference on electoral reform: letter from Mr Speaker to the Prime Minister, Cmnd 8463, 1917

Conference on electoral reform: letter from Viscount Ullswater to the Prime Minister, Cmd 3636, 1930

Conference on electoral reform and redistribution of seats: letter from Mr Speaker to the Prime Minister, Cmd 6534, 1944

Final report of the Committee on Electoral Law Reform, Cmd 7286, 1947

Conference on electoral law: letter dated thirty-first January, 1967 from Mr Speaker to the Prime Minister, Cmnd 3202, 1967

Report of the Committee on financial aid to political parties, Cmnd 6601, 1976

The funding of political parties in the United Kingdom: The Government's proposals for legislation in response to the Fifth Report of the Committee on Standards in Public Life, Cm 4413, 1999

The Government's response to the Electoral Commission Report: Delivering Democracy? – the future of postal voting, Cm 6436, 2004

The Jenkins Commission, *The Report of the Independent Commission on the Voting System,* Cm 4090-I &II, 1998

Hansard, House of Commons Debates

The House of Commons Research Paper 01/75 of 22 October 2001

Eighth Report of the 2003–04 Session of the Select Committee on Human Rights. Also at www.publications.parliament.uk/pa/jt200304/jtselect/jtrights/49/4906.htm

Hansard, Commons Vol 7 75, Col 1404, 18 December 1968

Electoral Commission Publications

All published by The Electoral Commission: London, in the year shown.

Electoral Commission's Circular EC29/2002

Electoral pilots at the June 2004 elections, 2003

Party political broadcasting: report and recommendations, 2003

Voting for Change: an electoral law modernisation programme, 2003

The shape of elections to come: a strategic evaluation of the 2003 electoral pilot schemes, 2003

Age of Electoral Majority: report and recommendations, 2004

An audit of political engagement, 2004

Delivering Democracy? the future of postal voting: the road ahead, 2004

Securing the Vote, 2005

Other Reports

Report of the Hansard Society Commission on Electoral Reform, 1976, London: Hansard Society

Electoral reform: fairer voting in natural communities: first report of the Joint Liberal/SDP Commission on Constitutional Reform, 1982, London: Poland St Pubs

Elections in the 21st Century: from paper ballot to e-voting. Report of the Independent Commission on Alternative Voting Methods, 2002, London: Electoral Reform Society

Pratchett, L, et al, *The implementation of electronic voting in the UK*, 2002, London: Dept for Local Govt & the Regions

Books and Articles

Bagehot, *Essays on Parliamentary Reform*, 1965–78, London: The Economist

Baker, JH, *Manual of Law French*, 1990, Aldershot: Scolar

Bamforth, N and Leyland, P, *Public Law in a Multi-Layered Constitution*, 2003, Oxford: Hart

Barendt, E, *Freedom of Speech*, 1985, Oxford: Clarendon

Barrett, P, 'The Tories swap vitriol for humour in bid to useat Blair', 23 March 2004, *Gaurdian*.

Baston, L and Ritchie, K, *An Analysis of Political Engagement and What can be Done About It*, 2004, London: Electoral Reform Society

Baudrillard, J, *The Consumer Society*, 1998, Thousand Oaks CA: Sage Publications Inc

Beckett, F, *Clem Attlee: A Biography*, 2000, London: Politico's

Belchem, J, *Popular Radicalism in 19th Century Britain*, 1996, Basingstoke: Macmillan

Belchem, J, *'Orator' Hunt: Henry Hunt and English Working Class Radicalism*, 1985, Oxford: OUP

Bellman, H, *The Building Society Movement*, 1927, London: Hutchinson.

Birch, S and Watt, B, 'Remote electronic voting: free fair and secret?' (2004) 75(1), *Political Quarterly* pp 60–72

Brailsford, HN and Hill, C (eds), *The Levellers and the English Revolution*, 1961, London: Cresset

Brennan, G and Lomasky, L, *Democracy and Decision: The Pure Theory of Electoral Preference*, 1997, Cambridge: CUP

Brennan, G and Pettit, P, 'Unveiling the vote', (1990) 20 *British Journal of Political Science*

Bromwich, D (ed), *On Empire, Liberty and Reform; Speeches and Letters of Edmund Burke*, 2000, New Haven: Yale UP

Butler, M and King, A, *The British General Election of 1964*, 1965, London: Macmillan

Calder, A, *The People's War: Britain 1939–1945*, 1969, London: Jonathan Cape

Calvert, C, 'The voyeurism value in First Amendment jurisprudence' (2000) 17 *Cardozo Arts and Entertainment Law Journal* 273

Clayton, R (ed), *Parker's Law and Conduct of Elections*, 1996, London: Butterworths (plus updates)

Crewe, I, 'Has the electorate become Thatcherite?', in Skidelsky R (ed), *Thatcherism*, 1988, London: Chatto & Windus

Curtice, J and Seyd, B, 'Is there a crisis of political participation?', in Park *et al* (eds), *British Social Attitudes: The 20th Report*, 2004, London: Sage

Dickens, C, *The Pickwick Papers*, 1992, London: Penguin

Dowd, K, 'Participation in civil society', in Lewis, DN and Campbell, D (eds), *Promoting Participation: Law or Politics?*, 1999, London: Cavendish Publishing

Dworkin, RM, *Law's Empire*, 1986, London: Fontana

Ewing, KD, *The Funding of Political Parties in Britain*, 1987, Cambridge: CUP

Feldman, D, *Civil Liberties and Human Rights in England and Wales*, 2002, Oxford: OUP

Foot, M, *Aneurin Bevan*, 1975, London: Granada

Forsyth, F, *The Fourth Protocol*, 1984, London: Hutchinson

Fox, A, *History and Heritage: The Social Origins of the British Industrial Relations System*, 1985, London: Allen & Unwin

Fredman, S, *Women and the Law*, 1997, Oxford: Clarendon

Freedland, M, 'Law, Public Services, and Citizenship – New Domains, New regimes?', in Freedland, M and Sciarra, S (eds), *Public Services and Citizenship in European Law*, 1998, Oxford: Clarendon

Glover, J, *Humanity: A Moral History of the 20th Century*, 1999, London: Jonathan Cape

Goodrich, LM, *The United Nations*, 1959, New York: Crowell

Goodwin-Gill, G, *Free and Fair Elections: International Law and Practice*, 1994, Geneva: Inter-Parliamentary Union

Graves, R, *The Anger of Achilles*, 1961, London: Cassell

Gray, K, *Elements of Land Law*, 2nd edn, 1993, London: Butterworths

Gray, K and Gray, SF, *Elements of Land Law*, 3rd edn, 2001, London: Butterworths

Griew, E, 'Dishonesty: the objections to *Feely* and *Ghosh*' (1985) *Criminal Law Review* 341

Hadfield, B, 'Does the devolved Northern Ireland need an independent judicial arbiter', in Bamforth, N and Leyland, P (eds), *Public Law in a Multi-Layered Constitution*, 2003, Oxford: Hart

Hailsham, (Lord), *The Dilemma of Democracy*, 1978, London: Collins

Halpin, A, 'The test for dishonesty' (1996) *Criminal Law Review* 283

Harrison, JFC, *The Common People: A History from the Norman Conquest to the Present*, 1984, London: Croom Helm

Harvey, C, 'It all started with Gunner James' (1986) *Denning LJ* 67

Hohfeld, WN, *Fundamental Legal Conceptions as Applied in Judicial Reasoning*, 1978, Westport, CT: Greenwood Press

Holdsworth, W, *A History of English Law Vol X*, 1966, London: Methuen

Homer, *Iliad*, 1992 (trans Fitzgerald), London: Everyman

Johnston, RJ, *Money and Votes: Constituency Campaign Spending and Election Results*, 1987, Beckenham: Croom Helm

Jones, N, *The Control Freaks: How New Labour Gets its Own Way*, 2001, London: Politico's

Jones, T, *Remaking the Labour Party: From Gaitskell to Blair*, 1996, London: Routledge

Kelman, M, 'Trashing', (1984) 36 *Stanford Law Review* 293

Lee, J, *My life with Nye*, 1980, London: Cape

Lees-Marshment, J, *Political Marketing and British Political Parties: The Party's Just Begun*, 2001, Manchester: Manchester UP

Leonard, T, 'Will ITV's search for an MP win viewer's votes?', 16 April 2004, *Daily Telegraph*

Little, W, Brown, L and Trumble, W (eds), *Shorter Oxford English Dictionary*, 2nd edn, 2002, Oxford: OUP

MacNeil, IR and Campbell, D (eds), *The Relational Theory of Contract: Selected Works of Ian MacNeil*, 2001, London: Sweet & Maxwell

Mandelson, P and Liddle, R, *The Blair Revolution: Can New Labour Deliver?*, 1996, London: Faber & Faber

Martin, JE, *Hanbury and Maudsley's Modern Equity*, 12th edn, 1985, London: Stevens

Mates, R, Scallan, A and Gribble, P (eds), *Schofield's Election Law*, 2nd edn, 1996, London: Shaw & Sons (plus updates)

McDonald, H, 'Tactical voting can save the peace', 3 June 2001, *Guardian*

McLean, I and Butler, D (eds), *Fixing the Boundaries: Defining and Redefining Single-member Electoral Districts*, 1996, Aldershot: Dartmouth

Mill, JS, *Considerations on Representative Government*, 1991, New York: Prometheus Books

Minford, P, 'Mrs Thatcher's Economic Reform Programme', in Skidelsky, R, *Thatcherism*, 1988, London: Chatto & Windus, pp 93-106,

Norris, P, *Digital Divide: Civic Engagement, Information Poverty and the Internet Worldwide*, 2001, Cambridge: CUP

Norris, P, 'The battle for the campaign agenda', in King, A (ed), *New Labour triumphs*, 1998, Chatham NJ: Chatham House

Pankhurst, ES, *The Suffragette Movement*, 1977, London: Virago

Parfit, D, *Reasons & Persons*, 1984, Oxford: Clarendon

Pickering, Statutes at large, 1762-1807, Cambridge: CUP

Pimlott, B, 'The future of the Left', in Skidelsky, R (ed), *Thatcherism*, 1988, London: Chatto and Windus

Pinto-Duchinsky, M, *British Political Finance 1830–1980*, 1981, Washington DC: Am Ent Inst

Plucknett, TFT, *A Concise History of the Common Law*, 5th edn, 1956, London: Butterworth

Plunkett, J, '"Political idol" loses Campbell's vote', 20 April 2004, *Media Guardian*

Rallings, M and Thrasher, C, *Public Opinion and the 2004 Elections*, 2003, London: Electoral Commission

Rallings, M and Thrasher, C, *British Electoral Facts 1832–1999*, 2000, Aldershot: Ashgate

Rawls, J, *A Theory of Justice*, 1972, Oxford: OUP

Raz, J, *The Morality of Freedom*, 1986, Oxford: Clarendon

Rossiter, CJ, Johnston, RJ and Pattie, CJ, *The Boundary Commissions: Redrawing the UK's Map of Parliamentary Constituencies*, 1999, Manchester: Manchester UP

Samuels, A, 'Is the Parliament Act 1949 valid? Could it be challenged?' (2003) 24 *Statute Law Review* 237–42

Seymour, C, *Electoral Reform in England and Wales: The Development and Operation of the Parliamentary Franchise 1832–1885*, 1915, New Haven: Yale UP

Sharp, A (ed), *The English Levellers*, 1998, Cambridge; CUP

Skidelsky, R (ed), *Thatcherism*, 1988, London: Chatto & Windus, pp 93–106

Stanley Holton, S, 'The making of suffrage history', in Purvis, J and Stanley Holton, S (eds), *Votes for Women*, 2000, London: Routledge

Sunstein, C, *Republic.com*, 2001, Princeton: Princeton UP

Taylor, AJP, *English History 1914–1945*, 1965, Oxford: OUP

Thomson, JAF, *The Transformation of Medieval England 1370–1529*, 1983, London: Longman

Thurlow, RC, *Fascism in Britain: A History, 1918–1985*, 1987, Oxford: Blackwell

Toynbee, P, 'It's the poor that matter', 6 June 2001, *Guardian*

Trietel, GH, *The Law of Contract*, 7th edn, 1987, London: Stevens

Valelly, R, 'Voting alone: the case against virtual ballot boxes', 13 September 1999, 221 (11/12) *New Republic*

Wade, HWR and Forsyth, CF, *Administrative Law*, 8th edn, 2000, Oxford: OUP

Watt, B, 'Justice', in Clarke, PB and Foweraker, J (eds), *Encyclopaedia of Democratic Thought*, 2001, London: Routledge

Watt, B, 'Legal issues concerning the implementation of electronic voting' http://www.local.regions.odpm.gov.uk/egov/e-voting/01/index.htm

Wedderburn, KW, 'Freedom of association and philosophies of labour law' (1989) 18 *Industrial Law Journal*

Williams, DGT, 'Lord Denning and Open Government' (1986) *Denning LJ* 117

Williams, F, *Fifty Years March: The Rise of the Labour Party*, 1950, London: Odhams

Williams, G, *Textbook of Criminal Law*, 2nd edn, 1983, London: Stevens

Woodward, L, *The Age of Reform: 1815–1870*, 2nd edn, 1962, Oxford: OUP

Index